EARNING MEDIA BPP

Becoming a Lawyer

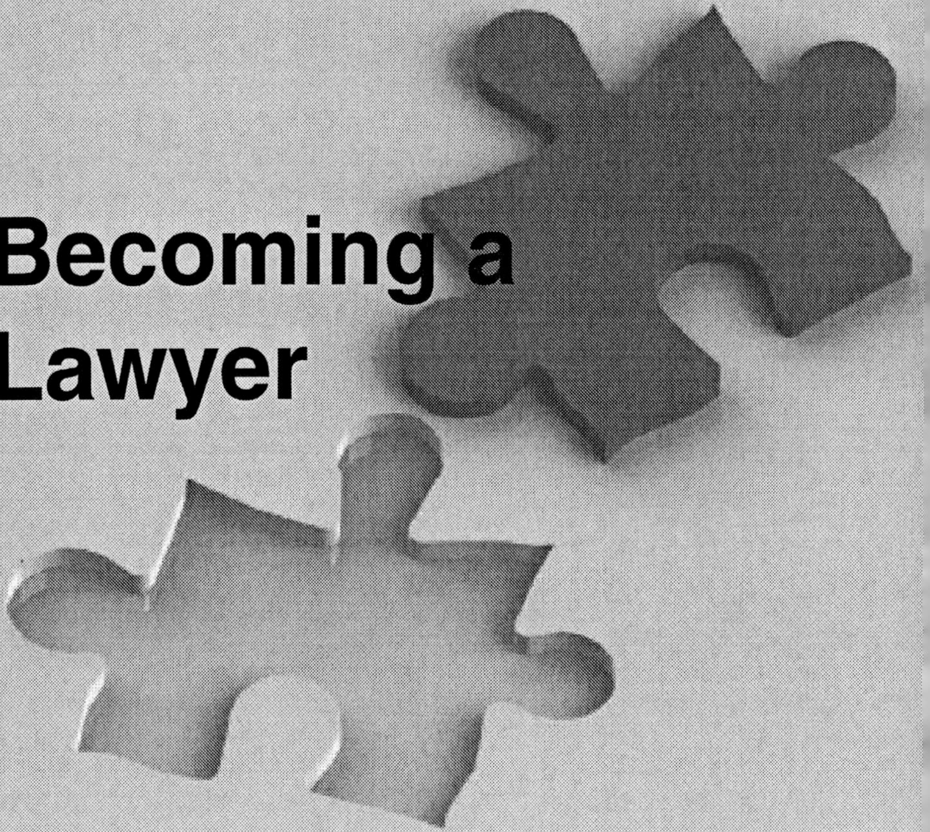

First edition

By Jonny Hurst

D1344446

BPP LEARNING MEDIA

First edition 2013

ISBN 9781 4453 9726 9
e-ISBN 9781 4453 9735 1

British Library Cataloguing-in-Publication Data
A catalogue record for this book is available from the British Library

Published by
BPP Learning Media Ltd
BPP House, Aldine Place
London W12 8AA

www.bpp.com/learning-media

Printed in the UK by
Ricoh
Ricoh House
Ullswater Crescent
Coulsdon
CR5 2HR

Your learning materials, published by BPP Learning Media Ltd, are printed on paper sourced from sustainable, managed forests.

The views expressed in this book are those of BPP Learning Media and not those of UCAS or any universities. BPP Learning Media are in no way associated with or endorsed by UCAS or any universities.

The contents of this book are intended as a guide and not professional advice. Although every effort has been made to ensure that the contents of this book are correct at the time of going to press, BPP Learning Media, makes no warranty that the information in this book is accurate or complete and accept no liability for any loss or damage suffered by any person acting or refraining from acting as a result of the material in this book.

Every effort has been made to contact the copyright holders of any material reproduced within this publication. If any have been inadvertently overlooked, BPP Learning Media will be pleased to make the appropriate credits in any subsequent reprints or editions.

BPP LEARNING MEDIA

Contents

Free companion material

Readers can access additional companion material for free online.

To access companion material please visit:
www.bpp.com/freelawresources.

About the publisher

BPP Learning Media is dedicated to supporting aspiring professionals with top quality learning material. BPP Learning Media's commitment to success is shown by our record of quality, innovation and market leadership in paper-based and e-learning resources. BPP Learning Media's study materials are written by professionally-qualified specialists who know from personal experience the importance of top quality materials for success.

About the author

Jonny Hurst read law at Manchester University in the mid 1980s, following which he trained and practised as a solicitor for the next twenty years, ending up as a partner in a Mid-size law firm in the City.

Jonny changed direction in 2007 when he joined BPP, where he is a senior lecturer and head of Property Law and Practice on the Legal Practice Course.

He lives in London with his wife and three children.

Foreword

The law has been kind to me.

I was the first person in my family to attend university and I came to the legal profession having no connections and not quite knowing if it would be right for me.

I loved the study of law, delving into the rich history of our fine nation and the development of our laws and legal system. The discipline of the study of law taught me great lessons in life which have stayed with me ever since: logical analysis, weighing up alternative outcomes, predictive judgment, the ability to put a coherent argument together and thinking on your feet. These skills are the core to success in so many jobs.

I was called to the bar as a fresh-faced 22 year old with a belief in my own ability and a conviction that despite the circumstances I had been born into, I would be given a chance to be successful. I now look back three decades later as a Professor of Law, having helped to create one of the leading providers of legal education in England, BPP University College, which helps so many students take their career journey into law.

I am not disappointed in the career I chose. But I learned things the hard way – through experience. I only wish that when I was making those career-defining decisions I could have done so with the benefit of Jonny Hurst's 'Becoming a Lawyer'. What Jonny has done is to give the reader a real flavour of what it is like to be a lawyer and how to get there. What you will be immediately struck by is that being a lawyer is not the same for everyone because the practice of law mirrors life itself. My practice was in the areas of personal injury law, employment law and medical negligence. My experience as a courtroom barrister was very different to the experience of a tax lawyer advising large corporate clients on the latest restructuring scheme. That is why I love the law so much; it becomes your own individual experience and the path takes you where you want to go.

The law produces more members of Parliament than any other profession, more business leaders (apart from the accountancy) and it is one of the UK's greatest export services. For example, English law is respected around the world as the most popular legal system for international commercial contracts. By entering the legal profession, you are acutely aware of the weight of history and expectation that you carry on your shoulders.

'*Becoming a Lawyer*' offers you a great insight into one of the world's most respected professions. It will prove to be an invaluable guide to anybody contemplating whether a career in law is right for them and how they should go about it.

Professor Carl Lygo LLB (Hons), LLM, Barrister, MBA, CCIM
Principal, BPP University College

Acknowledgements

My thanks extend to numerous colleagues and students, past and present, for their assistance and patience in helping to shape *Becoming a Lawyer.* Thanks in particular to Abi Flack, Andrew Chadwick, Anna Banfield, James Welsh, Keri Goddard and Olivia Cox, along with my family and friends both within and outside the profession, whose wise counsel and encouragement over the years have made me the lawyer, tutor and person I am today.

JSH, 2013

Note from the author

Congratulations! You have just made one of the first decisions of many you will make on your journey to becoming a lawyer.

The art to being a successful lawyer is getting the vast majority of your decisions right, because no one goes through their studies or their career without making one or two errors of judgment along the way. In fact, on some occasions, as a law student, you will be so puzzled by the apparent insanity of some of the judgments you read, you would be excused from wondering whether the judges were actually sitting in the right institution! But most of the time, you can only have the utmost respect and admiration for the way in which the judiciary reaches and rationalises its decisions. And it is that level of wisdom which you should aspire to when you eventually get the opportunity of dispensing your own learned legal advice.

At the moment, you could be in secondary education and are simply curious about what being a lawyer entails. Maybe you are pondering over your UCAS form as you contemplate your choice of degree. You could still be at university or perhaps you are a recent graduate, facing the huge variety of career choices you now have at your disposal. If you are any of the above, please read on.

But being a law student is not the exclusive domain of those in their late teens/early twenties who are taking the traditional route into the profession; the law is also open to those who may have had a career already (professionally, domestically or otherwise). Each year, many mature students achieve legal qualifications and successfully join the profession, because those who give them the opportunity appreciate that lawyers with life experience offer clients an added dimension.

So what decisions do you have ahead of you?

It depends on who you are and the stage you have reached in your life/ your studies. Some of the typical questions where decisions need to be made are listed below:

Secondary school/A level students

- At university, should I read law or choose a non-law degree?
- At which university should I study?
- Should I live at home with my family or in a different town or city?
- Should I take a gap year, and if so how should I spend it?

Undergraduates

- What elective subjects (options) should I choose during my studies?
- Do I want to be a solicitor or a barrister, or something else?
- When do I have to decide on whether I wish to be a solicitor or barrister?
- Where should I study for the relevant professional examinations (ie the BPTC or the LPC)?

Mature students

- Are there special entry requirements for mature students with an unconventional academic background?
- Should I study full-time or part-time?
- Will I be able to manage my law studies with my job and/or other commitments?
- What life experience do I have which will set me apart from younger law students?

LPC/BPTC students

- To which types of firm/chambers should I apply for a training contract/pupillage?
- How should I prepare for an interview?
- When do I need to specialise and what practice area should I specialise in?
- Is my overall LPC/BPTC grade as important as my degree classification?

All prospective lawyers

- What skills do I need to become a lawyer?
- How much will becoming a lawyer cost me?
- How important is the non-academic side of my CV?
- What work experience should I seek and when should I seek it?

Whoever you are, irrespective of your background, you should have many more questions, several of which are addressed in this book. In time, you will begin to appreciate that the route to becoming a lawyer reflects the practice of law: it is just as important to know the right questions to ask as it is to discover the answers to those questions. Hopefully, for you, this book will just be the start.

Jonny Hurst, 2013

Important note

The scope of this publication is limited to becoming a lawyer in England and Wales only as at 1 January 2013. The law and legal qualifications required to practise law outside England and Wales (including Scotland and Northern Ireland) are not covered in this title.

The start of the journey...

BPP LEARNING MEDIA

Chapter 1

Is the law for me?

BPP
LEARNING MEDIA

Introduction

'Is the law for me' and *'how do I know if I'll make a good lawyer?'* are two of the most common questions posed by prospective lawyers. The simple and honest answer to both questions is 'no one knows'. OK, that's not so helpful, but in this chapter, we will highlight the range of skills and attributes which many successful lawyers possess.

No university or employer expects you to be the 'finished product'. Most lawyers cultivate these skills throughout their professional careers, particularly in their early years in practice. Nevertheless, you should be able to recognise where your current strengths are, and use them as a springboard to develop in other areas during your studies and beyond.

The reality is no solicitor or barrister is brilliant at everything, even after a long and successful career. Most good lawyers will excel in their knowledge of the law in the area in which they specialise, but some may not possess the same practical and commercial instincts as their so-called 'less academic' colleagues. It may be that the most meticulous contract lawyer doesn't feel as comfortable presenting to clients or representing them in court. Whatever your current skill-set, if you can see you have the potential to develop in at least a few of these areas, you're on your way!

If you're still not sure whether you are capable of acquiring these skills, carry on reading: you may surprise yourself! Law tutors and employers prefer to see a more measured, cautious approach than blind arrogance or ill-judged self-confidence. On the other hand, if you don't see yourself being able to rise to the challenge of acquiring any of the skills required to be a lawyer, then maybe the law isn't for you. But the reality is you can probably identify with at least a few of the skills listed below. So, read on!

Top tip

Ask yourself: *'Can I see myself **acquiring and developing** these skills?'*

Rather than: *'Do I have these skills already?'*

The A to Z of a lawyer's key skills and attributes

A is for... Analytical mind

One of the most important skills you will need to develop is the ability to analyse a complex set of facts and apply the correct law to those facts before reaching a well-reasoned conclusion. Most students enjoy being introduced to new legal principles, but some struggle, at least initially, trying to apply them to a practical scenario. However, most get there in end!

As well as mastering legal analysis, lawyers will be required to analyse their own work objectively. In particular, when drafting legal documents, lawyers need to ensure their message will be clearly understood. First appearances can sometimes be deceiving.

Exercise 1.1

Analyse the following statement:

'Stephanie's mother said she was going to be late for her appointment with her solicitor.'

What does this mean?

The problem with the statement is that it is ambiguous. Who was late? Stephanie or her mother? Whose appointment was it? Stephanie's or her mother's? Whose solicitor was it? The fact the reader is left asking these questions means the writer has not effectively communicated the desired message. Effective communication lies at the heart of being a good, practical lawyer. If it's possible for there to be eight equally sensible interpretations of the same 15-word sentence (yes, eight!), imagine the number of problems there could be in a badly drafted 50-page document!

Top tip

- Analyse something you have written recently of around 500 words in length (or more). Can you spot any ambiguities? If not, ask someone else to read the same piece who is not familiar with the subject matter. You may be surprised what they find.
- Be more critical of what you write in future, and where you see possible ambiguities, correct them so you leave the reader with only one possible interpretation – the one you intended.

B is for... Business and commercial awareness

Prospective employers frequently explore whether their candidates have an appreciation of the business and commercial world, particularly if the work involves acting for corporate clients. Having such awareness doesn't just help you get a job, it will often give you an insight into how and why your clients function in the way they do. In turn, by developing such an understanding, you will be in a better position to deliver what your clients need. Even if you see yourself practising in a non-corporate area, the organisation you work for still needs to operate within a market place and you will have a significant part to play in at least preserving (if not improving) its position.

Top tip

Read the financial pages and follow the legal press on a regular basis. Get an idea of what the latest business deals are about and which law firms are acting. You will not understand everything you read, but the more you absorb, the quicker you will develop an understanding of business and commerce.

Another Top tip

Such background reading may be tempting to introduce during an interview, but proceed with caution: interviewees do sometimes get caught out when their apparently well-researched point is exposed as being out of date, or their understanding of it, misconceived. If you are still brave and confident enough to discuss what you have read, always assume your interviewer will know more about the subject than you!

C is for... Communication which is clear, concise, and to the point

Clients want you to use language they can understand, which addresses their issues in as few words as possible. Sometimes, this is incredibly difficult, particularly if you have to explain how several competing legal principles affect your client's interests. The art of communicating this message in a concise, client-friendly way presents different challenges, depending on whether you are communicating verbally or in writing.

Exercise 1.2

Re-write the following sentence in ten words or less without losing any of the meaning:

Abdul did not ever fail to attend his contract law lectures which were held each week on a Monday morning at 9.00 a.m.

There are a number of ways to re-write this sentence. It is possible to use less than half the number of words without losing any of the meaning:

Abdul always attended contract lectures at 9.00 a.m. on Mondays.

Simply replacing the double-negative '*did not ever fail...*' *with 'always'* saved three words and some words (eg *'which were held each week'*) could be removed completely. On the Legal Practice Course (known as the 'LPC'), which is the post-graduate course you need to pass if you wish to become a solicitor, prospective solicitors develop their verbal and written communication in the Advocacy, Interviewing and Advising, Drafting and Legal Writing modules.

Top tip

The 'ABC' of journalism is 'Accuracy, Brevity and Clarity'. The same applies to lawyers when drafting documents.

- **Accuracy:** is the statement true and complete? Does it reflect your client's instructions?
- **Brevity:** why use ten words if you can say the same in three?
- **Clarity:** did you make your point clear, or is it possible you could be misunderstood?

D is for... Discipline and dedication

Law students and practising lawyers spend considerable amounts of time working on their own researching, reading and writing. This requires you to maintain a sharp focus in order to meet deadlines while, at all times, achieving the highest of standards. Sometimes, you will be tired or distracted by matters outside your studies or work, and, occasionally, you may be tempted to persuade yourself 'that will do'. When that happens to you (and it will do, even if you are the most diligent of individuals), you will need to dig deep into your reserves to motivate yourself. The exacting, unforgiving nature of the legal profession will not accept a 'that will do' mentality. Saying 'no' to an evening with friends when you have an important tutorial or meeting which you need to prepare for the following day does sometimes take courage, particularly if some of your friends do not share the same ambitions as you. There will always be a 'next time' for seeing them, whereas you may only get one opportunity of attending the tutorial or impressing a potential client.

E is for... Excellence

Not only do universities and employers expect you to have an excellent academic record, your clients will as well. Clients, who can pay several hundred pounds per hour for the service of a lawyer, will expect to reap the benefits of your excellent education, as you skilfully guide them through their problems. Otherwise, what are they paying for?

The highest of standards is also expected of lawyers outside the workplace, and this extends to law students as well.

Case study

'Amy', an LPC student, found, to her cost, that travelling on a child's ticket on the London Underground was not considered conduct which the profession could condone. As a consequence of such dishonesty, she was not permitted to complete the course and qualify as a solicitor.

Any incident of criminal behaviour seriously risks jeopardising your career. We all hear of people (including some lawyers) who 'bend the rules' for an apparent 'justifiable' cause. If that is you, ask yourself whether, after all your years of study, you really want to put your chosen career on the line on the toss of coin (ie the risk of being caught)? Lawyers tend to be risk-averse, so most will quickly develop antennae which can detect the first sign of trouble, and then find a way of running as quickly as possible in the opposite direction.

Excellence in performance at work is the main gateway to promotion; this is usually assessed on both the quality of your work and, particularly in law firms, by the volume of income you generate for the business.

As a lawyer, you are not permitted to have an 'off-day'. On the day you let your standards drop, there will often be adverse consequences for your clients, and in today's 'claims culture' such clients aren't slow to complain if you under-achieve on their matters.

On the other hand, obsession with perfection can also get in the way of being a good lawyer, because you will not be able to operate profitably (both in a monetary and non-monetary sense) if you take too long creating a masterpiece, which compromises the delivery of the project. The trick is learning to be satisfied with achieving excellence (as opposed to perfection) in any given task, before moving onto the next one.

F is for... Fit and healthy

Although not actually a skill, we can all have an influence on our own mental and physical wellbeing. The negative impact which neglect of one's health can have on your relationships and your job can be considerable. Lawyers usually work in high-pressure environments, so it is not surprising that the profession has more than its fair share of alcoholics and workaholics. Maintaining healthy pursuits outside the workplace will produce a better performance at work, which is why so many employers offer cut-price gym membership.

I was horrified when I attended one meeting with three other lawyers and our respective clients. The clients were of varying ages between 30 and 50 (as were the lawyers) but while the clients were generally slim and well proportioned, the three other lawyers sported the grossest variety of protruding overhangs you would ever wish to see. It made me, who at the time was around two stone overweight, look like an Olympic athlete. Within two weeks of the meeting, one of the other lawyers had open heart surgery and I had joined a gym and given up smoking. The immediate effect on my energy levels and general performance at work by getting fitter was staggering – I was no longer tired at the end of the day, even the stress levels seemed to diminish a little.

The moral? One day you may wake up and find you haven't done any exercise for 20 years. If you want to perform at the highest level and achieve your potential as a lawyer, don't let that be you!

Jonny Hurst

G is for... Good listener

Taking instructions is an integral part of the role of a practising lawyer, but if you don't fully understand what your client is saying, or if you mishear them, you will lose rapport, which is essential to the lawyer-client relationship. More importantly, if you do not carefully process everything you are instructed, there is a danger that you will not end up acting in your clients' best interests. But being a good listener isn't just about what you hear, it's also recognising what your clients don't say, reading their body language and fully understanding the motivations behind their words and actions.

H is for... Hard-working

We all have those annoying friends who float into an exam having done minimal preparation and when you see their results, you find they do as well as you. They may even have done better than you, despite the fact that you worked twice as hard as they did. The reality is you are likely to last longer in the legal profession than they are. Eventually, whether it is in their university examinations, professional training or early years in practice, bright but lazy lawyers will get caught out, because the treadmill is usually revolving at such a pace, if you get too behind with your work, it can be impossible to catch up. Working hard is a way of life for all successful lawyers; those who tend to be more conscientious are ultimately more successful. The same applies to law students. So, if you're bright and you're used to coasting along, ask yourself whether you can 'up your game', which you probably can. Then ask yourself whether you honestly wish to do so.

I is for... Intelligence

At various stages of your journey to becoming a lawyer, you will be required to demonstrate your intelligence, which, not surprisingly, starts with your GCSE and A level examination results. Universities and employers don't expect Einstein, but they don't expect a philistine either. Most undergraduate law schools require their applicants to possess at the very least a solid 'A/B' profile at A level, with many universities operating a 'straight A' entry criteria. Large law firms require, in the vast majority of cases, their trainee solicitors to have gained at least an upper second class (2:1) degree (not necessarily in law). Securing a pupillage, which for barristers, is the equivalent of a training contract, is even more competitive; a first class degree no longer guarantees a career at the bar.

If your A level profile is no higher than Bs and Cs, you will be at a disadvantage from the outset. While it is not quite the case that such students should consider a different career, they should appreciate that they will have to work twice as hard and have twice the determination to succeed. Regrettably, many will fail to do so.

With so many excellent candidates vying for a limited number of places, academic intelligence is only part of the selection process. But, inevitably, as universities and employers seek to whittle down the volume of applications for their hugely over-subscribed vacancies, an applicant's academic record will invariably be the decisive factor, at least initially.

Academic ability is only one type of intelligence. Many law firms use asymmetric tests, teamwork exercises, as well as the traditional interview panel as part of the selection process for their trainees, which will be explored later on in this book in further detail.

J is for... Judgment

From the most minor of amendments in a document to a decision which could have huge implications on another person's liberty or financial wellbeing, there is a whole range of decisions which lawyers have to make on a daily basis. The exercise of sound judgment, which is the product of thoughtful, carefully considered analysis, lies at the heart of getting these decisions right, which is one of the keys to becoming a successful lawyer. Equally, having to live with an unpopular decision or one which, with hindsight you wished you hadn't made, is also part of professional life. Today's judges who preside over the gravest of charges and disputes learn from the judgments handed down by their predecessors. Likewise, throughout your career, when you exercise your judgment, your ultimate decision will be influenced not just by court decisions, but also the decisions of other lawyers – your law tutors, your supervisors in practice and your peers.

K is for... Knowledge

The practice of law does, of course, require the accumulation of a vast amount of knowledge, much of which you will need to retain and apply during your career. You will also be introduced to areas of the law which may, at first, seem a waste of time. For example, you may be certain that you never want to practise as a criminal lawyer. But consider this: athletes don't lift weights during a race or competition, yet they spend hours each week 'pumping iron' in the gym. Similarly, the time you spend studying seemingly irrelevant subjects will help to develop your legal brain, making you a fitter, stronger and better lawyer.

The early stages of your legal training will lay the foundations for your knowledge and understanding of the law as you are introduced to a whole variety of legal concepts, such as the law of contract, constitutional law and the law of torts. These areas will be the gateway to more specialist areas later in your studies, such as commercial law and employment law, which are two popular electives (options) frequently chosen by undergraduate law students.

Your accumulation of legal knowledge does not end with your professional qualifications; the law is continually evolving, so whatever area you end up specialising in, you will need to keep up to date with changes in legislation, recently reported cases and professional practice. Continuing Professional Development (known as 'CPD') is now a mandatory requirement for all qualified lawyers. For example, solicitors who work at least 32 hours per week are required to complete at least 16 hours of CPD each year, of which a minimum of 25% must be on accredited training courses (SRA, 2012). Most CPD will be in areas directly related to the lawyer's area of speciality, but there are many other useful courses which help lawyers improve their management skills, particularly in the context of managing a legal practice.

So, even when you become a practising lawyer, you never stop being a law student!

Top tip

Get into the habit of reading the law reports in the quality newspapers or online. Like reading the financial pages, some of the law reports will be difficult to follow, but others will be more straightforward. Most reported cases relate to civil proceedings (ie not criminal law).

If the subject matter of a case interests you, try to identify:

- The key facts
- The main issue which the parties were litigating over
- What the court/tribunal decided
- The point(s) of law or the relevant facts upon which the main decision of the court/tribunal was based
- The implications of the court/tribunal's decision on the parties

L is for... Likeable

Most of us would prefer to be popular than despised. But is likeability key to being a successful lawyer? Some practitioners would argue that earning the respect of the people you work with is more important. Perhaps it is, because without it, you are not going to last long in any job. However, an 'awkward personality' can frustrate the progress of an otherwise successful legal career. Lawyers are sometimes portrayed as aloof or arrogant, but ask yourself whether such a detachment is ultimately helpful to your clients, or, for that matter, you.

Within a few sessions of teaching a group of LPC students, a tutor can usually identify one or two of them who clients will love and a similar number of the class who clients may have difficulty taking to. In both cases, these students appear outwardly confident, but whereas the former possess self-awareness, the latter can sometimes be unaware of the negative impression they are creating.

M is for... Management skills

As soon as you qualify, you will be managing clients. As a barrister, there is a certain amount of management required in your relationships with your instructing solicitors, your clerks and pupils. As a solicitor, you will, in time, manage junior fee earners, and unqualified support staff. To assist, the Solicitors Regulation Authority ('SRA') requires solicitors to complete a compulsory management course before the end of their third year in practice, which covers the management of:

- Finance
- The firm
- Client relations
- Information
- People

N is for... Natural curiosity

An ability not to accept things at face value – an instinct to question and keep seeking information until you have the 'full picture' is a prerequisite of any good lawyer. The information you need will rarely fall into your lap. You will, on occasions, have to use your initiative to complete your information-gathering exercise before being able to advise a client. This may involve being creative in both *where* you look and *how* you look. In fact, your clients may have much of the information you need, but they may not be aware you need it.

O is for... Organisational skills

You need to be able to cope with a large volume of work, often in situations where there are competing priorities. Should you do some extra reading to prepare for tomorrow's tutorial or give the essay which has to be handed in tomorrow one last read through? Or can you afford the time to see the latest blockbuster movie, because, after all, you deserve some pleasure after working hard all week? Alternatively, which of the many emails you have received overnight from different clients should you answer first? There will be some days when you'll start with the best intentions, with an ambitious 'to do' list, which is just about achievable, provided nothing gets in the way. Inevitably, something does happen which consumes a significant chunk of your time meaning that you have to re-prioritise, and re-re-prioritise when the day takes another unexpected turn!

Being organised isn't just about prioritising. You need to ensure your working environment is conducive to maximising your output, and that starts with keeping your room, desk, files and papers in order. *'Cluttered desk, cluttered mind'* is a view often taken by managers when appraising junior staff. Those who wish to defend their chaotic working environment might think they need look no further than Einstein whose clever retort was:

'*If a cluttered desk is a sign of a cluttered mind, of what, then, is an empty desk a sign?*'

But the reality for almost all lawyers is your desk is never clear, and your head is usually full of one work-related issue or another. So there's little chance of your mind being empty. Most of us aren't working out the theory of relativity, so we need sound organisation systems which succeed not just in our head, but also in practice, in order to work effectively and efficiently.

Exercise 1.3

- Do you have a pile of papers somewhere which need sorting or filing?
- Should you have put those papers in a folder by now? Or maybe thrown them away?
- Do you admit to not remembering everything you have put in that pile?

If your answer to any of the above questions is 'yes', ask yourself how long it would actually take to resolve. You know there is a benefit to sorting through that pile of papers, so ask yourself why you don't do it.

Instead of a physical pile of papers, is there a metaphorical one? Are there tasks you know you need to complete, but which you have put off because you can't face them or perhaps you've convinced yourself you don't have the time? Multiply these tasks by the number of clients you will have as a lawyer and that will give you an idea of what it's like trying to juggle your priorities and how being organised helps you get things done.

P is for... Political awareness

Wherever you end up in the legal profession, you need to have an awareness of how the world around you operates. As lawyers, neither we nor our clients operate in a vacuum, although, on occasions, you may wish one or two of your clients did!

What does political awareness mean for aspiring lawyers? Keeping up with current affairs by watching the news and reading quality newspapers is a good start. Awareness of the political issues of the day may be particularly important if you end up specialising in an area which is regularly affected by legislative changes, such as tax issues, which will impact on most transactional lawyers (ie those operating in the corporate, commercial and property worlds).

Top tip

To help develop your political awareness, take an interest in the next budget (March) or autumn statement (December) delivered in the House of Commons by the Chancellor of the Exchequer. Ask yourself how any tax changes impact on:

- Lawyers
- Their clients

Q is for... Quick on your feet

The ability to 'think on your feet' – that is, to think quickly and creatively – is often required as a lawyer. This may mean responding immediately and effectively to a surprising turn of events, such as when your client's witness gives unexpectedly hostile or prejudicial evidence. It may mean that the whole of your previous advice was based on a premise, which now turns out to be false. When the unexpected does arise, your client will require you to deal with it; so you will need to become adaptable to changing circumstances.

R is for... Reading

Becoming a lawyer involves a phenomenal amount of reading. There's no getting away from it: you will spend hours digesting the contents of all of the following as you build up your understanding of law:

- Legislation
- Reported cases
- Statutory instruments
- Various rules and regulations
- Articles in legal journals
- Practice guidelines
- Text books

As practitioners, you will also be required to read an array of correspondence and other documents, not always written by other lawyers. Most trial bundles for court run to at least several hundred pages.

Top tip

If consuming large amounts of reading is not your strength, recognise that this is the case and increase your consumption now, so you regularly read something which is challenging every day. It doesn't necessarily have to be law-related, as long as you challenge yourself to read something more 'difficult', so you can practise more analytical thinking.

S is for... Sensitivity and emotional intelligence

The lawyer-client relationship isn't just about giving good advice – it's about appreciating and recognising who and what your clients are, and how you communicate that advice to them. Being sensitive to the needs of your clients will avoid embarrassing moments. It can also help cement your relationships with them. Although a 'bedside manner' is more commonly recognised in the context of a doctor-patient relationship, a successful lawyer will need to develop a way of communicating with a variety of clients from different backgrounds. This may require subtle changes in the type of language you use with clients (eg formal or informal), or having a particular sensibility and sensitivity to your client's particular needs. For example, ordering a full English breakfast with orthodox Jewish clients or arranging sandwiches to be served for a meeting with Islamic clients during Ramadan are simple mistakes, which are easily avoided.

One type of sensitivity lawyers need is 'emotional intelligence', which is an ability to read and understand the emotions of their work colleagues, clients and fellow professionals. This is a skill most lawyers develop during their careers. Emotional intelligence can be innate in the personality of the individual, but it can be learned, as it frequently is, in the workplace.

Top tip

Observe someone you know in their working environment who you regard to have good emotional intelligence. This may be a teacher, a tutor, a leader or someone else you have an opportunity of spending time with at their workplace. Making a point of noting:

- Their body language, including eye contact when communicating with others
- The tone of their voice and any variety they use in such tone
- The speed at which they speak
- The choice of words they use
- How they tackle problems with 'difficult' people
- How and why they speak in a different way to:
  - More junior members of staff
  - Staff at the same level as they are in their organisation
  - More senior members off staff
  - Their clients or customers (or if in an educational institution, the students)

T is for... Thorough

Attention to detail (the need to be thorough) is essential or you won't give the best possible service to your client. As part of your review of any document, you need to discover all the important detail which may be buried in an ocean of less relevant text. There may be a key fact in a witness statement upon which the whole case may turn, or a punitive clause which the other side has buried in the middle of draft contract which you are reviewing. Ultimately, if you are thorough, you should spot where the pots of gold are hiding and where the potential bombs are buried. That is a significant part of the service your client is paying for – to meticulously review the 'small-print' so that any prejudicial provisions are diluted or negotiated away and anything advantageous can be seized upon for the benefit of your client.

U is for... Unflappable, calm in a crisis

Lawyers rarely go through their careers without one or two crises along the way. It could be the loss of a valuable client, a complaint or a claim made against you/the firm, or simply an overload of work. Whatever the crisis, it is important to share your concerns with people of influence, however difficult you may perceive that to be, as we all need help to get through the more trying times in our lives. Maintaining a clear head and sharing the burden is normally the quickest route to resolving the problem. Frequently, when you talk it over with a more experienced colleague or manager, you discover someone else has had or is having a similar issue, which paints a different perspective on your problem. Knowing that it's 'not just you' is sometimes all you need to hear for the anxiety to begin to recede. There will be crises you will experience as a lawyer, but they will rarely compare to the life or death issues a medic faces on a daily basis. So, do try to remain calm and measured; if you don't get the mark you thought you deserved or if you find a particular client extremely difficult to deal with, work your way through the issue and move on. It may feel like 'the end of the world', but it rarely is.

V is for... Versatile

Versatility, adaptability and flexibility are essential in any trade or profession nowadays. Although it is true that solicitors, in particular, have become increasingly more specialised in the areas of the law they practise, to do well, it does help to be an 'all rounder' – eg someone who has good IT skills but is also happy to represent or promote the firm at conferences, marketing events and client receptions. Equally, an ambitious solicitor must have an awareness and understanding of how the firm functions economically, practically and politically. In other words, you should know who to go to in order get things done, whether it is to replace the toner in the photocopier, to deal with a client complaint or an idea how to make the firm's working practices more efficient.

Top tip

Make yourself more versatile! Learn to touch type if you don't know already. It will double the speed you produce documents and genuinely impresses your bosses, even if it frightens the secretaries!

W is for... Work-life balance

You will need to juggle your work, social and family/private life in such a way that each is given space and time in your diary. Failing to keep a healthy work-life balance is a common complaint of both law students and practising lawyers. Planning how and when you are going to spend your time to serve both these masters can take a career to conquer – and some never do. Good organisational skills will lie at heart of winning this battle!

When I started working for a busy solicitor who was continually juggling child care with her work duties, I noticed there were regular, identical entries in her diary, marked 'MET'. They tended to be at lunchtime or at the end of the working day. When I needed to schedule a meeting which clashed with 'MET', I plucked up the courage to ask her what these entries were. I found out that 'MET' stood for 'me time'. In other words, my boss made a point of scheduling time in her busy life for herself. She said it didn't really matter whether it was going to the gym, retail therapy or going to an art gallery. She believed 'me time' kept her sane!

Linda, legal secretary

X is for... eXpect the unexpected (and prepare for it!)

Even in transactional areas of the law (eg the sale and purchase of companies and properties) where the procedure of the deal normally follows a relatively predictable path, it is almost inevitable that complications will arise at some stage. Your job is to tell the client to 'expect the unexpected' and then to adapt to any complication which does arise. This means ensuring you plan for the unexpected, which includes forewarning your clients of what can 'go wrong', so your client has realistic expectations. Litigators, unless they are very lucky, will only win around half of their cases, but it doesn't necessarily follow that they perform any worse in the cases they lose. Litigators will rarely advise that the prospects of succeeding in court are much better than 75%, even if they are privately much more confident of victory. Experience teaches us not to take anything in the law for granted.

Y is for... Yourself

Be yourself! And recognise what your strengths and weaknesses are as an individual. Some lawyers are too arrogant or too busy to reflect on their personal performance. Taking the time to periodically assess 'what went well' and 'what you would do differently next time' is time invested in your own personal development.

Many students feel under pressure to study particular subjects because it will 'look good' on their CV or because of family pressure, despite having little or no interest in the area. If you have a passion for family law, then follow your passion – it's your career, no one else's.

Z is for... Zest (or enthusiasm) for the law

Don't feel at this stage you have to possess a burning ambition to resolve complex disputes, draft complex commercial documents or wish to use the law as a vehicle to 'do good' by 'giving something back' to society. If you do, then great, you're reading the right book. That said, all you need is enthusiasm for and/or a genuine interest in the law. But if your main motivation is to make money, to acquire social status or to please your family, you should ask yourself whether the law really is for you.

Case study

Alison, Christina, James, Robert and Stuart all trained at the same time and qualified as solicitors in the early 1990s. Alison is now a partner in a law firm, but is the only one of the five who is still in private practice in England. Christina works as an 'in house' lawyer for an NHS Trust, James is a university lecturer, Robert works for the Government Legal Service and Stuart emigrated to Australia, where, following an extended break from legal practice, he re-qualified and set up his own law firm in Queensland.

Apart from Alison, each of their 'reasons' for choosing the law have changed at least once during their careers and yours may do as well. Not every aspiring lawyer has a clear vision of where they are going and how they will end up, so don't feel like you should, particularly if other prospective lawyers have a clearer personal vision than you do. Once you qualify, as long as you retain an underlying interest in the intellectual application of the law and how it works, there will be plenty of opportunities for you both in private practice and beyond.

Assess your skills

Ask yourself the following questions:

- Which of the above skills have I started to acquire already?
- How can I continue to develop those skills further?
- Which other skills am I able to work towards acquiring?
- How can I start to acquire those skills?

Once per week, try working, on:

1. An area you have begun to make progress already; and
2. A new skill, like, perhaps reading the law reports if you don't already.

Once these become part of your routine, you will find it easier to work on other skills you also need to add or develop.

Chapter summary

You can begin to develop some key skills now by following the Top tips in this chapter. Try not to do too much too quickly or you will not achieve much of substance.

Key points

- Take your studies seriously.
- Good study lays the foundation to your acquisition of the key skills and attributes of a successful lawyer.
- Some of the skills can only be acquired while you are in legal practice, and most will develop over a long period of time.

Useful resources

www.lawgazette.co.uk

www.thelawyer.com

www.thetimes.co.uk/tto/law *

*This is a subscription-based service

References

Solicitors Regulation Authority (2012) Continuing professional development. [Online] Available at: http://www.sra.org.uk/solicitors/cpd.page [Accessed December 2012]

Becoming a law student...

BPP
LEARNING MEDIA

Chapter 2

What is a lawyer?

Introduction

The word *lawyer* is a generic term for someone who practises law in England and Wales. However, the legal profession rarely refers to one of its own as a 'lawyer'. Instead, practitioners tend to be described with reference to their specific professional qualification, which, in the vast majority of cases, will be one of the following:

- Solicitor
- Barrister
- Legal executive

In England and Wales, as at 1 January 2013, there were around 170,000 people practising as qualified lawyers or training in the workplace to become lawyers. The approximate breakdown is as follows:

- 128,419 solicitors (as at December 2012) plus around 5,441 trainee solicitors registered with the SRA (as at October 2012) (known as 'trainees') (SRA, 2012)
- 15,387 barristers (as at 2010) plus 444 pupil barristers (as at 2010/11) (known as 'pupils'), (The Bar Council, 2012). At the time of publication of this book, the bar had only published statistics up to 2010 - not the only thing which some people may say is a little out of date with the bar! Having said that, the current numbers are not believed to be radically different.
- 7,500 chartered legal executives (who are fully qualified lawyers) and around a further 12,500 members of the Chartered Institute of Legal Executives who are in various stages of training and/or have not yet become chartered legal executives. (CILEx, 2012)

None of the above figures include paralegals.

That's not a lot of jobs, considering the law is such a highly sought after career option, and the population of England and Wales surpassed 56 million in the 2011 census. That works out at around one lawyer/trainee lawyer for every 329 people in England and Wales.

Only a very small proportion of the population regularly engages a lawyer, but most people will do so at some stage of their lives for personal matters, such as drafting wills, moving house, or matrimonial breakdown. Most work undertaken by lawyers is undertaken for the public sector clients and business organisations, the largest of which will regularly engage several firms of solicitors in relation to all aspects of their business – eg employment contracts, sales contracts, litigation for unpaid good/services, renting leasehold business premises, and so on.

So, where do solicitors, barristers and legal executives fit in? And what's the difference between them?

The usual focus of a barrister's work is acting as an advocate, in contested legal proceedings, in respect of which barristers will also draft documents and write legal opinions as to the prospects of success.

Solicitors and legal executives work together at law firms to provide a much broader range of services than barristers; as well as advising and representing clients in court, tribunals and other litigious matters, collectively, solicitors provide almost every other type of legal service as well. A non-exhaustive list of some of the non-contentious/transactional areas covered by law firms includes:

- Banking and Finance
- Corporate Law (eg mergers and acquisitions of companies)
- Commercial contracts
- Entertainment Law
- Financial Services
- Intellectual Property
- Media Law
- Real Property
- Regulatory Compliance
- Tax and Financial Planning
- Wills, Probate and the Administration of Estates

Whereas barristers are usually self-employed, solicitors (at least at the beginning of their careers) and legal executives will be employed. The vast majority of solicitors and legal executives work in private practice for a law firm, but there are also jobs for qualified lawyers working in the public sector, in commerce and in industry.

Most of this book will focus on the traditional route to becoming a lawyer by becoming a barrister or a solicitor via tertiary education. However, it is important at this stage to spend a little time looking at legal executives and other career options in the legal profession, such as that of barristers' clerks, legal secretaries, solicitors' clerks, paralegals and legal apprentices.

Barristers' clerks

Barristers in private practice work from a set of shared rooms (often referred to as a '**set**' or '**chambers**'), sharing expenses and support staff, the most important of whom are their clerks. Barristers' clerks are responsible for the management and administration of a set of barristers' chambers. They will begin by assisting barristers with their papers to and from court and managing barristers' diaries. In time, they will progress to negotiating fees on behalf of their barristers, managing the chambers' finances and counselling the junior barristers on their career progression. The point of entry is usually after leaving school at 16 or 18. At the top end, senior clerks can earn a significantly higher salary than some of their chambers' junior tenants.

Legal secretaries

Historically, law firms employed significant numbers of legal secretaries whose primary function would be to type correspondence and legal documents on behalf of one to three solicitors and take messages on their behalf. Indeed this is still the case to a certain extent, although some legal secretaries take on more of a 'PA' role (eg to a particular partner), organising the partner's diary and accompanying the partner to meetings. Other legal secretaries sometimes take on more of a paralegal role, some of whom end up studying law part-time and eventually become legal executives or solicitors.

In recent years, the IT revolution has undoubtedly threatened the sustained future of legal secretaries – at least in the same numbers they enjoyed in the 1980s and 1990s, because many of the partners of tomorrow join law firms today as trainees with good IT skills and being able to touch-type. There will still be a need for fast and accurate word-processing specialists, but it is already evident that the typing pool of the past is being seen as the most cost-effective way of mass-producing documents in larger law firms. So, the legal secretaries of the future are unlikely to enjoy a close working relationship with just one or two of the solicitors at their law firm unless they fulfil more of a paralegal or PA role, or work in a small law firm.

Solicitors' clerks

In addition to qualified lawyers and those in training, law firms also employ a number of support staff without any legal qualifications, such as solicitors' clerks. Solicitors' clerks carry out a range of administrative and clerical functions, some of whom eventually take on a fee-earning role.

A solicitors' clerk in a litigation department will start by delivering briefs to counsel, issuing court applications, collecting and filing papers at court, as well as generally assisting the qualified fee earners in the firm's litigation department – eg in the preparation of bundles for court. In time, if they show ability, solicitors' clerks may interview witnesses in preparation for a court hearing, prepare witness statements and even attend interim court applications in a representative capacity.

The title 'solicitors' clerk' is becoming increasingly old-fashioned. Traditional clerking duties are already becoming absorbed in a variety of paralegal roles and this trend is set to continue with the recent advent of legal apprenticeships (see below).

Paralegals

Another recent trend is for law firms to employ paralegals in low-grade fee-earning work, which, in the past, may have been given to trainee solicitors. Firms are currently employing paralegals in unprecedented numbers, mainly for economic reasons. Although there are no accurate published figures, it is believed that there are over 200,000 paralegals working in England and Wales, which is well over the combined number of practising solicitors, barristers and legal executives!

As firms take advantage of the more flexible labour market, the increase in the number of paralegals is likely to continue: law firms do not have to commit to employing paralegals for as a long as a trainee's two-year training contract and paralegals are generally cheaper to employ than trainee solicitors. In addition, once paralegals are trained in the narrow tasks they are required to perform, law firms will need to spend considerably less management time and resources supporting and managing them when compared to the investment (both in time and money) which law firms are required to make in respect of their trainee solicitors.

Many paralegal roles are filled by people with no legal background at all. For example, in real estate departments, some law firms train unqualified members of staff to administer property completions and ensure all the post-completion formalities are achieved within the prescribed time limits, such as registration at the Land Registry.

In recent years, aspiring trainee solicitors who have passed the Legal Practice Course, but have been unable to secure a training contract, have taken paralegal positions in law firms in the hope that a training contract may follow if they make a good impression. It is certainly a 'step in the door' and not a bad short-term career move to plug a gap in your CV and to acquire more experience at the same time, but unfortunately, most paralegal roles do not, in the end, lead to a training contract at the same firm.

Unlike barristers, solicitors and legal executives, paralegals are not separately regulated. However, career paralegals may join representative bodies like the Institute of Paralegals or the National Association of Licensed Paralegals, but that is not a legal requirement.

Legal executives

After this chapter, the remainder of this book will focus on the more conventional route to becoming a lawyer: qualifying as a solicitor or barrister by way of the conventional academic route – ie via university and the relevant vocational examinations. However, before focusing on that area, you should not dismiss becoming a legal executive as an alternative career option.

Most legal executives work for firms of solicitors. The main difference between solicitors and legal executives is that the traditional route to becoming a legal executive is not via university. In fact, most legal executives start off life in a law firm as a legal secretary, paralegal or solicitors' clerk, often straight from school or college. Over time, many of them become highly proficient in the area of the law in which they work, and can become fee earners in their own right without needing to sit a single law examination. Indeed, as you may have surmised, paralegals can happily spend the majority of their working lives doing a very similar job to their legally qualified colleagues whom they work alongside. There are, however, limitations to being a solicitors' clerk or paralegal – not least the salary you can command and the positions you can hold, the most significant of which is that an unqualified paralegal is not able to be a partner in a traditional law firm. Consequently, many of them go on to study to and become legal executives or solicitors.

Qualifying as a legal executive (which you can do while you are working), provides opportunities for progression to more prestigious and better-paid positions. You are able to qualify as a legal executive over the same four-year period as someone who studies full-time for a law degree and then takes the Legal Practice Course, known as the 'LPC' (to qualify as a solicitor), or the Bar Professional Training Course, known as the 'BPTC' (to qualify as a barrister). One of the obvious benefits of taking the legal executive route is that you will be 'earning while you're learning'. It is, of course, possible to work and study for a law degree and the relevant vocational examinations on a part-time basis, but that is a much more expensive option and will normally take you around six years or more to complete.

If you are thinking of combining a full-time job with being a law student on a part-time basis, make sure you have some 'armbands', because, at times, you will feel like you're coming close to drowning. What keeps me afloat are discipline and good time management.

Discipline is crucial for a number of reasons. You will need to be comfortable telling your friends on numerous occasions that you can't go to the pub or go out shopping with them as you have 'work to do'. You will also need to regularly tell your boss that you 'really need to leave the office now to get to college'. Time management is also vital in order to anticipate busy periods in your life and to ensure that you stay on top of all your various commitments, both in relation to the course and outside.

There is light at the end of the tunnel though, even if it may feel never-ending at times! Prospective employers really do value your work experience, whether it be in the legal sector or not. You may also find that you have picked up some of that magic dust - 'commercial awareness' that you can apply to your studies.

Any law course you undertake is a huge commitment and will have a big impact on your life. However I have always found that everyone in my part-time classes are in exactly in the same boat as I am and the tutors are acutely aware that part-time students may need to be cut some slack at times and thrown a life buoy or two.

Richard Turner, part-time GDL graduate and part-time LPC student

The total tuition fees for a typical three-year law degree followed by a full-time place on the LPC or BPTC will be upwards of £35,000 to £40,000 excluding living costs, which can double that figure. The CILEx (Chartered Institute of Legal Executives) course and examination fees to qualify as a legal executive are only a few thousand pounds, which is a fraction of the cost of the traditional route to qualify as a solicitor or barrister. Furthermore, if you work for a law firm, your employer may pay these costs for you. Why? Because once you qualify as a chartered legal executive, although your qualification will attract a higher salary, your firm will usually be able to charge your time to clients at a higher rate.

So why doesn't everyone take the legal executive route? The main reason is that the legal profession generally expects most of its qualified staff to have a depth of legal education which simply isn't possible to cover on CILEx courses. Consequently, qualifying as a solicitor or a barrister is considered a higher and more versatile professional qualification, with more career options. Nevertheless, the content and level of difficulty of CILEx modules is in many respects very similar to parts of an undergraduate law degree course and the LPC, and the ability to acquire the qualification while earning a salary in legal practice without accumulating huge debts is appealing, particularly in the current economic climate. If you have ambitions to become a lawyer, but you do not have a conventional academic background, or if you need an income as you study, then maybe becoming a legal executive is the best career option for you.

Advantages of becoming a legal executive	Disadvantages of becoming a legal executive
1. You can 'earn and learn'.	1. Less formal legal education.
2. Flexible timings to qualify.	2. Less prestigious qualification.
3. High A level results are not essential.	3. Career progression generally slower and lower.
4. No university degree generally required.	4. Will not always command the same salary as a solicitor for doing the same work.
5. Considerably cheaper to qualify, so less debt!	5. Limited rights of audience to appear in court.
6. Can still be a partner in a law firm and can use as a stepping stone to qualify as a solicitor.	6. Currently not able to set up in business on your own account.

Table 2.1: Becoming a legal executive (as opposed to a solicitor): advantages and disadvantages

Case study

Tracey joined a law firm from secretarial college in the early 1990s, aged 18. After a little over a year as a legal secretary in the firm's litigation department, the firm could see Tracey had potential and started to give her greater responsibility drafting simple court applications and lists of documents, alongside her secretarial duties. After three years, she began working for one of the litigation partners, often accompanying him to meetings with clients, and her role developed into a combined PA/secretary/paralegal.

The recognition which Tracey received from her employers gave her confidence to apply for a place at college, to study for the legal executive exams two evenings per week, which she did over five years. Initially, she found combining a demanding job with her studies a challenge to manage; there never seemed to be time to do everything. Eventually, she found a routine which worked well for her – always ensuring she studied for one full day at weekends and at least an hour per day during the week – sometimes before work, sometimes during her lunch break (if she had time) or in the evening. She found the modules which had relevance to her day job, like Tort, Contract and Civil Litigation, more straightforward, as she could relate to them. However she found Land Law very difficult, but managed to scape through that exam on her second sit.

Now, twenty years on, as well as getting married and giving birth to two children in the interim, Tracey works as a personal injury lawyer for a firm which specialises in representing insurance companies. And, by the way, in the intervening time, she also qualified as a solicitor as well!

Recent developments: legal apprenticeships

The government, in partnership with the legal profession, intends to create 750 legal apprenticeships by 2015 and is committing £1m from the public purse to kick-start the process. Both law firms and the government have recognised that there is a need for some of the lawyers of tomorrow to have an alternative route to train as lawyers without going to university, and, of course, without accumulating a vast debt along the way.

At the time of publishing this title, a Level 2 intermediate apprenticeship in legal administration is available, but rather than covering the law itself, the qualification focuses more on the business and mechanics of a law firm. Level 3 and Level 4 apprenticeships in legal services are in the process of being developed as work and education training programmes.

It is hoped that the introduction of legal apprenticeships will be for the mutual benefit of firms and apprentices alike: firms will be able to develop and nurture talent in return for a more loyal, committed employee. Quite how legal apprenticeships will sit alongside CILEx qualifications remains to be seen. What is certain is that non-graduate and paralegal recruitment to law firms is going through a process of change. So, if you are seriously contemplating a non-graduate route into the legal profession, it is strongly recommended that you research the up-to-date position on the websites listed at the end of this chapter.

The road map to becoming a lawyer

The diagram below at Figure 2.1 shows the road map to becoming a lawyer in England and Wales. In the remainder of this book, you will explore each stage of the journey to the two most popular destinations: the solicitor and the barrister. You will observe that the career progression for solicitors and barristers overlaps at the undergraduate stage, but diverges when it comes to taking the relevant vocational examinations: ie once you have decided to become either a solicitor or a barrister.

Solicitor or barrister? When should I decide?

The simple answer is 'when you know'. In other words, don't make the decision until you feel ready and properly informed to reach that decision. Some law students have a clearer vision than others at a much earlier stage of their studies. The majority start their law degree with an open mind but do manage to come to a decision sooner rather than later, partly because the choice has an influence on the work experience opportunities they should be seeking. When non-law graduates start the Graduate Diploma in Law (GDL) which is the one-year graduate conversion course, there is significantly less lead-time before they are able to start their training contract or pupillage. So, if you are a non-law graduate, you should, ideally, have an idea before you start your GDL of whether you see yourself wearing a wig and gown as part of the day job, or maybe just part of your extra-curricular activities at weekends!

The largest law firms begin courting potential trainees during their first and second year at university, which is when you should be seriously considering:

- Whether you want to be a barrister or solicitor
- The practice area(s) in which you might wish to specialise; and
- The type of law firm or set where you may wish to end up.

Offers for training contracts are rarely made before the beginning of an undergraduate's final year at university, but in order to get yourself to the stage where you actually receive a job offer it's never too early to start getting experience and boosting your CV. The same applies if you want to be a barrister, although applications for pupillage are not generally invited from undergraduates.

What if I make the wrong decision?

A small minority of lawyers take one route, practice for a few years, and then re-qualify for 'the other side'. Don't worry, you won't feel like Henry VIII being excommunicated following his rejection of Catholicism. And you won't get the hate mail which Carlos Tevez received when he turned his back on the 'reds' in favour of the 'blues' of Manchester. Although you will have to re-qualify, you will be exempt from taking some of the LPC/BPTC assessments.

Whichever decision you take, it is always reversible. That said, you will want to try to get it right first time. So, the aim of the rest of this chapter is to give you some guidance to help you arrive at a reasoned, well-informed decision, and above all, the one which is right for you.

Top tip

It's never too early to get work experience in law firms and in barristers' chambers either informally or via more formal Vac Schemes (for large law firms) and mini-pupillages at barristers' chambers. For more details, see the later chapters. It boosts your CV by showing your interest in the law and may help to shape some of the important decisions you will need to make.

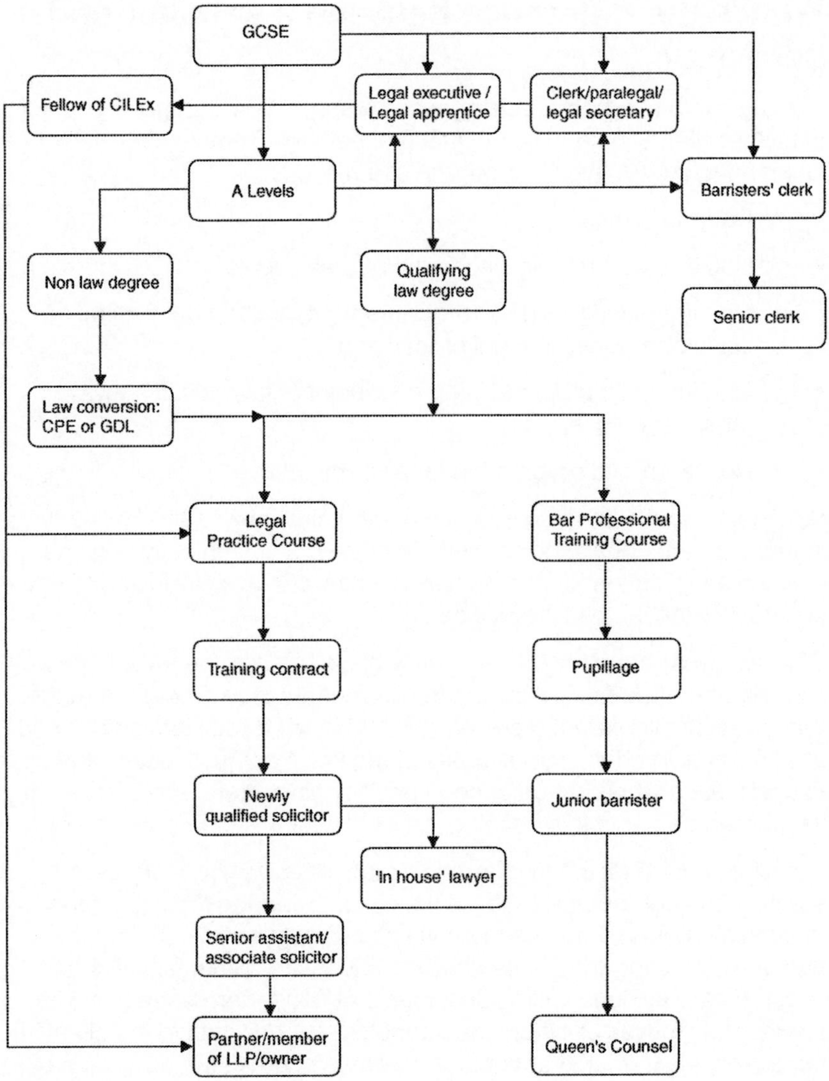

Figure 2.1: The road map to becoming a lawyer in England and Wales

What's the difference between a solicitor and a barrister?

The main role of a barrister is to act as a specialist advocate on behalf of his/her clients in court or tribunal proceedings. The working week of a junior barrister will, typically, consist of a mix of:

- Court hearings
- Conferences with solicitors and/or their clients
- Drafting pleadings (ie formal statements setting out a client's claim or defence in legal proceedings)
- Drafting written opinions (eg on a point of law or a litigant's prospects of success)
- Research and preparation for all of the above

Barristers choose to specialise in either criminal law or civil law early in their careers. Most who choose the latter route eventually begin to develop a reputation for certain types of cases (eg family law) and end up specialising in that type of work.

Whereas what barristers do on a daily basis tends to be a variation on a similar theme (albeit in relation to different practice areas) the range and diversity of different types of solicitors is vast: solicitors advise and assist clients in relation to all areas of the law – not just cases which go to court, but a whole range of non-contentious matters, some of which were listed earlier in this chapter.

In litigation matters, the first lawyer a client sees will normally be a solicitor. The solicitor will prepare the case, preparing the claim form, drafting the court pleadings (sometimes possibly with the help of a barrister), proofing witnesses, drafting witness statements, collating documentary evidence, filing documents at court, corresponding with the representatives of other side and regularly reporting to the client. If the case goes to trial, that solicitor may also conduct the advocacy, but usually that's where the barrister – the specialist trial lawyer – comes in. Even if counsel (ie a barrister) is instructed to conduct the advocacy, a solicitor or a representative of the law firm will usually attend court as well to support both counsel and the client. After the trial, unless there is the prospect of an appeal, any remaining matters relating to the case will be dealt with by the solicitor/law firm. So, whereas solicitors have a continuous relationship with the client, a barrister only tends to get involved at certain key points.

All solicitors have rights of audience (ie the right to represent clients) in the 'lower' courts, such as the magistrates' court, the county court and all tribunals. However, most solicitors will recommend that a specialist advocate represents their clients at important hearings, especially trials. However, solicitors and trainees will represent their clients more frequently at interim hearings which often relate to procedural issues in the litigation. An example of such a hearing is given in the 'Day in the life of a trainee solicitor at a small firm', which you will find later in this book.

A minority of litigation solicitors obtain a further qualification to represent clients as advocates in the higher courts, which are the Crown Court, the High Court, the Court of Appeal and the Supreme Court.

Solicitors who do not practise litigation rarely go anywhere near a court: their main place of work will usually be in the office, or perhaps, occasionally, visiting clients or counsel in chambers. Barristers will spend their working days in court or working from chambers or home.

	Solicitor in a law firm	Barrister in chambers
Personality	Suits all types, because of the variety of roles. Can be 'client-facing' or 'back office'.	Needs supreme self-confidence or at least excellent acting skills! First-class public speaker.
Team work/ working on your own	Usually works as part of a team, particularly in larger firms, although for large parts of the job you will be working on your own.	Must be comfortable to work on your own most of the time, but junior counsel may work in a supporting capacity assisting leading counsel in a large case.
Employed/ self-employed	Starts as an employee. Equity partners are self-employed. Salaried partners are employees.	Self-employed from the outset, although there are some opportunities to work at the employed bar (see later in the book).
Prospects	Very competitive to get a training contract.	Even more competitive to secure pupillage!
Research/ reading skills	Research plays a part, but can often be delegated to trainees or outsourced to counsel.	Excellent research skills and ability to absorb quickly the contents of lengthy documents essential.
Client contact	Ongoing relationship with clients from start to end of a matter.	Only meets clients at critical stages – at conferences and court.
Responsibility	Responsibility for your own files comes earlier at smaller firms. Trainees at larger firms don't tend to get their own files until after they qualify.	You are fully responsible for your own briefs, which will happen once you start the 'second six' of your pupillage.
Supervision	Law firms must supervise how trainees and recently-qualified solicitors conduct their client files on a risk-sensitive basis.	Although barristers recently called to the bar will usually be assigned a mentor in their set, there is no formal supervision.

	Solicitor in a law firm	Barrister in chambers
Financial security	Regular wage, no overheads. Salary normally rises year on year quite sharply in the first few years after qualification.	Can be infuriating if you have done the work and you're still waiting to be paid! Financially insecure at the start of your career. Overheads to pay as a tenant.
Hours	Working a 'regular' day – ie between 9.00 and 18.00 five days per week is possible, although many solicitors will work much longer hours including weekends.	Working hours are less predictable and will often involve working late into the evening preparing for hearings the following day. Working part of the weekend is common.
Career progression	Quicker rise to partner level in smaller firms. Larger firms may promote you to 'senior associate' after around three or so years, as a stepping-stone to a possible partnership. Promotion is largely dependent on the value of work you bill and the clients you bring to the firm.	Taking silk' – becoming a Queen's Counsel ('QC') or being appointed in a judicial capacity takes at least ten years. Recognition of excellence by your peers, senior colleagues and judges is essential to achieve these lofty heights.
Financial support during training	Large law firms may pay your LPC fees if you they offer you a training contract which you accept. Mid-size firms may offer an interest-free loan.	Some chambers sponsor students on the BPTC, although there is considerably more funding available for BPTC students from the Inns of Court.

Table 2.2: Solicitor v barrister: Key differences.

Exercise 2.1

Could you be a potential barrister? Test your reading, memory, listening and recall skills with the help of a friend:

- Ask your friend to write down detailed answers to the 10 questions which appear at the end of this Exercise. Encourage your friend to write expansively – ie not to write short sentences for every answer.
- Make a copy of your friend's answers – keeping one for yourself and handing back the other copy to your friend.
- Next, study your friend's answers to the 10 questions for a maximum of five minutes.
- While you read your friend's answers, instruct your friend to prepare to be asked those questions as if he/she was a witness, but ensure that your friend plans to deliberately change small parts of his/her previous answers on around 8 to 12 occasions. Your friend should ensure that at least one or more answers are unamended. Instruct your friend that some changes to the details should be major, but most of them should be relatively small, but significant nonetheless.
- Then role-play a barrister (you) interviewing a witness (your friend) by asking the same 10 questions. You are only permitted to have the questions in front of you (not your friend's written answers) – you can you can use this book if you like. You may not take any notes. Your friend should have their amended answers to hand, but to make the role-play authentic, your friend should try not to use the prepared answers as a script. Your task is to spot your friend's inconsistencies while you are asking the questions.
- Once you have finished asking the questions, you have five minutes (maximum) to write down the inconsistencies between your friend's written and oral answers to each question. Your only prompt will be the questions themselves and what you can remember from your friend's answers.
- Then, finally, compare what you have written with your friend's amended written answers.

Questions

1. Describe where you were and what it felt like when you first learned to ride a bicycle.
2. Describe your favourite bicycle from your childhood. What did it look like? (eg make, style, colour, wheel size, type of handlebars, bell, horn, basket, water bottle etc)
3. How old were you when you rode it?
4. Who gave the bicycle to you?
5. Where did you regularly ride your bicycle to and from?
6. How far was that journey?
7. What was the best thing about the bicycle?
8. Did you ever have an accident or fall off the bicycle? If so, describe the incident.
9. What happened to the bicycle after you stopped riding it?
10. How many bicycles did you own as a child?

You may find that you can spot what's new but not remember all of the detail which it has replaced. You will probably spot some, but not all of the discrepancies in the discrete information (eg some of the numbers). Now imagine how much information barristers have to retain from the volumes of documents they read, and how difficult it can be to recognise inconsistencies between those documents and a witness' evidence during a lengthy trial.

Chapter summary

At some stage you will need to answer the eternal question: 'do I want to be a solicitor or a barrister?' Make sure you invest sufficient time to research both wings of the legal profession. The skills you need to become a solicitor or a barrister overlap considerably. Although very high academic success, an outgoing personality and excellent reading and comprehension skills are present in most good solicitors, they are particularly important if you wish to become a barrister. It is hard enough to find a training contract these days, so unless you see yourself in the top 10% of your law degree or GDL cohort, you will find it even more difficult to make it as a barrister.

Key points

- Qualifying as a lawyer means qualifying as a solicitor, barrister or legal executive.
- You normally need a degree to become a solicitor or a barrister.
- There are more job opportunities for solicitors in private practice than barristers.
- Start getting experience of the legal profession now. It's never too early!

Useful resources

www.sra.org.uk

www.barstandardsboard.org.uk

www.cilex.org.uk

www.ibc.org.uk

www.legalhigherapprenticeships.com

References

SRA (2012), Regulated population statistics. [Online]
Available at: http://www.sra.org.uk/sra/how-we-work/reports/data/population-solicitors.page [Accessed December 2012]

The Bar Council (2012), Statistics. [Online]
Available at: http://www.barcouncil.org.uk/about-the-bar/facts-and-figures/statistics/ [Accessed December 2012]

CILEx (2012), Interesting Facts. [Online]
Available at: http://cilex.org.uk/media/facts_figures.aspx.

Chapter 3

Your secondary education: getting ready for the law

BPP LEARNING MEDIA

Introduction

This chapter discusses the issues you need to bear in mind when contemplating your secondary education choices, and in particular, the subjects you should study at:

- GCSE (or equivalent)
- A level (or equivalent)

We will also highlight some of the opportunities that are available to aspiring law students while they complete their secondary education.

GCSEs: what should I study?

It is recommended that your set of GCSEs includes **all** of the following:

- Maths
- English
- A language (classical or modern)
- A humanity (ie History or Geography, or both)
- Two (or more) sciences

These subjects make up the core of the English Baccalaureate ('Ebacc'), which is a performance indicator used in school league tables. The above combination of subjects should, wherever possible, be studied at GCSE by any student who harbours ambitions of becoming a lawyer. This is because a full set of Ebacc subjects offers maximum flexibility in terms of your A level choices, which, in turn, will mean you have a wider range of degrees open to you.

And while you're at it, you'll need to achieve high grades (generally, A*s, As and Bs) in the vast majority of your subjects to keep you at the front of the pack of aspiring potential lawyers.

You may think that good GCSE grades in Maths and science subjects are not that important for potential law students, but you would be wrong! The logical reasoning and organisation skills required to do well in Maths and the ability to make sense of complex scientific theories will stand you in good stead when you have to break down a complicated legal problem, understand it and then apply it to a set of facts.

Vocational/'non-academic' GCSE subjects

Many bright students are advised not to study any vocational or so-called 'non-academic' subjects at GCSE. There is no doubt that a full Ebacc GCSE profile is considered academically stronger than one which lacks a science, a humanity or language, at the expense of, say, Dance or Textiles. However, it should still be possible in most schools to study one or two vocational GCSEs without prejudicing your GCSE profile. For example, choosing GCSE Drama together with other GCSEs which fulfil the Ebacc criteria, should be absolutely fine if you are looking at law as a career option. Indeed, your acting training could be particularly useful in a courtroom if you need to persuade a judge or a jury, especially if you're not convinced of your client's case yourself!

Schools frequently encourage their brightest students to choose a complete 'academic' set of GCSEs – after all, it looks better for the school's results if their most able students select as many traditionally academic subjects as possible, particularly because those students will invariably pick up a shower of A*s and As. Just because it's good for the school, it doesn't make it good for you, so don't feel pressured into dropping a subject you have passion or talent for, like Music. Law firms and chambers are often impressed by a high level of achievement in Music, because it suggests you may have the self-discipline and dedication required to become a lawyer.

GCSEs are usually your first intense academic pressure-point, so choosing a subject which you think will provide some light relief, both during the regular timetable and examination periods, has its benefits. So, if you have a burning desire to study one of these subjects, then do so! Just make sure you strike a balance by choosing no more than two vocational subjects at GCSE.

You will need to attain a minimum grade C at GCSE (or equivalent) in Maths and English Language, and some universities require you to have attained at least a grade B in both subjects as well as a GCSE in a modern language. Universities normally publish their minimum GCSE criteria, especially for overseas students, which is usually based on equivalent qualifications in the European or International Baccalaureate. In addition, if English is not your first language, you may be required by a university to demonstrate your written and oral ability in English. For example, such students may be required to demonstrate their competence by sitting the university's own English Language test or one of the internationally recognised alternatives.

Advantages of choosing a 'less academic subject'	Disadvantages of choosing a 'less academic subject'
1. Enjoyment and can provide light relief from other subjects.	1. May give a 'non-academic' impression to universities and employers if you choose too many.
2. Expected high grade.	2. Some schools may put you under pressure to select more 'academic' subjects.
3. May allow more time for your other studies.	3. Choice of more than two of such subjects may harm your academic profile.
4. Shows you are an 'all-rounder'.	4. May put a little more pressure on you to achieve A or A* grades in your other GCSEs.
5. One or two choices should not adversely affect your academic profile if you still collect the full Ebacc 'set' of GCSEs with good grades.	5. Other students studying this GCSE may be less focused on achieving a good result, which may have an effect on how effectively the subject is delivered in the classroom at your school.

Table 3.1: Advantages and disadvantages of choosing a 'less academic' subject at GCSE

A levels: what should I study?

Most aspiring lawyers will choose to study four or five subjects at A/S level (ie in their 'lower sixth') and they then drop one of these subjects in their 'upper sixth', and will ultimately sit three or four full A Levels in their second year of sixth form.

The competition for places on law degree courses is intense, and, not surprisingly, your A level grades will be critical in whether, ultimately, you win that coveted place. So, the subjects you choose to study will require careful consideration. Any offer you receive to read law is likely to be made conditional on achieving high grades in three A level subjects, typically A*AA, AAA or AAB. However, because most students complete their UCAS form before sitting their A levels, universities will also scrutinise your GCSE performance and the grades your teachers expect you to achieve at A level.

The Russell Group's guidance on A levels

The Russell Group represents 24 leading universities in the United Kingdom. In its literature, it members are '*committed to maintaining the very best research, an outstanding teaching and learning experience and unrivalled links with business and the public sector* (Russell Group, 2012). A list of the members of the Russell Group is found in Table 3.2 below.

If you are considering applying to study on any degree course at a Russell Group university, you need to be aware that, generally, these 24 universities prefer to see students with three good A levels, at least two of which are a 'facilitating subject'. The facilitating subjects are:

- Maths and Further Maths
- English Literature
- History
- Geography
- Chemistry
- Physics
- Biology
- Any modern or classical language(s)

These subjects are considered to be the building blocks for undergraduate study because they equip students with the skills and/or knowledge which may be required to read a whole range of subjects at university. A levels in essay-based subjects, such as History and English Literature, are commonly chosen by prospective law undergraduates at Russell Group universities, because they demonstrate an ability to discuss, argue and research ideas. However, for law, the Russell Group also values other essay-based A levels like Economics, Politics and Religious Education, which all require some of the skills required to do well in History and English.

Choosing at least two of the Russell Group's facilitating subjects at A level will also keep more options open if you are still not sure what subject you wish to read at university. For more information, read the Russell Group's guide entitled *Informed Choices*, the details of which you will find at the end of this chapter.

University of Birmingham
University of Bristol
University of Cambridge
Cardiff University
Durham University
University of Edinburgh
University of Exeter
University of Glasgow
Imperial College London
Kings College London
University of Leeds
University of Liverpool
London School of Economics and Political Science
University of Manchester
Newcastle University
University of Nottingham
University of Oxford
Queen Mary University of London
Queen's University Belfast
University of Sheffield
University of Southampton
University College London
University of Warwick
University of York

Table 3.2: The Russell Group

Although some other universities may have a more flexible approach to A levels choices, many non-Russell Group universities have similar admissions policies to those highlighted above, so it is not recommended to depart from the Russell Group's guidance in your A level choices.

Should you choose a 'new' subject at A level?

Choosing a subject you have already studied	
Advantages	**Disadvantages**
1. You have an idea of what is involved when studying this subject.	1. Playing 'safe' by choosing subjects already studied at GCSE may suggest that you have a narrow focus.
2. A high grade at GCSE indicates a potential for (but no guarantee of) a high grade at A level.	2. You may feel like a 'change': some students need a fresh challenge to kick-start their A levels after five years of the 'same old' subjects.
3. Less risk of your not enjoying the subject at A level if you had a happy experience at GCSE.	3. You may perform better at A level in a new subject than one you have studied before.

Choosing a 'new' subject	
Advantages	**Disadvantages**
1. Shows you are interested in learning something new (which law is likely to be at university).	1. Not knowing whether you will enjoy the subject.
2. An opportunity to study a new subject in which you have an interest.	2. Not knowing whether you will have ability in the subject.
3. A chance to show you are an 'all-rounder'.	3. A levels in 1) General Studies and 2) Critical Thinking are not recognised by many institutions. Your top three grades should be in three other A level subjects.

Table 3.3: Advantages and disadvantages of choosing a 'new' subject at A level

Your choice of A levels should demonstrate a strong academic background, like your GCSEs. However, don't feel your A level choices should be strictly limited to the subjects you studied at GCSE. Most schools and colleges offer a number of additional subjects at A level which are not traditionally studied at GCSE, like Economics and Politics, which are commonly chosen by prospective law students. As well as choosing subjects you think you will score the highest grades in, choose ones which interest and challenge you.

Most A levels give you the opportunity of developing some of a lawyer's basic skills, such as analytical and critical thinking. Essay-based subjects give students the regular opportunity to develop their analytical skills in longer written assignments, which you will find useful if you are required to sit the LNAT (National Admissions Test for Law) as part of the university admissions procedure (see Chapter 4).

A level Law

Some schools and colleges offer A level Law, but choosing to study it does not confer any advantage on students when applying for places on law degree courses. All undergraduate law degrees assume students have had no previous legal education. So, the benefit of studying law at A level is, at best, marginal, especially since, from the outset, there is a sharp rise in the level and depth of understanding required in a law degree.

Arts and languages v social sciences v pure sciences

Most A levels will give you some help on your way to becoming a lawyer. A levels are, by definition, a more advanced level than GCSEs, and you will be expected to focus more on analysis than the facts. So, there is no single combination of A level subjects which universities and employers expect to see. Traditionally, law undergraduates lean more to the arts and languages than sciences at A level, but that is not as important as securing high grades. In fact, a science background (especially if you go on to a science degree and then take the GDL) can be a significant asset, particularly in areas of the law which require a more scientific mind, such as certain aspects of intellectual property (eg patents relating to complex machinery).

However, if you are a student contemplating studying three sciences at A level, you would certainly benefit from your fourth A level choice being an essay-based subject if you have not yet made up your mind whether you wish to read law or a science-based degree at university.

When selecting A levels, most students do not have a clear idea of what subject they will read at University in two years' time, let alone what career they see themselves going into. Some 16 year-old students get labelled 'scientists' because they have a record of high achievement in scientific subjects. Others have done better in the arts and languages, and of course, there are many very able students who have performed consistently well across all subjects.

Only you know what interests you most. Don't feel you have to study sciences at A level because you go to a school which has a science bias or English and History if you go to a school which has specialist arts funding or status. Like GCSEs, some schools have a vested interest in encouraging their most able students to select particular A levels because it reflects better in their statistics. Don't feel pressurised to choose a subject which you would rather not study. Whose A levels are they anyway? But, at the same time always listen to the advice you receive from your teachers and parents. Most practising lawyers will be able to recall instances where a client said 'thanks, but no thanks' to their wise counsel – only to see the client walk into a metaphorical car crash. You haven't been there before, but your teachers certainly have, and while you may not always wish to follow their advice, you need to be clear in your own mind why you choose to reject it. Bouncing these issues off friends and current law students will always give you a different perspective and is worth doing if you're finding it hard to commit to a decision one way or the other.

Schools offer much help and support in your choice of A levels. There will be timetable constraints on which A level combinations your school or college may permit you to choose, which you won't be able to do anything about apart from taking your A levels at a different institution. But that is a pretty drastic move and one not to entertain lightly.

Languages can, undoubtedly, be a long-term asset, but only significantly so if you 'keep them up' after your A levels. Despite Boris Johnson's unofficial one-man marketing campaign, A level Latin is not a subject which will give you any tangible advantage as a lawyer. However, there are a few legal principles which are known by their Latin names, such as '*habeus corpus*'

Definition – 'Habeus Corpus'

A writ used to require '*production of the body*' of a prisoner in court who may have been unlawfully detained, in order to test the legality of that prisoner's continued detention.

.

As a law student, you just learn these Latin phrases. You don't need to quote Virgil to make it as a lawyer. The ability to speak a modern language fluently is much more useful. Most large firms have offices in several cities overseas, where your ability to speak the local language will certainly be an asset in your training contract application.

Top tip

Think twice before selecting Latin ahead of a modern language at A level, as there aren't any training contracts in the Vatican!

Case study

Simon's school didn't have a sixth form, so he studied for his A levels at the local sixth form college. It took him most of the lower sixth to realise that his new teachers weren't going to spoon-feed him what he needed to get good grades in his A levels, which was a bit of a shock to the system, as he had coasted through his GCSEs by rote-learning.

When Simon asked his A level History teacher why he wasn't getting high grades for his course work, she advised him to 'read around the subject' more. Actually, he wasn't reading anything else other than the hand-outs and notes he took in class, which the teacher well knew. The teacher told Simon to read the text book he had been given at the start of the course, which had been sitting on his bookshelf at home gathering dust all year. Simon did open the book, but it wasn't easy. The text was more formal than he was used to, but he slowly became drawn to the richness of the language and the depth of the content, so much so that, ultimately, it gave him a whole new insight into what studying History was all about. Simon had, rather naively, thought that History was just a bunch of interesting facts, but discovered that, sometimes, versions of historical events are challenged and the reasons for them happening in the first place are hotly debated. Studying History at A level empowered Simon to become a truly independent learner, an approach which he followed in his other A levels and later studies. History also started to equip him with the skills and confidence he needed to process complex legal arguments in the reported cases, text books and journals he read during his law degree.

Opportunities to experience the law during GCSEs and A levels

Work experience

Many schools run work experience at the end of Year 10. This is an early opportunity to learn about the legal profession and boost your CV at the same time by starting to demonstrate you are seriously interested in pursuing a career in the law. It's not easy, though, trying to persuade a law firm to allow you to spend a week or two in their office. Most schools do not have direct links with law firms, so you may have to use any connections you have through your family or friends' parents, or try a more personal approach – either in writing or in person.

If you come from a 'disadvantaged background', you may be eligible to apply for work experience via PRIME. To qualify, you must satisfy all of the following:

- Attend a state (non fee-paying) school
- Be in school year 9 to 13
- Be entitled to free school meals (or have been so entitled in the past) or attend a school which has a significantly higher than average proportion of students who receive free school meals
- Be in the first generation of your family to attend university (should you get there!)

PRIME is a nationwide initiative by a number of leading law firms to provide at least 30 to 35 hours of work experience to school-age students who, according to PRIME's website, 'come from a less privileged background or don't have the right contacts to call on'. Financial assistance in the form of travel expenses and refreshments are provided as part of PRIME, which has a 'headline target for the wider profession [of] 2,500 places by 2015' (PRIME, 2011).

As well as providing work experience, participating firms will be committed to developing the '... key personal and business skills that are essential to entry in to the legal profession and wider business world (e.g. team working, communication, presentation/impact, negotiation, networking).' (PRIME, 2011).

If you are serious about exploring the possibility of becoming a lawyer and you satisfy PRIME's qualification criteria, you have little to lose by applying for a place now!

Having decided early in my education that I wanted to become a lawyer, I started applying for relevant work experience. After a couple of letters to local law firms and other organisations I landed my first placement. This was my first opportunity to see what 'legal people' do. I was placed with the legal team at the offices of my local authority, where the majority of the work was focused on land and planning law. During this placement I had the opportunity to draft both acknowledgements and response letters, conduct legal research and was introduced to the structure of the legal system and what role a local authority plays within it. I would recommend obtaining relevant work experience before starting a law degree. Be persistent in seeking such opportunities, even if this is just a spare afternoon observing a case in court, as this shows commitment, initiative and proactivity .

Alia Campbell, LPC Student

My legal work experience has given me context to my legal studies and has made me realise how much more methodical the law is in practice than in theory. Experiencing different legal working environments is extremely helpful for writing training contract applications because it has enabled me to prove important qualities, such my communication skills and attention to detail, by giving me the opportunity of referring to specific examples from my own personal experience.

Corina Demeter, LPC student

Visiting courts

Visiting your local magistrates' or crown court is a great experience for an aspiring lawyer. You'll tend to get longer, more lurid cases at the crown court, but if you want to see summary justice getting through long and varied lists of prosecutions, then try the magistrates' court.

Exercise 3.1

During the school holidays, wearing a smart set of clothes, attend the local magistrates' or crown court and observe the proceedings. Explain to the usher that you are a student interested in becoming a lawyer and ask which court (as there will usually be several in the same building) is hearing the most interesting case that day. If you get a chance, try to get talking to one of the advocates after the hearing or at the lunch adjournment. It's a bit like asking a stranger out for a date, because you don't know how they're going to react, but you could try the following 'chat-up line' (or one of your own):

- *Excuse me Mr/Ms [Name] – I'm [Name].*
- *I'm looking to study law in the near future.*
- *I found the proceedings this morning: interesting because [reason]/difficult to follow because [reason].*
- *Do you have a few minutes to answer a few questions? It won't take long ...*
- *You seem to be in a hurry: do you mind if I call you to discuss a few questions if you can't answer them now?*

You never know, striking up a conversation may make it easier to ask the same lawyer a similar question a day or two later if and when they come back to the same court. If you make a good impression, they may be prepared to allow you to shadow them for a few days in other courts or at their office or chambers (as long as your enthusiasm isn't misjudged for being a stalker!).

Whilst on a mini-pupillage as a non-law undergraduate, I attended the crown court to witness a high profile terrorism case, the 2006 transatlantic aircraft plot. The crown alleged that the accused planned to blow up several planes using liquid explosives hidden in soft drink bottles. Prior to this occasion, I had never visited a criminal court, and the gravity of the case and high level of security were somewhat intimating at first. However, I soon found the case to be a thrilling introduction to Criminal Law in practice.

The trial was reaching its conclusion and so I heard the summing up regarding one of the accused, a man who was subsequently acquitted. The defence revealed the man's background with meticulous detail, and I began to appreciate the volume of work which goes into a long trial. The logistical problems associated with such a trial also became apparent, as many jurors were struggling to attend court every day to hear all the evidence. I managed to follow the case by taking plenty of notes - a notebook is essential for any court visit - but it did require concentration.

This court visit sparked an interest in Criminal Law which remained with me throughout my GDL and LPC, and informed my decision to apply to firms with a criminal practice, one of which I look forward to joining as a trainee later this year. When I was at university, I felt there was a trend towards applying to the largest law firms and expressing a particular interest in their non-contentious departments, but I would urge anyone considering a career in the law to visit their local crown court and witness a criminal trial as part of the decision making process. It was an invaluable experience for me.

Maryam Masalha, LPC graduate

Conferences, taster days and open days

Most (if not all) law schools at universities hold sixth-form conferences, taster days or open days, mainly targeted at Year 12 students before they complete their UCAS forms. For example, Cambridge University has been running its three to four day residential conference for prospective law undergraduates since the 1970s, which combines an impressive array of speakers, with lectures, workshops, debates, moots and social events.

Cambridge's conference may be longer and more formal than most outreach events, and while the others may be branded slightly differently with variable programmes, in their own way, they are all extremely useful information-gathering exercises and experiences for potential law students. You may have the opportunity to:

- Find out what it's like to study law
- Discover what it's like to study at that particular university
- Meet similar-minded Year 12 and Year 13 students
- Meet current law undergraduates
- Have the opportunity of experiencing a law lecture

I attended several open day events, all of which provided me with similar information about the teaching, library facilities and how their alumni had succeeded, followed by a discussion with current students and teaching staff.

One of the universities which I was seriously considering only provided a site tour followed by an orthodox introduction by administrative staff and an opportunity to have a chat with current students about the course and university life. I felt there was no real snapshot of how I would study, which would have enabled me to picture being there.

In contrast, when it came to selecting my preferred university, one of the decisive factors was attending a demonstration lecture at the open day. I was greatly impressed by the lecturer, who was very charismatic and explained difficult concepts in a novel way, and included several intellectual jokes. Because I was given a real taste of the learning environment, I could clearly imagine studying there.

Mami Ueno

Pathways to Law

This is an ongoing programme which is jointly delivered by University College London ('UCL') and the London School of Economics. The programme runs for each cohort between September of Year 12 and April of Year 13 and UCL describes it as providing '*ongoing support to its members in Years 12 and 13, through a structured series of information, advice and guidance sessions'*. (UCL, 2012)

Pathways to Law is a programme open to students who are committed to a career in law and who satisfy all of the following criteria:

- They attend a state school.
- They have a mostly A*/A/B profile at GCSE.
- They are the first in their family (other than siblings) to attend higher education.

The programme aims to attract as many students as possible who satisfy the above criteria and:

- Reside within 50 miles of the relevant university
- Come from relatively disadvantaged backgrounds

There are 400 places available for 2012/13:

- 50 at Bristol University
- 50 at Leeds University
- 75 at the London School of Economics
- 50 at Manchester University
- 50 at Southampton University
- 50 at Warwick University
- 75 at University College London

If you meet the qualifying criteria, the experience you would gain from the programme (which can also include e-mentoring and a three to five day placement with a law firm) would be invaluable experience, even if you do not end up reading law at any of the participating universities.

Chapter summary

Choose your GCSE and A level subjects carefully. Getting high grades in traditionally academic subjects is generally more important than choosing arts subjects over social sciences or pure sciences. However, having at least one essay-based subject on the Russell Group's list of facilitating subjects is strongly recommended in any A level combination.

Key points

- At A level, an AAB profile (or better) in so-called 'academic' subjects is almost essential if you wish to read law at university.
- Start to build up your experience of the legal profession now

Useful resources

www.russellgroup.ac.uk/informed-choices.aspx

www.pathwaystolaw.org

www.primecommitment.org/home

www.judiciary.gov.uk/you-and-the-judiciary/going-to-court

References

The Russell Group (2012) [Online] Available at: http://www.russellgroup.ac.uk/ [Accessed December 2012]

Prime (2011) About. [Online] Available at: http://www.primecommitment.org/about [Accessed December 2012]

Prime (2011) The Commitment. [Online] Available at: http://www.primecommitment.org/the-commitment [Accessed December 2012]

Chapter 4

Applying to university

BPP LEARNING MEDIA

Introduction

For most of this chapter, we will assume that you intend to apply for a place on a qualifying law degree ('QLD') in England or Wales, rather than any other degree. However, it is important to note that you can study a non-law subject at degree level and still become a lawyer. Non-law graduates who want to become lawyers will need to complete a one-year graduate conversion course (if studying full-time) to reach the same stage as a law graduate – the completion of your academic stage of training. The one-year conversion course is known as the Graduate Diploma in Law ('GDL') (sometimes referred to as the Common Professional Examination or 'CPE') and is referred to in more detail in the next chapter.

Definition – Qualifying law degree ('QLD')

A QLD is a law degree which qualifies you to start the relevant vocational examinations. In other words, a QLD contains all the exempting subjects which the Solicitors Regulation Authority and the Bar Standards Board require you to pass before permitting you to commence the Legal Practice Course (to become a solicitor) or the Bar Professional Training Course (to become a barrister).

Not every law degree is a QLD. If you study for a law degree from a university outside England and Wales, you may still have to complete the GDL in full. However, a law degree from a university in Scotland, Northern Ireland or the Republic or Ireland, *may* give you a full or partial exemption from the GDL.

Top tip

If you intend studying for a law degree outside England and Wales, find out now whether that law degree is a QLD, or you may find your journey to become a lawyer is up to a year longer than you expected!

For the rest of this book, unless the contrary is shown, all further reference to 'law degree(s)' will mean QLD(s).

There are a variety of ways of studying for a law degree, the most common of which is to take the 'straight' LLB route. This is a single honours degree for which you exclusively study the law and law-related modules. However, joint honours degrees are also popular, such as Law and Accountancy, Law and Business, and Law and Politics. If you carefully select your modules on a joint honours degree, the degree can also amount to a QLD. Indeed, the provider often ensures that such degrees are capable of becoming QLDs by making the required exempting modules compulsory, or at least making them available to study as an option.

I chose to read Law and Business for my degree, as it gave me 'the best of both worlds', especially because I wasn't sure which field I wanted to go into and I didn't want to limit myself. It meant that I could combine my two interests, while still studying them independently.

I didn't realise it at the time of applying, but what has subsequently become apparent is that that my joint honours degree has given me greater breadth and an insight into the law from a perspective which most law students do not get to experience. The flexibility I had was enormous: I could pick and choose modules which really interested me from a long list of options.

However, as with all joint degrees, there is an element of trying to cope with two subjects simultaneously and being expected to attain the same level in both as those just studying the one subject. The first year is probably the hardest when everything is new, but you soon learn to adapt.

I have never regretted my degree choice and I think I will be a better lawyer for it.

Raashi Jain,
Law and Business graduate, LPC graduate

Top tip

Choosing a joint honours degree gives you exposure to more than one major area, which is useful if you wish to keep other options open. But be warned, some joint honours degrees may take an extra year to complete at undergraduate level (typically, four years instead of three), so at a job interview, be prepared for the question: 'Why didn't you study for a "pure" law degree?'

Where should I study for my law degree?

When you are faced with over 100 different institutions to choose between, and some are based in multiple locations, it can be a daunting prospect to whittle them down to the five you need to nominate on your UCAS form. So what's important? What should you take into account when nominating a particular law school?

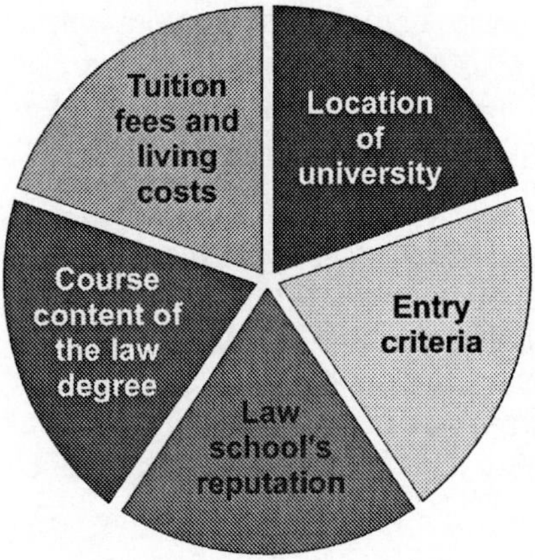

The weight you decide to give to each of these criteria will depend on your individual circumstances and preferences.

Figure 4.1: Choice of law school – factors to take into account

Tuition fees and living costs

Most full-time law degree courses at English and Welsh universities in the 2012/13 academic year are charging the maximum tuition fee of £9,000 per annum, for which a 100% tuition fee loan from the UK government is generally available to UK students and those from the EU. Part-time UK and EU students may borrow up to £6,750 per annum for tuition fees.

If you are from Wales and are studying for your first degree, you may also be entitled to a non-refundable new fee grant, as well as the tuition fee loan.

Some private universities and colleges charge tuition fees significantly below £9,000, partly because the maximum tuition loan available for students who study at such institutions is £6,000 and £4,500 for full-time and part-time students respectively.

Higher fees are generally payable by non-EU overseas students.

In addition to tuition fee loans, maintenance loans and maintenance grants are also available, the latter of which are strictly means-tested. Maintenance grants of any substance are only available to full-time students from UK families with combined incomes below £40,000 (which takes into account the income of parents and the student). The maximum maintenance grant for students starting a degree course in England in September 2013 is £3,354, which is for a student who comes from a family with a combined income of less than £25,000. The grant reduces significantly for each subsequent bracket of £5,000 of family income up to £40,000. The lowest annual maintenance grant of any substance is £540 for a student who comes from a family with an income of between £35,000 and £40,000. If you come from a family whose total income exceeds £40,000, no grants are available except a token £50 if family income is in the £40,000 to £42,611 bracket, which must cost more to administer than is ultimately paid to the student!

Given the cost of tuition fees and rising living costs, some providers are offering more intense law degree courses over two years, where the overall tuition fee is substantially less than a traditional three-year law degree course. So, if minimising student debt is a significant factor for you, consider a shorter degree, where you will work much more intensely, maybe at the expense of missing some of the 'student experience'. But with less debt!

Location of university

Traditionally, students have combined the opportunity of going to university with leaving home, at least during term time or until they've run out of clean clothes! Many, understandably, would prefer to do so if they, or more likely, their parents have the resources to cover the student's additional living costs. However, with tuition fees having risen sharply in 2012/13, more students are likely to choose to live at home in order to save accommodation costs, which means they select a more local university. Travel time and the cost of travel may also come into the equation in your choice of university, as well as your ability to work part-time in the area while you are a student.

Entry criteria

A significant proportion of law degrees require at least three A grades (or equivalent) at A level with a minimum Grade C at GCSE in English and Maths. A number of leading universities also require applicants to sit the National Admissions Test for Law (see later on in this chapter). Others have their own dedicated test, which they require students to take as part of the application process.

Reputation of the law school

There are various league tables, such as those published by the *Guardian* and the *Times*. It may be helpful to your future career prospects to attend one of the top 50 institutions listed in these league tables, because employers do consider some universities to be 'better' than others.

Course content of law degree

Law students are required to study a number of core subjects for their law degrees to be a QLD:

- Law of Torts
- Contract Law
- Public/constitutional Law
- Criminal Law
- Land Law
- EU Law
- Equity and Trusts

You will also be able to choose a number of optional modules, mainly during the last two years of a typical three-year law degree. There are a huge number of optional law modules, which vary considerably between universities. Most (but not all) universities give students the opportunity of studying the following popular modules:

- Child Law
- Commercial Law
- Company Law
- Employment Law
- Evidence
- Family Law
- Human Rights
- International Law
- Medicine and the Law

However, there are many other modules, some of which you can only study at a handful of institutions, like Roman Law or 'Women and the Law'. Take time to research the full range of subjects which are on offer.

You won't select your elective options until you have completed an undergraduate term or two, by which time you may have a better idea of what options are available and desirable from your point of view – not least from talking to your tutors and other students who are further progressed in their studies. If you have a burning desire to study a particular module at degree level, make sure it is offered by the universities that you nominate on your UCAS form. Even if it isn't, there is always the option of studying that subject as a postgraduate at Masters' level, as part of an LLM, should you wish to extend your academic learning after your degree.

Top tip

Inclusion of a module in a university prospectus merely indicates that such subject has been taught recently at the relevant university. Universities rarely guarantee all modules will run in any future academic year, because their timetabling is dependent on staff availability, student demand and law school policy. Consequently, it is normally not recommended for your choice of university to be swayed exclusively by the possible provision of a single elective module.

Nevertheless, you should still familiarise yourself with the options which are available at the time of your UCAS application, as the chances are that most of them are still likely to be offered when the time comes later in your studies.

Comparing law degrees – league tables

So who is best?

To a certain extent, there is some independent, objective help at hand, in the form of the various university league tables, which are published each year (details of which you will find in the website links listed at the end of this chapter). Not only are universities compared, so are their respective law schools.

Like school league tables, the detail and the data in university league tables is not universally accepted. Most (but not all) universities get an overall rating for their law degrees, but since the compilers of the tables use different criteria to rank the courses, their results are rarely consistent. So, don't feel you're wasting your time and your money in applying to a university which is outside the 'top 10' in any table.

Having said that, the Russell Group universities and those other universities which consistently make the top half of each table don't get there by chance, and they do tend to be the institutions which most chambers and many law firms (particularly the largest ones) prefer to see on the CVs of students applying for pupillage and training contracts. Although, in theory, an upper second-class degree in law should have equal value wherever it is gained from, unfortunately, that view is not always held by employers. But don't think your career is over before it starts if you don't get a place at a so-called 'top' or 'leading' university. It isn't, but you must be looking to achieve at least an upper second-class degree to give yourself a reasonable chance of developing your career in the way you may have envisaged.

It is important for you to note that the university league tables for law degrees have not, historically, included the two heavyweight market leaders of postgraduate legal education – the University of Law (formerly the College of Law) and BPP University College. These two institutions train more solicitors and barristers than all other institutions in England and Wales put together. Since obtaining degree-awarding powers in 2006 and 2007 respectively, both 'the College' (as it was known) and BPP have invested significantly in the undergraduate law degree market. BPP has been so successful in recent years that it now teaches more LLB students at multiple sites across England than any other LLB provider in England and Wales, except for the Open University. When it comes to the University of Law and BPP, it is clear that prospective law students are attracted by:

- The reputation for excellence which both institutions have built up and consistently delivered in their other legal programmes – especially the LPC and the BPTC, which most LLB graduates move onto.
- Unrivalled (apart from against each other) connections with leading law firms who practise in England and Wales; a significant majority of top UK and several top American law firms send their UK trainees to either the University of Law or BPP.
- Cheaper undergraduate tuition fees compared to most three-year degree courses run by more traditional universities.
- Guaranteed places, sometimes at a discount, on a BPTC or LPC course at the same institution.
- Multiple locations – unlike most traditional universities, they are not just based in one city.
- Continuity from law degrees to the LPC or BPTC.

There is no doubt that the landscape for the provision of undergraduate legal education has changed in recent years with these two powerhouses looking to take an increasing share of the undergraduate law degree market. For future university law school league tables to have any credibility, they will need to feature the University of Law and BPP University College, and, in turn, you should be considering what they have to offer you as a law student as well as the more traditional universities.

So, other than league tables, how do you rule out 95% of law degree providers? Try Exercise 4.1.

Exercise 4.1 – choosing your law degree

1. Print off a list of law degree providers in England and Wales from the UCAS website.
2. Cross out the names of those you feel can rule out absolutely, for whatever reason: your decisions may be based on location, entry criteria, reputation, or a combination of all three, or something else. Hopefully, you can rule out at least half of them at this stage.
3. With the ones you have left, research the institutions in much more detail, by, for example, reading their websites, their prospectus and the information on the UCAS website. You should slowly be able to develop a 'yes', 'no' or 'maybe' approach and whittle them down to around 10 to 20 institutions.
4. Make a note of when the relevant open days, fairs or conferences are for each law faculty and try to attend at least four or five of them. Ideally, try to visit most (if not all) of what you think will be your final five UCAS choices.

Applying to UCAS

The Universities and Colleges Admissions Service ('UCAS') is the organisation which processes applications for places on degree courses, including almost all law degrees in England and Wales.

You will need to be thinking about and researching your choice of course and university options as soon as you start your A levels, if you haven't started already.

Applications for places on degree courses at Oxford and Cambridge need to be made a year in advance by mid-October of your upper sixth. Apart from a handful of art and design courses, all other degree applications need to be lodged with UCAS by mid-January for courses starting in the following September/October. You can apply to up to five universities for a place on one of their courses.

Figure 4.2 shows some of the key dates in the UCAS timeline for 2012-13. There are other significant dates, but this snapshot shows that if you applied before 15 January 2013, you ought to have received offers (or rejections) from all your nominated universities by 31 March 2013, and if so, you had until 8 May 2013 to accept any offer. These dates are a guide as to the various timescales, but they will vary year on year and so you will need to research and diarise the key dates which apply at the time of your UCAS application

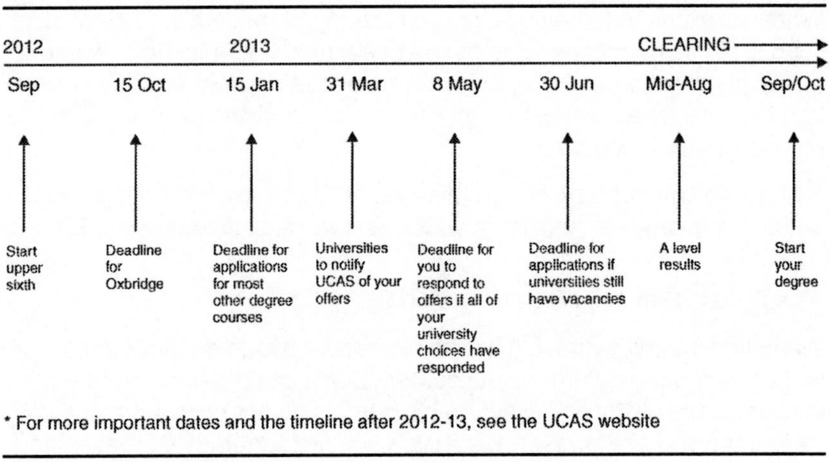

Figure 4.2: UCAS application main timeline: 2012-13

If universities still have vacancies after having considered the first round of applications (ie the ones received by 15 January), they will consider later applications up to 30 June. Any applications received by UCAS after 30 June go into 'clearing' which lasts until the end of September when universities try to fill their remaining places. That is when students who didn't get an offer first time round or if they don't receive the grades they required for a place on one course, try to find a place on another.

Top tip

These deadlines are strict, so make sure you leave enough time to complete and submit your application to UCAS, including time to sort out your references.

So, how do you distinguish yourself from other applicants chasing the same place on the same law degree? Prove you're bright? Of course! But, there aren't many prospective law students who don't have at least a few A grades at GCSE and a sprinkling of A*s. Indeed, there will be many who treat their only 'plain' A as a disappointment.

So do you have to demonstrate that you're 'interested' in the law and how the legal system works? Yes, absolutely! But every potential law student should hold such an interest or at least a curiosity. So do you need to show how that you're 'motivated', 'enthusiastic', a 'hard worker' and 'focused'? Again, what potential law student isn't all these things?

When you're used to being at or near the top of most of your classes at school, it's easy to get a false sense of security. You may have worked terrifically hard to get there, or it may be something which you've never had to break sweat for. Either way, you have no divine right to a place on a law degree course.

So how do you get a place? In this part of Chapter 4, we will give you some tips in order to maximise your chances of succeeding in this goal.

Your UCAS personal statement

When you submit your UCAS form, you may have to do something you haven't done before – sell yourself! Some people don't need any excuse to 'big up' their achievements, and if you are one of them, just make sure you are measured and you don't exaggerate. Or maybe you are aware which of your personal achievements would be of interest to universities, but perhaps you feel uncomfortable 'bragging' about them. If that is you, start getting used to discussing your achievements or you may appear to lack confidence in an interview situation. There is a fine line between modesty and shyness, which some people take longer to find than others. At this stage try to recognise how you project yourself to the outside world and/or get someone to give you their honest opinion.

Or maybe you think you haven't achieved anything of note worth telling anyone. Is that you? If so, you must be the only bright student who hasn't achieved or experienced something else in your life apart from academic success. The reality is you are likely to have achieved at least one the following:

- A position of responsibility at school, home, or in the community
- Shown leadership skills (eg youth leader) or management skills (eg been responsible for delivering a project, with or without other persons)
- Performed music or drama (at any level)
- Represented your school at sport or a non-sporting event (eg debating)
- Attended clubs in or outside school
- Won awards (in or out of school)
- Met an inspirational figure
- Had a life-changing experience which has shaped you into the person you are today

Selling yourself starts with your UCAS personal statement, because as well as selecting specific courses at up to five different universities on your UCAS form, you are required to complete a statement in support of your application, in no more than 4,000 characters (including spaces) or 47 lines – whichever comes first.

The UCAS website provides much general guidance and there is plenty more help (and hindrance) just a few clicks away all over the internet. There are numerous examples of personal statements accompanying applications to law degree courses on the internet ranging from excellent to the incredibly poor. If you feel you have to check them out, learn from the good ones and make a mental note of not replicating the mistakes in the poorer ones. But most importantly, don't use any of the apparently fabulous examples you may read online as a template for your own personal statement.

Top tip

There is incredibly sophisticated software which universities use to check for plagiarism in applicants' personal statements. Similar software is also used to check for plagiarism in degree level and postgraduate work, like dissertations. Don't think changing a few words around, adding a synonym or two or extra adjectives will throw the software off the scent. It won't. Principle 2 of the SRA Code of Conduct 2011 requires solicitors to act with integrity, so perhaps it's not the brightest of moves to cut and paste someone else's work into your UCAS form! You don't want your legal career to be curtailed before it's even got off the ground!

The clue is in the word *'personal'*! It's a statement about you, and no one else. The mistake many students make is to write what they expect universities want to read. The moment you do that, you will end up writing something which looks like hundreds of other statements – which end up in the pile of rejected applications.

Remember, your life experience is unique, so explain what makes you stand out compared to your rival applicants. Imagine you're on the Apprentice and you are taking a new product (ie you) 'to market': what is your USP (unique selling point)? Your academic achievements will be covered elsewhere in the form, and in any case, they only put you on the starting line with other able candidates. You need to dig deeper. What follows is a non-exclusive list of questions you may wish to address. The limited space available on the UCAS form will mean you can't deal with all of them, but your personal statement should deal with the questions below which resonate with you more than the others.

Suggestions for your UCAS personal statement

- What motivates you to want to study law? Is it a life-changing experience you have had? An inspirational person in your life? Someone or something you have read about? Or is there an issue you feel particularly passionate about?
- Which areas of the law interest you in particular? Why are they of interest to you?
- What skills do you have (eg a foreign language)? How might you use these skills as a practising lawyer?
- What experience of the law do you have? (It's probably best that you do not refer to the time you were breathalysed, even if you were under the limit!)
- What skills do you wish to acquire by studying law?
- Have you achieved anything relatively unusual which will make you stand out against most other candidates? (eg have you won an award, or been head boy or head girl at school?) What did you learn from your achievement?
- How may you use your legal education in the future?
- What do you do/have you done outside school which may be of interest to your university? How might these interests or achievements help you in your study of the law?

Your statement must demonstrate your motivation, commitment and enthusiasm for studying law. You can start preparing for this from Year 10 by making links with the legal profession (see Chapter 3) or getting experience of the law in action by visiting courts or observing lawyers in practice – either at firms of solicitors, barristers' chambers, Citizens Advice Bureaux, law centres or legal advice centres.

Your UCAS personal statement – what NOT to do

In order to get you in the right frame of mind to draft your personal statement, attempt Exercise 4.2. This is a fictitious **badly drafted** personal statement in support of a UCAS application for a place on a law degree course. Not only is this exercise useful to learn from before you prepare your own personal statement, it also tests the analytical and deductive skills which were mentioned in Chapter 1. Identify and explain as many issues as you can with the following personal statement. What makes the statement a poor one?

Exercise 4.2 – a badly drafted UCAS personal statement

Like Martin Luther-King Junior, 'I have a dream!' My dream is to become a lawyer. I have always wanted to be a lawyer since I was a kid. I've read loads about the law and think I have a lot to offer. I'm intelligent (I have 2 A*s, 5 As and 2 Bs at GCSE) and I'm expected to get an A and two Bs in my A levels and I know I'll be interested in the law. Who wouldn't? It's fascinating!

My Mum has a law degree and says that I'll be a 'natural' as I am very passionate when arguing a point, invariably coming out on top, which I have often been at my school's debating society.

I have done voluntary work from time to time which proves I have a social conscience, although I had to stop when I started my upper sixth to concentrate on my A levels.

I have had the opportunity of gaining a couple of days' work experience in my mother's law firm. Photocopying and taking notes in meetings is only the start, but it was invaluable experience. I also went on a school trip to watch a case in the Crown Court. Having had that experience, although it was interesting, I don't see myself as a barrister. Dealing with criminals 'day in, day out', is not what I want to do. I could never defend someone who I think is guilty. Who could?

Lawyers are hard workers and so am I. I am ambitious and hope to become the senior partner at a large firm in the City specialising in equity finance. I have an inner drive which is lacking in most of my friends, which explains why they will never earn a six figure salary before me.

If you were to ask me the one event which has led me to decide to become a lawyer, it has to be the abuse of the privacy of the individual by big organisations like the News of the World, because I took great pleasure in the inevitable demise of such a disreputable publication, what they did was nothing short of scandalous and the grilling Murdochs senior and junior got from the MPs was well-deserved since no one deserves to get away with the intrusion into people's lives even if they are some of the richest people in the world, so, I will certainly want to study human rights as one of my options during my law degree as it is something I am intensely passionate about.

I'm particularly interested in choosing to study subjects like contract law because I want to deal with commercial contracts when I qualify as a lawyer. I regularly read the Sunday Times, Sunday Telegraph, the Observer and most quality newspapers. I particularly enjoy reading the law reports and can't wait until a case I'm involved in gets reported. The cases illustrate how the law works in practice and how the whole outcome of a case can turn on something so small. I don't always agree with the decisions I read about but like politics, the law is a broad church, and there is room for more than one point of view.

Their are many other reasons which motivate me to wanting to study law, so if you like what you see, please interview me because I have impressive presentation skills.

UCAS personal statement – commentary on Exercise 4.2

Like Martin Luther-King Junior, 'I have a dream!'[1] My dream is to become a lawyer[2]. I have always wanted to be a lawyer since I was a kid[3]. I've read loads about the law[4] and think I have a lot to offer[5]. I'm intelligent (I have 2 A*s, 5 As and 2 Bs at GCSE) and I'm expected to get an A and two Bs in my A levels[6] and I know I'll be interested in the law[7]. Who wouldn't?[8] It's fascinating![9]

---

1 Using a quote at the start of your statement is risky, particularly if the connection is gratuitous (as it is here).

2 Too clichéd! An admissions departments could be put off this statement already. If Martin Luther King Junior inspires you so much you want to talk about him in your personal statement, maybe you should be talking about the civil rights movement in 1960s America and linking it with something more recent like the riots in the UK in the summer of 2011.

3 '... since I was a kid' is a little too casual. Try to use less colloquial language.

4 This statement is vacuous unless it is supported. What have you read? What did it teach you?

5 Like what? This point is not supported by any evidence. It almost smacks of desperation to impress.

6 Don't repeat your qualifications in your personal statement. We've read the other parts of your UCAS form!

7 Why? Don't just make a significant statement like that without explaining why the law interests you.

8 Quite a lot of people actually!

9 Of course it is! But the reader isn't going to believe you mean this unless you explain why. Don't just say what you think the admissions department wants to read!

My Mum[10] has a law degree and says that I'll be a 'natural'[11] as I am very passionate when arguing a point, invariably coming out on top[12], which I have often been at my school's debating society[13].

I have done voluntary work from time to time[14] which proves I have a social conscience[15], although I had to stop when I started my upper sixth to concentrate on my A levels.[16]

I have had the opportunity of gaining a couple of days' work experience in my mother's law firm[17]. Photocopying and taking notes in meetings is only the start, but it was invaluable experience[18]. I also went on a school trip to watch a case in the Crown Court. Having had that experience, although it was interesting[19], I don't see myself as a barrister[20]. Dealing with criminals 'day in, day out', is not what I want to do[21]. I could never defend someone who I think is guilty. Who could?[22]

---

10 'Mother' is more formal and better than 'Mum' on your UCAS form.

11 How does she know? What do you mean by this? If you have genuine skills which you wish to highlight, explain them! But if you think you're really no different than most other applicants, don't bother talking about it!

12 A little too big-headed – sounds like a nightmare of a student to teach!

13 OK – something relevant at last: you like debating, but you don't explain what it is about debating which you enjoy – other than winning. Give an example of where you won a debate and explain, with reference to how you structured your argument, and why you believe you were successful in persuading the audience to agree with your point of view.

14 Delete 'from time to time' – it doesn't add much and saves you a few words on the word count.

15 Does it prove a social conscience? Or is it evidence that you did some voluntary work just to 'tick the box' so you could refer to it in your statement? You don't even say what you did and what you learned from it.

16 You didn't have to say this. Concentrate on the positives, rather than the negatives.

17 Only a couple of days? If it's your mother's firm, why didn't you spend at least a week there? It shows a lack of commitment on your part or a lack of trust from your mother! What did you learn from your experience?

18 What did you learn about being a solicitor or the law from your work experience?

19 How? Did you really find it interesting? You don't explain why.

20 Why not? It's a little premature to completely rule out that option based on one day in court, particularly for someone who is a self-proclaimed excellent public speaker!

21 This is a mistake. You may have explained why you don't want to be a barrister who specialises in criminal law. But what about being a barrister who specialises in civil law?

22 Plenty of people, actually. As long as you do not know the defendant is guilty (as opposed to merely thinking he is likely to be guilty) barristers will be normally be obliged defend someone who pleads 'not guilty'.

Lawyers are hard workers[23] and so am I[24]. I am ambitious and hope to become the senior partner at a large firm in the City[25] specialising in equity finance[26]. I have an inner drive which is lacking in most of my friends, which explains why they will never earn a six figure salary before me.[27]

[28]If you were to ask me the one event which has led me to decide to become a lawyer, it has to be the abuse of the privacy of the individual by big organisations like the News of the World, because I took great pleasure in the inevitable demise of such a disreputable publication. What they did was nothing short of scandalous and the grilling Murdochs senior and junior got from the MPs was well-deserved since no one deserves to get away with the intrusion into people's lives even if they are two of the richest people in the world, so, I will certainly want to study human rights[29] as one of my options during my law degree as it is something I am intensely passionate about.[30]

I'm particularly interested in choosing to study subjects like contract law[31] because I want to deal with commercial contracts[32] when I qualify as a lawyer. I regularly read the Sunday Times, Sunday Telegraph, the Observer and most quality newspapers[33]. I particularly enjoy reading the law reports and can't wait until a case I'm involved in gets reported. The cases illustrate how the law works in practice and how the whole

---

23 Tell the reader something they don't know.

24 That's all well and good, but if it's so important to demonstrate dedication and commitment, do so with reference to a project outside your school work.

25 Even if you harbour this ambition, it rarely pays to express it in your statement, unless, perhaps you know or have shadowed someone who holds such a position. An interview would expose you to know very little about what such a role involves.

26 Why? This is a highly complicated area of the law, which you cannot possibly 'know' you want to specialise in until you have studied the subject and had some practical experience.

27 OK – you're motivated by the money you think you can make, rather than the law itself. No thanks!

28 This is one long rambling sentence which should have been broken down into several shorter ones.

29 A mistake again! Human Rights law is a much broader branch of the law than the law of privacy, although the right to privacy is arguably a human right. Make sure your technical references are correct!

30 What was the relevance of this paragraph to the application? It shows you have a view on an important issue, but what you haven't done at all is to link this to your application to study law or your possible career as a lawyer.

31 Another mistake. In any QLD, you won't choose to study the law of contract, because it is a compulsory subject in all QLDs.

32 Didn't you just say you wanted to specialise in equity finance? Make your mind up, or, better still, don't pretend you have a vision as to where you see your career going, when you don't really have one – that's perfectly normal at this stage.

33 That many newspapers? An exaggeration at best, if not an outright lie. Or perhaps you want to be a journalist?

outcome of a case can turn on something so small.[34] I don't always agree with the decisions I read about but like politics, the law is a broad church, and there is room for more than one point of view.[35]

Their[36] are many other reasons which motivate me to wanting to study law, so if you like what you see, please interview me because I have impressive presentation skills.[37]

Top tip

- Lawyers are drilled from an early stage when writing any email, letter or document to assume one day the document may come before the court. In other words, don't write anything that you won't feel comfortable defending or explaining under stiff cross-examination! The same applies to your personal statement: treat anything you write as something that you are prepared to be questioned on during an admissions interview.
- If you quote from or refer to any text, such as a law report, make sure you have read the whole piece. And don't exaggerate or lie about your achievements. Untruths and half-truths are likely to be exposed and blow your chances of a highly coveted place, which up to that point you may have been on target to achieve.

National Admissions Test for Law ('LNAT')

You will be required to sit the LNAT if you apply to read law at any of the following English universities ('**LNAT participating universities**'):

- Birmingham
- Bristol
- Durham
- Kings College, London
- Nottingham
- Oxford
- University College London

Why do these universities use the LNAT?

34 This point does not work without an example, but make sure you have really grasped the issues or your ignorance is likely to be exposed at interview (if it isn't already).

35 Too glib and arrogant. It's more likely that you didn't really understand the main reasons for the court's decision.

36 Proof-read everything and get someone else to check it too. Spell-check won't pick up all errors like the wrong 'there'.

37 It is extremely unlikely that anyone would want to interview such an applicant whose application lacks substance, motivation and genuine enthusiasm for the law!

The LNAT was designed as a way of assessing a candidate's aptitude to study law. Those who run the LNAT say their test is used by participating university admissions departments:

'... alongside standard methods of selection such as A level (or their global equivalent) results, university applications, and admissions interviews, to give a more accurate and rounded impression of the student's abilities.'

Previous academic achievement (particularly in areas which have little to do with the skills needed to be a good lawyer) is no longer considered the only way in which to assess a student's suitability. Consequently, the LNAT has been designed to test the skills you will need to succeed in your legal education.

LNAT participating universities do not all use LNAT in the same way.

'The use of LNAT essays varies and is dependent on each participating university's admissions policy. Some universities may use it, for example, as the basis for interview questions. Others may compare it with the personal statement and school/college report on UCAS forms, or use it as a means of distinguishing between borderline candidates.'

(LNAT website, 2012)

Top tip

If you do not intend to apply to any of the LNAT universities to read law, it is unlikely that you will need to take the LNAT because non-LNAT participating universities do not have access to any LNAT information. However, please do double-check the up to date position with LNAT and the universities you are considering applying to at the time you submit your UCAS application, because law faculty admissions departments do review their admissions policies from time to time.

What does the LNAT assess you on?

The LNAT does not require you to have any legal knowledge, nor is it testing you for any such knowledge. Instead, you will be assessed on various aspects of your verbal reasoning skills.

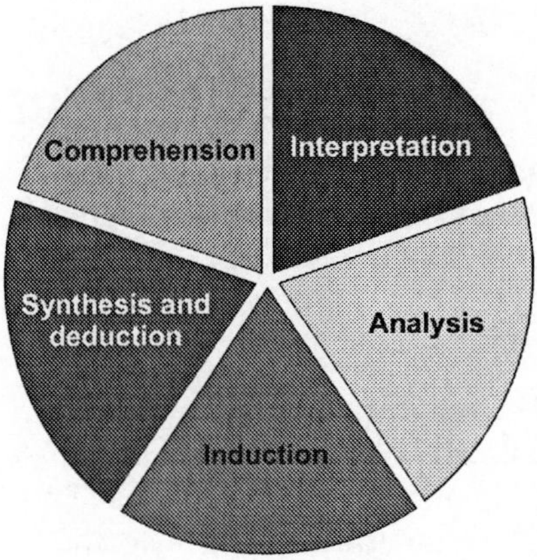

Interpretation: the intended (and sometimes unintended) meaning of a word, phrase or passage.

Analysis: the study of separate parts of the text: how and why they make up the whole.

Induction: logical reasoning from the facts.

Synthesis and deduction: the combination of separate points to form a conclusion.

Comprehension: understanding of the text.

Figure 4.3: Skills tested in the LNAT

What is the structure of the LNAT?

- Part A: (1 hour 35 mins) – 42 multiple choice questions ('MCQs')
- Part B: (40 mins) – an essay

The MCQs in 2011-12 were based on 12 argumentative passages, three or four of them relating to each passage. Students were required to select the correct answer from five options for each MCQ. The passages came from a variety of sources, such as literature or newspaper articles. The MCQs, which were equally weighted, were electronically marked out of 42. This MCQ mark is your LNAT score.

For the essay, you will be required to answer one of three questions. You will be required to write 500 to 600 words, usually on a contentious subject. When writing the essay, LNAT participating universities are generally looking for:

- Structure:
  - A clear introduction
  - A middle section where the main issues are discussed; and
  - A clear conclusion
- Balance between competing points of view – not a one-sided argument
- Clarity of expression – making yourself understood; and
- Good spelling, grammar and punctuation

What happens after I sit the LNAT?

Your LNAT score will be supplied to LNAT participating universities together with your essay, which will not be marked. In 2012, candidates were separately emailed their LNAT scores at two points in the year: in early February 2012 for those who sat before 15 January 2012, and for later sitters who sat before 30 June 2012, in early July 2012.

How can I prepare for the LNAT?

Although you cannot revise for it, any student who is serious about maximising their chances of getting onto a law degree course at an LNAT participating university, will need to prepare fully for the test. This preparation should not only involve getting familiar with the style and format of the test from the LNAT website, you should also regularly read the editorials of quality newspapers because the text you may be required to read and the essays you will be required to write should follow a similar style.

> *Reading a quality daily newspaper will help you to be aware of the world around you. The LNAT essay topics will not be specifically about current affairs, and you will not be judged by what facts you know. But knowing how the world ticks,. in general terms, will help you to write intelligently about a host of different topics.*
>
> LNAT website, 2012

Exercise 4.3

Read a quality newspaper editorial and:

- Identify the main issue(s) being discussed.
- Analyse what facts and assumptions the editorial is based on.

Then, write a 500 to 600-word essay taking a different point of view (even if it is not one you hold personally!), explaining what facts and assumptions you base your counter-argument on. Alternatively, practise for the essay by attempting some of the following questions, which are examples given on the LNAT website:

- – Make the best case you can for public funding of the arts.
- – Does it matter if some animal and plant species die out?
- – What is 'political correctness' and why does it matter?

How many students sit the LNAT?

Over 7,000 students sat the LNAT in 2010-11.

Where do I sit?

You can sit the LNAT in any one of LNAT's 150 test centres in the UK or at any one of the 500 test centres overseas. You cannot sit the test at your school or college.

When do I sit?

Between 1 September and 30 June in the UCAS year in which you are applying. Each LNAT participating university has its own deadline to sit the LNAT (which you should check separately on the relevant university's website). Most will be at or around the deadline for UCAS applications, which is in the middle of January each year for UK/EU nationals and 30 June for non-EU nationals.

How many times can you sit?

You are only permitted to sit the LNAT once in each application round (ie once per academic year) and you cannot carry forward your result from one year to the next – you would have to sit the LNAT again.

How much does the test cost?

In 2012-13, the fee was £50 if you sat in the UK and £70 for those sitting abroad. There are some bursaries available.

Who is responsible for registering me with LNAT and booking my test?

You are! But before you do, check what help (if any) your school or college may provide.

Top tip

Think twice before hiring a private tutor in an attempt to boost your LNAT score. While private tutors can make a significant difference to your GCSE or A level grades, that is because they (and you) know what sort of questions you will be asked. Paying someone to prepare you for the LNAT is not likely to make a significant difference because you will be tested more on the way you think than what you know. At best, a private tutor may help you to structure your thoughts and answers, but the significance of their help is likely to be marginal. The money would be better spent on hiring a suitable private tutor to boost your A level grades.

Chapter summary

When selecting the five choices for your UCAS form, thoroughly research each university and the course online and/or read the prospectus and attend their open days. Make sure your application stands out, by ensuring your personal statement reflects your unique characteristics and your motivation and commitment for studying the law.

Key points

- Most (but not all) law degrees in England and Wales will charge UK and EU students £9,000 per annum in tuition fees.
- Diarise the key deadline dates in the UCAS timetable so you don't miss them.
- Get feedback from people who know you well on your UCAS personal statement.
- Make sure the final version of your UCAS personal statement is proof-read by at least two people other than yourself. Carefully proof-read it at least three times yourself!
- If you apply to a LNAT participating university, visit the LNAT website, attempt their sample questions and essays, and practise for the LNAT test by writing in the style of newspaper editorials which you should be regularly reading.

Useful resources

UCAS (2012) *UCAS Guide to getting in University and College.* Second revised edition. Cheltenham: UCAS

Hutton R, Hutton G and Simpson F (2011) *Passing the National Admissions Test for Law* 3rd edition. Exeter: Learning Matters.

Barnard C, O'Sullivan J and Virgo G (2011) *What about Law? Studying Law at University.* 2nd revised edition. Oxford: Hart Publishing.

www.gov.uk/student-finance/loans-and-grants

www.ucas.ac.uk

www.lnat.ac.uk

www.guardian.co.uk/education/table/2013/june/04/university-guide-law

www.thecompleteuniversityguide.co.uk

www.thetimes.co.uk/tto/public/gug

www.whatuni.com

References

LNAT (2012) About the Test. [Online] Available at: http://www.lnat.ac.uk/lnat-exam.aspx [Accessed May 2013]

LNAT (2012) Results. [Online] Available at: http://www.lnat.ac.uk/lnat-exam/lnat-results.aspx [Accessed May 2013]

LNAT (2012) Preparing for your LNAT. [Online] Available at: http://www.ucl.ac.uk/lnat-preparation.aspx

UCL (2012) Pathways to law. [Online] Available at: http://www.ucl.ac.uk/laws/prospective/pathways-to-law/index.shtml?home [Accessed December 2012]

Being a law student...

BPP
LEARNING MEDIA

Chapter 5

Studying the law for the first time

With contributions from
Olivia Cox

BPP
LEARNING MEDIA

Introduction

A first-time law student will, in most cases, be studying for either:

- A qualifying law degree ('QLD' – see Chapter 4), the most popular of which is the LLB, which is read typically by undergraduates after they complete their A levels; or
- The Graduate Diploma in Law ('GDL'), which is sometimes also referred to as the Common Professional Examination or 'CPE'. The GDL is a graduate conversion course, which is taken by non-law graduates who wish to pursue a career in the law, after they have completed a non-law degree.

There is a significant overlap in the content of a QLD and the GDL, because they both contain the necessary modules which you need to study and pass before progressing to the vocational or practical stage of your training:

- The LPC (if you wish to qualify as a solicitor); or
- The BPTC (if you wish to qualify as a barrister).

In this chapter, we will compare and contrast what it's like to study for a QLD and the GDL, explain the difference between the courses, but mainly focus on their many common characteristics and the challenges faced by first-time law students.

In case you've lost track of where each of these courses come in your career progression, you may wish to refer back to Figure 2.1 in Chapter 2 – *The road map to becoming a lawyer in England and Wales.*

Almost every university in England and Wales is validated to run law degree courses, which means you have over 100 institutions to choose from for your law degree! In contrast, there are less than half that number of providers who run the GDL, although the two largest, BPP University College and the University of Law, run their LLB and GDL courses from multiple sites across England.

Qualifying law degrees and the GDL – core course content

The Bar Standards Board and the Solicitors Regulation Authority set the standards which are required to be met by students on QLDs and on the GDL to complete the first (academic) stage of their legal training. Specifically, these standards include the requirement for all such students to study the '**Foundations for Legal Knowledge**', which are:

- Public Law (including Constitutional Law, Administrative Law and Human Rights)
- Law of the European Union
- Criminal Law
- Obligations including Contract, Restitution and Tort
- Property Law
- Equity and the Law of Trusts

In order to give you a flavour of the Foundations for Legal Knowledge, we have set out below a brief summary of each subject.

Students on a QLD and the GDL will also receive training in legal research, as well as the structure and institutions which make up the English Legal System.

Case study

Before beginning the LPC, Lucy was worried about studying alongside those who had law degrees because they had studied law for at least two years more than her. However, in the early weeks of the LPC, Lucy actually began to feel the advantages of doing the GDL. Both the GDL and the LPC courses are heavily focused on the practical application of law to clients. In contrast, what Lucy understood from her fellow students who have law degrees, is that their legal education before the LPC had much more of an academic approach.

Because the GDL is very issues-based and in most of the classes students focus on a particular fictional client and their problems, this helped Lucy to see the picture as a whole, rather than as separate strands of law. Her degree in Politics developed many of the same skills she would have acquired on a law degree, but her study of law through the GDL allowed her to keep the client at the forefront of her mind, rather than as an academic hypothetical.

Public Law (including Constitutional Law, Administrative Law and Human Rights)

This includes the study of the UK constitution, the separation of powers (ie between parliament, the government and the judiciary), the rule of law, human rights and judicial review. Unlike most other modules, this one is light on cases but you need to know and understand them in greater depth than the more case-heavy modules like contract law and the law of torts (both of which are described below). Exam questions can be a combination of essay discussions and scenario-based problems. Students often struggle with some of the concepts, so you will require a thorough knowledge and understanding of your course materials and text books, parts of which students report having to read several times over in order to master them. Mooting (ie a hypothetical case which is debated by students) is sometimes used as a way to teach this subject.

Law of the European Union

You will study the legal structure of the European Union and its relationship with member states, the EU's legislative process and structure. EU law is full of complex concepts which law students often find hard to relate to, especially as the reported cases tend to be more complicated and hence more difficult to follow than the common law cases.

Criminal Law

Many first-time law students consider Criminal Law to be the most interesting. You will spend hours pouring over the details of the leading cases, the facts of which often appear to resemble an *Eastenders* plot. For example, topics such as burglary leave the classroom open to a variety of 'what if' scenarios because to commit burglary, the accused must have entered the building. There are several cases where part (but not all) of the accused's body (eg an arm, hand or foot) has crossed the threshold of a building, and so the court has to decide whether 'entry' has taken place for the offence of burglary to have been committed. This leaves students debating 'what if the accused poked his head through the window?' Or perhaps only his nose? You will soon appreciate that there are sometimes very fine margins between guilt and innocence, which makes studying this module more challenging than students initially appreciate.

> *Despite the interesting stories behind the cases and heated debates in the classroom, I found Criminal Law to be one of the harder modules. This was because there are so many different factors which could determine the outcome of the case study/exam answers.*
>
> Olivia Cox, trainee solicitor.

To give you a flavour of the sort of analysis you will undertake when studying Criminal Law, take a look at Exercise 5.1 below, which deals with the definition of 'provocation', which is one of the defences to murder.

Exercise 5.1:

'Where on a charge of murder there is evidence ... that the person charged was provoked (whether by things done or things said or by both together) to lose self-control, the question whether the provocation was enough to make the reasonable man do as he did shall be... determined by the jury; and in determining that question the jury shall take into account everything both done and said according to the effect which, in their opinion, it would have on a reasonable man.'

Section 3 Homicide Act 1957

Now consider the following scenario:

A battered wife, who was subjected to ten years of domestic violence from her husband buys some petrol, takes it home and throws it into the bedroom and then sets the room alight, knowing her husband to be there. The husband suffers serious burns and dies from his injuries a few days later.

The wife is charged with murder and in her defence, she pleads provocation (on grounds of a long history of domestic violence) and loss of self-control.

Now take 5 to 10 minutes to consider how the wife might construct her defence on the basis of provocation. What arguments might the prosecution try to run to claim that the defence of provocation under Section 3 Homicide Act 1957 should not apply?

If you were discussing Exercise 5.1 in a Criminal Law class, you are likely to debate the following questions to analyse when the defence of provocation applies:

- Does the loss of 'self-control' under Section 3 have to immediately follow the act of provocation (ie the domestic violence)? Or does the wife's planning and pre-meditation completely rule out the defence?
- How much delay (if any) can there be between the last incident of domestic violence and the killing?
- Does it matter that the defendant did not react in such a way in the past despite being subjected to similar provocation?
- Should the court take into account any particular important characteristics about the defendant (eg that she was a 'battered wife') which may have influenced her behaviour? In other words, is the 'reasonable man' test mentioned in Section 3 an objective or a subjective test?

The purpose of this exercise is not to teach you or fully explain the defence of provocation – we will leave that to your Criminal Law lecturers, tutors and text books. Instead, you should begin to appreciate how complex the law can be. It is impossible for the law to be 'black' or 'white' on every set of facts. There are just too many variables for legislators and judges to cover. Consequently, you will spend much of your law degree or GDL analysing these 'grey' areas. You will also face competing arguments that sometimes point you in different directions, which makes arriving at the 'right' answer a challenge! Consequently, it is the quality of your analysis rather than getting the 'right' answer, which is where most of the marks will be.

If you can't wait until you study Criminal Law and want to know what happened to the wife in the above case, Exercise 5.1 was based on the case of *R v Ahluwalia* (1992), in which the wife's initial conviction for murder was overturned on appeal, but not because the court accepted the defence of provocation – the court considered but side-stepped the problems with running that defence, some of which we began to identify above. Instead, the court of appeal accepted new medical evidence that the defendant was suffering from 'battered wife's syndrome' (a depressive disorder) and ordered a retrial, at which she pleaded guilty to manslaughter by way of diminished responsibility. The defendant was still sentenced to three years and four months' imprisonment, but because this was precisely the time she had already served, following the re-trial, she left the Old Bailey a free woman.

What should strike any potential law student from the decision in *R v Ahluwalia* (1992) is that one line of argument (the defence of provocation) was debated and analysed in depth, only, ultimately, to be rejected in favour of an alternative, even more compelling argument. Legal arguments (especially claims and defences in litigation) are often framed 'in the alternative'. In other words, the lawyers are saying to the court 'if you don't agree with me on that point, consider what I'm about to say "in the alternative" (ie instead).'

Obligations including Contract, Restitution and Tort

Contract Law

Having a grasp of this core subject is essential for all law students, because you will follow through several principles of Contract Law in your later studies. In addition, you, yourself, may be entering into contracts regularly with your clients (eg on behalf of your law firm if you become a solicitor). Many of the main areas of legal practice involve drafting or negotiating contracts or advising a party with regard to their rights or liabilities under a contract. Contract law is case-heavy but students do find that there are clear structures to problem-solving contract issues. So, Contract Law is easier to understand and prepare than other subjects, if you are good at working to and applying a structure. However, this module can still be terribly dry and complicated: you won't come across as many of the tabloid fact patterns as the Criminal Law cases. Instead, you will find yourself deconstructing a series of events to work out:

- Whether there actually is a contract between the parties.
- What the terms of that contract actually are.
- Whether there has been a breach of contract.
- Whether the innocent party has suffered loss as a consequence of the breach, and if so, how that loss should be quantified.
- What remedy (or restitution) the innocent party is entitled to.

Sometimes the whole outcome of a contract case can depend on seemingly insignificant points, like how and when an important document was sent by one party to the other: you will left agonising over when and how letters are sent (ie the difference between personal service and postal service). Putting a letter in a red or gold box will no longer seem so simple!

Law of Torts

'Tort' is a word most law students never come across until their law degree or the GDL, unless it was in the form of an incorrectly spelled dessert menu! Like Criminal Law, this is another module full of colourful stories and many more reported cases to learn. A 'tort' is a wrongdoing, but, generally speaking, not one which is covered by either Criminal or Contract Law. The Law of Torts includes a host of wrongdoings, such as the controversial rule in *Rylands v Fletcher* (1868), which is a case which examined the liability of a landowner whose reservoir flooded the neighbour's mines and caused significant damage. The court decided that if a landowner brings onto their land something which is likely to cause a mischief if it were to escape, the landowner may be liable for any damage it causes. This usually causes great consternation in class when students explore precisely what falls under the rule in *Rylands v Fletcher* (1868). For example, if you brought children onto your land and they escaped causing damage to your neighbour's land, would that fall inside or outside the rule?

The law of negligence is one of the most significant areas of the Law of Torts. Once you read the case of *Donoghue v Stevenson* (1932), you may never want to drink a bottle of ginger beer ever again for fear of choking on a decomposing slug! Negligence is the area of the law under which victims are compensated for their losses in circumstances where the so-called 'guilty' party ('T'), who is known as the 'tortfeasor', owes a duty of care to the victim ('V'), who suffers loss as a consequence of T's actions (or omission).

Personal injury cases are negligence actions. Supposing there was a collision between two vehicles and it was reasonably clear who was 'negligent' or 'to blame' for the accident. Your Tort tutor may ask you to consider a number of 'what if?' scenarios:

- What would be the effect of T's liability (or the amount of compensation payable) if V was driving under the influence of alcohol?
- Suppose it was a minor collision which would not have injured most people, but because V suffered from osteoporosis (brittle bones), V suffered multiple fractures? Should T take the victim as he finds her or just compensate her for the injuries most people would have sustained had they been injured in the same accident?
- How far should the compensation go? Should V be entitled to be compensated for the loss of her expensive foreign holiday which she cannot now take because of her injuries?
- Can she recover all of her loss of wages (ie before deductions for income tax and national insurance)?
- Suppose V lost the opportunity of exploiting a potentially lucrative business contract as a consequence of her injuries. Could she be compensated for the potential loss of earnings had such opportunity been successfully pursued?

Land Law

When studying Land Law, you will steadily acquire the vocabulary associated with the rights and obligations which come with land ownership and the circumstances in which you are entitled to enjoy rights over someone else's land. Much of the 'modern' land law was written in the 1920s, which presents its own challenges because the Law of Property Act 1925, the Land Registration Act 1925 and the Landlord and Tenant Act 1927 aren't the most student-friendly of statutes. There are, of course, plenty of reported cases to get familiar with as well, but unfortunately, their details are much drier than the more exciting fact patterns of Criminal Law and Tort. Land Law isn't the most riveting of reads – it can sometimes be like wading through treacle. Yet to some (including the author who was a Real Estate specialist in practice), having a logical structure as to how the law should be applied is part of what appeals, even if, at times, it may seem uninspiring.

In a Land Law exam, you may, for example, be given a description of a property, details of its neighbours and the surrounding area, and you are then asked to identify the different rights (easements) which third parties have over the property in question. Issues in relation to shared driveways are relatively easy to spot, but when it comes down to who can hang signs on what parts of buildings and whether they have a right to light or a right to a television signal, the position gets trickier.

Most students find the Property Law and Practice module on the LPC more interesting as it has more practical application and is less theoretical. However, a good grounding in Land Law in your QLD or GDL is an essential foundation for the next part of your studies, even if you don't want to become a property lawyer.

Top tip

Plotting diagrams to transfer the description of a Land Law problem into pictures often helps students get to the bottom of a Land Law fact pattern.

Equity and the Law of Trusts

This is a module which looks at the creation and operation of trusts both in relation to family gifts and the commercial world. Part of the module examines the role of the trustee, when they may be in breach of trust and the remedies available to the beneficiaries of the trust in such circumstances. Like Land Law, 'Equity', as it is often referred to, does have the tendency to be dry and intellectually challenging, so an engaging tutor can make all the difference to your experience of the subject.

Of the core areas in my law degree, my favourite was definitely Tort. Areas such as loss of chance, where the law has to assess hypothetical outcomes and examine the effect of delayed diagnoses on survival rates, and public policy issues within occupiers' liability gave me food for thought. I enjoyed the challenge of developing arguments and answering essay questions on those topics. My interest in these and other concepts introduced in the Law of Tort led me to choose Medical Law as an optional module in my final year.

Contract Law had a very heavy reading list and crammed a lot of information in. In particular, I enjoyed reading the frustration cases where the factual background was often entertaining. Who would have thought that a whole body of Contract cases could come out of the delayed coronation of King Edward VII, which was initially postponed because he contracted appendicitis!

During my first and second year, Land Law was my demon. Whether it was not enjoying the teaching or struggling to get to grips with difficult concepts, I found it difficult to achieve high marks. But I would definitely advise law students to keep an open mind and not to develop a negative attitude towards modules they don't take to. In fact, I loved the Law of Trusts, which has a similar feel to the Law of Property, and did very well in it in my final year.

Grace Cassidy, LPC student

Legal Research

You never stop being a law student. Whether you are a trainee solicitor or a learned QC, you will still come across areas of the law which you don't know 'the answer' to and you need to look up. Consequently, it is essential that you are given the tools of how to research a legal problem, which involves training in the use of a law library and electronic legal databases. This essential skill is revisited in both the LPC and the BPTC courses, because of its fundamental importance to any practising lawyer.

Top tip

Take your Legal Research training seriously. It's not just about using indices and search engines efficiently. It's more about understanding what resources you have available, how to get the best out of them, and where to find what you need in the quickest possible time.

Qualifying law degrees and the GDL – other subjects of study

QLD options

As well as the Foundations for Legal Knowledge, if you are studying for a law degree, you will be required to choose a handful of elective subjects to make up the rest of your degree. The range of subjects on offer will vary considerably between institutions. Some subjects are of pure academic interest such as 'Literature and the Law', whereas others have a much more practical focus like 'Family Law' and 'Employment Law'. Most universities also offer the opportunity of writing a dissertation (research project) in an area of your choice, instead of one of your elective modules.

Your choice of elective modules is important, but the choice itself is rarely fatal to your career prospects. That said, employers will not only be interested in your marks for each module, but also the subjects in which they were attained. Employers will expect your CV to show those marks, which are particularly important in the screening process of applications to top law firms and chambers.

Subject to timetabling constraints, the choice of elective modules will ultimately rest with you. Choosing too many pure academic options may indicate to an employer that you are more interested in the academic approach to the law, rather than being a practising lawyer, but there is no point studying subjects which don't interest you, just because you believe they may enhance your career prospects. It's a question of balance: if you have a clear vision of the type of law firm or chambers you think you want to apply to, then it will be helpful if most of your options 'fit' with the firm or chambers' practice areas. That said, choosing a single pure academic subject won't do you any harm if you have a passion or genuine interest in it, but be prepared for an interviewer to ask 'Why did you study Medieval Law?', particularly if the rest of your options suggest a corporate profile.

Around half-way through the first and second year of your law degree, you will be asked to select your elective subjects for the next year of your studies. So what do you do if you still do not have a strong vision of where you see yourself going? This situation is perfectly normal. Many students select a broad range of modules, so they can discover what areas appeal to them as they are learning. In time, this wide exposure to a variety of subjects will start to help to shape your career options.

GDL options

Non-law graduates on a full-time GDL course only spend a year studying the law, most of which is spent on the Foundations for Legal Knowledge. In fact, most GDL students will only be given the opportunity of studying a maximum of two other modules (one of which may be a research essay or project), because there simply isn't time for anything else. So, by the time law graduates and GDL graduates meet on the LPC or BPTC, the former will, inevitably, have had exposure to several more areas of the law than their non-law graduate counterparts. However, this doesn't prevent non-law graduates who take the GDL from being recruited in large numbers by top law firms and chambers. So, it is important not to overstate the significance of an LLB student's options, but be prepared to explain why you chose any particular subject.

Top tip

When it comes to elective subjects, choose what interests you and what you think you will do well at, but always have your CV in mind when doing so.

Top tip

Look out for ways of to upgrade your GDL to an LLB degree (which is not strictly necessary, but may help to improve the CV of a mature applicant who does not have an undergraduate degree). Also look out for ways to combine your law degree with an LPC. Some institutions run a combined LLB and LPC (which is known as an 'Exempting Law Degree'), typically over four years. This also has the advantage of staying in the same location. The SRA also permits a combined GDL and LPC (known as an 'Integrated Course').

These combined courses may not be suitable for all students: some students feel ready to 'move on' to other institutions for a different experience and perspective for their LPC after their law degree or GDL. Just because an academic institution provides an excellent LLB or GDL, it does not necessarily follow that they are as well placed to deliver professional postgraduate law courses such as the LPC or BPTC. The proportion of staff who are experienced former legal professionals (as opposed to pure legal academics) can vary considerably from provider to provider, and, ideally, you want to be taught by former/current practitioners on the LPC or BPTC, rather than career academics.

	Common to both QLDs and the GDL	QLDs only	The GDL only
Course content	The Foundations for Legal Knowledge (see above).	You will also choose a number of additional modules to make up the rest of your law degree. QLD providers vary considerably in the range of modules they offer on their law degree courses. For more details, consult the websites of UCAS and the relevant universities.	The GDL is a gateway to the LPC and the BPTC. Apart from the Foundations for Legal Knowledge, your additional studies on the GDL will tend to be limited to a maximum of one or two other subjects, which may include a research essay or project.
Admission requirements	Both normally require applicants to demonstrate their academic ability from the results of their previous studies. There may be flexibility in some cases for mature students and those students whose backgrounds are less conventional.	Admission onto most QLD courses is usually dependent on the candidate's A level performance. Typical conditional offers are given to students, subject to their attaining AAB or better in their A levels.	You usually need a non-law degree to take the GDL. Remember, if you have a qualifying law degree, you can skip the GDL and go straight to the LPC or the BPTC. Students whose first language is not English may be required to sit an English language test.

	Common to both QLDs and the GDL	QLDs only	The GDL only
Admissions procedure	In most cases, providers do not take applications directly from members of the public – applicants are directed to the relevant intermediary which processes all the applications centrally before referring them to the providers.	Almost all university applications for QLD courses must be made via UCAS.	All applications for places on full-time GDL and LPC courses must be made via Lawcabs (see below). Part-time applicants apply directly to the provider.
Length of courses.	A QLD will take two or three times longer than the GDL.	A full-time student can complete a QLD in two years, but most full-time QLD courses are three years long. A part-time student may take four to six years.	A full-time student passing all modules at the first attempt is able to complete the GDL within a year. A part-time student will, typically, take just less than two years.

Table 5.1: QLDs and the GDL compared and contrasted

Top tip

It might be tempting to read ahead before you start your LLB or GDL, but if you do, go to a law library: don't buy any text books unless you are told to do so by your LLB or GDL provider, because publishers often print new editions in August/September each year, just before you are likely to start your course. The last thing you want to do is to spend £40 on a text book and find out that everyone else has bought a more up to date edition.

Chapter summary

A first-time law student's studies will include the Foundations of Legal Knowledge, whether the student is an undergraduate on a law degree course or on the GDL. These subjects are varied and will consequently not appeal to all law students: some will prefer the case-heavy subjects, others will enjoy the more concept-heavy, academic areas. A grasp of the key concepts is essential in any law module, which is often underpinned by detailed knowledge and understanding of the relevant case law and legislation. But the way you approach the study of some modules will be different to others. Be prepared to try out different methods of study – don't just read on your own, discuss the concepts and the cases with your fellow students as it will develop your understanding and will help you to explore the subjects in greater depth.

Key points

- Law graduates are exposed to a wider variety of subjects than those who take the GDL, but the depth covered in the Foundations of Legal Knowledge is broadly the same.
- Although different areas sometimes require a different approach, whatever the subject is, you still need a rounded analysis of the issues and concepts, rather than a one-sided view.

Useful resources

Wilson S and Kenny P (2010) *The Law Student's Handbook.* 2nd edition. Oxford OUP.

Donoghue v Stevenson [1932] AC 532

R v Ahluwalia [1992] 4 AER 889

Rylands v Fletcher [1868] LR 3 HL 330

Chapter 6

How to study the law

BPP
LEARNING MEDIA

The A to Z of how to study the law

Rather than spending pages discussing academic theories about studying law, it is, perhaps, more beneficial to the reader of this book to introduce you to a snappy list of practical tips which may be useful to a first-time law student. Having said that, these tips apply not just to LLB and GDL students but also to those taking their vocational examinations (the LPC and the BPTC). You will have to work at each and every one of these areas. Being aware of these tips is just the start.

A is for... Argue both sides

Don't be dogmatic. Academic study would be pointless if there was only ever one argument and one 'correct' answer. In fact, there are often several competing considerations which you need to make sense of in your analysis. Some arguments may be better than others, but you still have to discuss the relative merits of all relevant points of view before reaching your conclusion. Part of being a good lawyer is anticipating the other side's arguments and having your counter-arguments 'ready and waiting'. Learning where your weaknesses are is just as important as exploiting your strengths.

B is for... Breaks

Take regular study breaks. Sitting in a law library for 16 hours each day is not going to get the best out of you. Some studies say the optimum learning time is as low as 20 minutes! You might think that is a little extreme, but you should build regular breaks into your study days, such as lunch with a friend, a walk, a trip to the gym, some retail therapy or even a power-nap. You will find that you will probably achieve more in four or five 90-minute study sessions which are interspersed with pre-planned breaks (not just a cup of coffee), than you will by putting yourself through a marathon 12-hour session during which you only pause for a comfort break. No one can maintain a consistent level of concentration and focus for more than a few hours at a time, particularly when you're dealing with complex legal concepts. That is why your law exams will be around three hours long, as opposed to five or six!

C is for... Consolidate your learning

Most law modules are incremental in terms of how a student's understanding is built up. It is therefore essential that you achieve the learning outcomes for each and every session as you go along. If you're struggling with a concept, ask a tutor or a fellow student, or look it up. Don't leave it until you start revising. Your small group sessions (eg tutorials) and lectures will be carefully designed; the next session will often follow on from the last and if you didn't 'get it' yesterday first time round, you may struggle when next week's session takes you to the 'next stage'. Consolidating your learning means going over what you have learned, checking that you:

- Have understood the concepts
- Can apply those concepts to a variety of scenarios
- Can confidently write and talk about those concepts

You can do this in many ways (eg writing revision notes of key points, writing up key cards (see below), and drawing flowcharts or diagrams which package the information you need to know for your exams in a memorable way. Consolidating isn't revising – it is making sense of what you have learned and organising that information in such a way so that when it comes to revise (ie committing that material to memory and attempting past exam questions) you have done much of the ground work.

> *I consolidate by re-reading all of the notes I have taken from lectures and seminars and condense them into something I can use for revision. It also gives me the chance to contact my tutors questions if there is something I don't understand, or if I want to ask more about the subject. If you don't consolidate as you go along, there is too much to do later on, when there is never enough time to properly consolidate from scratch and then to revise.*
>
> *In order to test how effective my consolidation has been, I attempt as many exam-style questions, mocks and practice papers as possible. There is no better way of preparing for your assessments: it helps you identify where your strengths and weaknesses are.*
>
> Rosina Hough, GDL graduate, LPC student

D is for... Debate

Debate out loud with others and if no one is around, debate the issues with yourself! It is just as important to express your ideas orally, as it is to do so in writing and 'in your head'. You may think you have absorbed and understood a legal concept by reading about it, but until you have tested your understanding by way of a discussion (or writing about it), you can't be sure. As part of their training, aspiring barristers are encouraged to record themselves on video to see how they present themselves and how they speak. You learn a lot about your debating style this way, whether you want to become a solicitor or a barrister. But don't be too hard on yourself when you hear the playback! Only you will hear your hesitations, your 'ums' and 'errs'. Instead, when watching and listening to the playback, you should focus on:

- The substance of what you're saying
- The language you use (is the formality or lack of formality appropriate to the discussion?)
- Your tone of voice (do you vary the pitch and volume?)
- How fast (or slow) you are speaking
- Observe your body language – are you giving anything away when you get to the more 'difficult' parts of your argument: if you don't think you're convincing, how will you persuade anyone else?
- Where are your eyes focused?
- How confident do you appear?
- Get someone else to comment on the video for an objective assessment of your performance. You will be surprised that they won't spot all your insecurities!

E is for... Exam papers

Your university will provide its law students with examples of past papers to give you an idea of the sort of questions you will be asked. Sometimes these papers are published online, and if there are examiners' reports and/or suggested answers, make sure you use those papers as informal mock exams under exam conditions during your revision period. Replicating the conditions of an exam by sitting mocks for each subject and attempting to answer past papers is an essential part of your preparation for the exam. You will learn a huge amount about your examination technique – eg how well you manage your time, whether you are answering the question (or misunderstanding it!), and whether you write with clarity and with sufficient detail and depth.

F is for... the Future

While you're studying the law on your law degree or the GDL, you should be thinking about and planning for the future as an on-going project. This means you should be:

- Considering which career path you may wish to go down – ie solicitor, barrister, or a career outside the legal profession.
- Deciding where you wish to study the LPC or BPTC if you have decided you want to be a solicitor or barrister, and making the relevant application in the final year of your LPC or during your GDL.

- Pursuing opportunities for work experience, law firm workshops, vacation schemes and mini-pupillage opportunities (see later chapters). It is never too early to start. In fact, the longer you leave it, the less committed you may appear to a career in the law.

H is for... Home

Have a regular 'home' where you study. This can, literally, be at home, but if it isn't, make sure you study in an environment which is conducive to working. Familiarity with your surroundings may mean you feel comfortable and you don't get distracted by something 'new' in your eye-line. To some people, this is simply a desk at home, but to others, with all the distractions there are at home, the best place to study is a quiet law library. Work out which environment suits you best.

I is for... Identify what type of learner you are

Do you absorb information and learn best from reading, listening, discussion, re-writing what you read, typing up notes, drawing diagrams, preparing lists of bullet points or simply by drawing pictures? Most of us would answer 'a combination of all the above' but there are clearly some methods which lend themselves more readily to getting the information across and retaining it than others, depending on the subject matter. So what happens when you come across concepts which are too difficult to understand in the way they are presented in your course materials or text books? If no one is around to give you a hand, try to break down that information into its constituent parts and then to re-package it, for example, by way of a flow diagram. But flow diagrams don't suit every student's way of learning and they may not always be appropriate. If so, try something else. Analyse how you best learn and repeat your successes.

J is for... Jargon

Being a student of the law is almost like learning a new language. You will come across concepts and terminology, all of which you will need to fully understand in order to be able to use them with confidence. Some of the jargon you will come across isn't even English. You will probably have heard of the Latin phrase '*caveat emptor*', which means *'buyer beware!'* – in other words, if you're buying something and you don't get it properly checked out beforehand, if something goes wrong later on, it's your problem, not the seller's. If you use complex terminology in the wrong context, it is worse than not having used it at all. So, keep a book (or create an electronic document) of the legal jargon you come across, recording examples of how to use such words and phrases in the correct context.

Top tip

When studying the law, you will come across new legal jargon, almost on a daily basis. You can, of course, use an internet search engine to provide you with definitions, but such a solution is not always reliable. Consequently, many students buy a legal dictionary, because it is a cheap, cost-effective way of giving you a speedy reliable translation of the legal lexicon.

K is for... Key cards and Keywords

You will come across dozens of reported cases and legal concepts. You need to have an efficient way of recording and summarising them so that you can commit them to memory in readiness for your exams. Key cards (often known as 'flash cards'), which are small postcard-sized cards, may help in this respect. Write the case name or legal principle in capitals in one colour at the top of the card and underneath write the definition or case summary, underlining any keywords which may help you ultimately commit the details to memory. You can share these key cards with fellow students during your revision if you are part of a study group. And there's no reason why a family member or non-law student couldn't test you on the contents either.

L is for... Learn the law and legal principles

Because of the number of reported cases which first-time law students are required to learn, some feel the need to memorise the entire fact pattern which gave rise to the litigation in question. While it is important to understand the context of a court's judgment by knowing the relevant facts, it is more important to remember the points of law or legal principles which the court clarified or made a ruling on, because that is what you need to know and apply both in your exams and in practice.

Exercise 6.1

Salomon v A Salomon & Co Ltd

Mr Aron Salomon formed a limited company through which he ran his business.

He owned 20,001 of the 20,007 shares, the remaining six being held by five of his children and his wife.

The company went insolvent.

The Companies Act 1862 made it clear that a limited company is a separate legal entity (ie it is a separate 'person' in the eyes of the law, distinct from its shareholders.)

The Court of Appeal held that a creditor of the company was able to sue Mr Salomon (in person) for his company's debts. The Court of Appeal considered the six minority shareholders to be 'mere puppets' and that Mr Salomon had used the company as a vehicle to avoid personal liability for the debts of his business.

The House of Lords overturned the Court of Appeal's decision, holding that a creditor of the company had no claim against Mr Salomon personally, even though he owned 99.97% of the company. A creditor of the company could have no claim against Mr Salomon because he and the company were separate personalities.

What do you need to remember from this case?

Can you neatly and concisely summarise the point of law which comes out of this case?

Answer to Exercise 6.1

The shareholders of a limited company cannot be liable for the company's debts because limited companies have a separate legal personality. This still applies even if there is one substantial shareholder, who is effectively, a 'one man company'. From the case summary above, that's all you need to remember in terms of the main point of law which was clarified.

M is for... Memorise

Law students have to commit to memory a huge amount of information. There are many techniques for doing this ranging from mnemonics, acrostics and 'rote learning' to more sophisticated methods of memorising information through flowcharts and diagrams. Use a variety of methods, because by the time you've use the same memory aid half a dozen times, it may be hard to distinguish one set of information from the other!

> *When revising, I prefer not having to flick through pages and pages of notes, so I use my previously consolidated notes to create a structure or a 'map' for each subject on one side of A3 paper. I try to avoid using long sentences, preferring instead to use bullet points to prompt the information in the detailed notes. In these 'maps' I incorporate diagrams, drawings and colour. For example, I use highlighters to colour code my notes; yellow for things I know, orange for things that I need to revisit, and pink for things I don't know and need to learn. Revision then consists of memorising each structure for each subject and being able to expand on the bullet points. The use of colour and diagrams will assist in this memorising process.*
>
> Joe Defalco, LPC student

N is for... Notes

You listen. Then you write it down. Anyone can take notes can't they? That's true to an extent, but taking useful notes in a way which helps you study is a different matter altogether. Hopefully, whenever you have missed a class in the past, you have been conscientious enough to ask for a copy of the notes from someone who attended. Sometimes the notes are clear, but on other occasions they could be a combination of doodles, scribbles and the odd keyword but with little cohesion to them as a whole. So, fast-forward three months when you're revising for an exam and you come across your own notes from a session which you did turn up to, but can't remember what was covered in any detail. How useful are your doodles, scribbles and keywords now? The reality is that your text books, lecture hand-outs and other course materials will contain much of the information and explanations you need, and, yes, you may (and should) spend time extracting the important parts to make your own notes. That makes sense, but you also need to take notes in lectures, tutorials and small group sessions which should, generally, be supplementary to the course materials – in other words your notes should be clarification of the important concepts, explanations, examples and diagrams to help your learning, but not the actual law itself (unless it's breaking down a complicated concept into smaller parts).

Some students find it helpful to take notes on a laptop or tablet in class, whereas others go over what they wrote in the sessions they attended and type up the key points, which will be easier to revisit later in the year when it comes to revise the same material. So, take notes intelligently, which also means regularly using headings, sub-headings, bullet points, numbered points and diagrams to give clarity. Some students write in different coloured pens (eg they write the name of a case or a statutory citation in red and the summary in blue or black). See how others take notes and learn from them too!

O is for... Organisation

Organise your:

- Course materials (eg in a separate ring-binder for each subject)
- Notes
- Electronic files
- Diary
- Your private study time
- Your social life!

Planning how, what, where and when you do all the above will really help you maximise your potential as a law student. Spreading out volumes of loose papers onto a table (rather than perusing the same material which has been neatly filed in a ring binder) demonstrates to your tutor that you're not organised – so how prepared are you for the session you're now in?

Don't be late for class. Students who consistently roll in 15 or 20 minutes late disrupt the session for the tutor and their fellow students who bothered to turn up on time. You wouldn't (or at least shouldn't) turn up late for work, so why is it any different when you're studying? Tutors will remember those who can't get in on time – particularly because employers are interested in your punctuality as well as your intellectual ability and commitment. If there is a genuine reason for being late (or not attending at all) speak to or email your tutor. Doing nothing is discourteous and not an option.

P is for... 'Prep'

Never turn up to class unprepared. It's disrespectful to your tutor, but also lets down your classmates if your lack of preparation means you cannot contribute to class discussions in the way expected. And, of course, you're not doing yourself any favours either. Tutors are incredibly adept at spotting a student who is unprepared. Hopefully, they won't humiliate you. They shouldn't, although some do. More importantly, your tutor will remember your lack of preparation, which may count against you when it comes to giving a reference. Employers aren't just interested in your grades; they want to know how diligent you are in your preparation for class. Don't get labelled 'lazy but bright'.

This won't come as a surprise, but legal study involves a lot of reading. As a non-law graduate I took the GDL-LPC route, and the modules on both courses were structured with a designated amount of preparation work on each topic, including background reading, a lecture and practical exercises (typically between 2 – 4 hours work), followed by a taught class, in which the topic is tackled through group exercises and discussion.

The reality is that, for a number of reasons, be it time pressure, other commitments, or just plain sloth, it's pretty unlikely that you'll be able to prepare for every class in as much depth as you'd like. The good news is that the class tutor won't shout at you if you haven't done all the prescribed reading – they will work with what you've got. And there's definitely a lot to be gained from turning up, whatever state of preparation you're in: the face to face classes put the legal concepts and procedures you've been learning about into a practical context, usually by working through a fictional case with your tutor's help, and that's really useful for getting it clear in your mind, and obviously for practice too.

The more you put in, the more you get out. And in each module, there will be classes which build on what you've learnt before, so missing one or preparing inadequately will make the next harder to follow; the danger is allowing it to snowball. These courses involve a lot of independent study, so the key is organisation: be realistic about the amount of time you need to prepare, and then go and do it!

Will Russell, GDL graduate and LPC student

Case study

In the first week of his law degree, Ian attended all of his tutorials but rarely prepared for class, despite being given a manageable reading list, which should have been achievable, even with the new attractions and distractions of university life. Ian got away without contributing anything to any of his first week's tutorials, leaving other members of the group to answer the tutor's questions and discuss the various points of law. Thinking he'd found a revolutionary method of learning which worked for him (ie being a passive bystander, and using the tutorial sessions to pick things up for the first time), Ian continued to party hard into week two of his law degree and turned up to watch (rather than engage in) his second week of tutorials. However, in his second Contract Law class, Ian's tutor asked him a number of direct questions to which Ian had no reply. Ian felt stupid. Other students' eyes rolled when the tutor tried (albeit in vain) to extract an answer from Ian to the simplest of questions, after having drawn a number of blanks. But, by then, Ian would have struggled to answer his name, such was the embarrassment he felt.

Ian's tutor spoke to him privately at the end of the session and explained that he had asked several straightforward questions, in respect of which Ian should have been able to offer something sensible in reply if he'd done any of the preparation for the tutorial. Ian's experience ensured he was fully prepared for his remaining Contact Law tutorials as well as those in all of his other subjects.

Q is for... Question-spotting

Question-spotting is when you try and second-guess what questions are going to come up in your exams. Don't do it! It's a recipe for disaster! Question-spotting has two main pitfalls. First, the temptation is not to revise a subject which you're not comfortable with or you don't give it the attention it deserves in the hope that the question doesn't come up. In some exams, you are required to answer all of the questions, whereas in others, you will have a choice. There is no scope for manoeuvre if you have to answer every question, but even if there is a choice, wouldn't you prefer to have as wide a choice as possible of questions to answer, so you can select the ones at which you think you will do best, rather than gambling and perhaps being forced to answer a question which you are not properly prepared for?

If you 'expect' a topic to be examined in a particular way but the question in the exam approaches the subject from a different angle, you may not be in a position to answer it properly. Simply writing 'everything

I know about' or rehashing the model answer you've crafted to the question you wish they would have asked you isn't going to score you high marks. By all means, prepare for the sort of questions you expect you may be asked, but be prepared to have to think about the subject matter in a different way. That means getting a deeper understanding of the concepts, rather than simply learning a model answer.

R is for... Routine

Have a routine to your days, and have a routine to how you study – eg the times you study, when you don't study, where you study and who you study with. Familiarity with your routine breeds efficiency. That doesn't mean to say you should always study the same way, as that can get boring – you should introduce variation to how you study – if you're a slave to the material which your college provides you, try to read round the subject by looking at articles in law periodicals or law journals. But above all, try to work at regular times, like a job, so you build in pre-planned leisure time.

S is for... Study groups

Being part of a study group will not only enhance your learning, it will also develop your teamwork and presentation skills. Having 'study buddies' is a great way to learn, consolidate and revise. The ideal number to have in a study group is four, and while you should meet regularly (maybe once a fortnight initially), the first meetings should be informal as you simply get to know each other, swap experiences and generally support each other as you settle into life as law students. It's worthwhile trying to form such a group very early on in your studies, but make sure each member is committed to the principle, rather than treating the group as a social club.

Be prepared for members of the group to have strengths and weaknesses – that's part of the value of belonging to such a group: each member will bring different qualities to the study table. Just because you're breezing through the contract law module and one or two members of the group are not, it doesn't mean that you will be spending the rest of the course as their informal private tutor. If, from time to time, you do assume that role, take encouragement from it and appreciate the value in explaining the areas which your colleagues are finding difficult – it's great practice for what you'll be doing in the exam! And of course, it is just as likely that the roles will be reversed in a few weeks' time when you're struggling to get your head around the basics of an EU Directive which the rest of your study buddies have spent hours debating without your understanding a word of it.

When studying the GDL you will find that different subjects suit different backgrounds. For example as a result of the process-led nature of equity, those with a slightly more logical and scientific background may be able to grasp it a little faster than those who studied the arts. However, the opposite can be said for subjects such as constitutional and administrative law. People grasp concepts at different paces in any learning environment and it is certainly the case in law. But you just have to be patient (even though it can be frustrating that someone isn't getting something you think is blatantly obvious) because it's you will be the one struggling 15 minutes later.

Olivia Cox, trainee solicitor

T is for... Tabbing

Law students soon get into the habit of tabbing, highlighting and underlining the important parts of their reference materials (eg statute books), which is quite handy as it means you don't have to memorise the wording of every section of every relevant statutory provision. That's what statute books are for! Flagging those sections with 'Post-it' style tabs and/or using fluorescent highlighters, and/or underlining important words or subsections will make it easier to find those provisions again when you have to look them up later on in your studies or during the exam.

Top tip

Before marking any of your statute books or other materials which you are permitted to take into your law exams, familiarise yourself with your university/college's annotation rules. There is likely to be detailed guidance as to what you can and can't do when it comes to tabbing, highlighting, underlining and so on. The last thing you want is, having spent £40 on a book, to have to buy another clean copy for the exam because the markings on your original copy can't be taken into an exam. Worse still, don't taken an 'illegally' annotated statute book into an exam, which is likely to be treated as a serious examination offence, to the extent that your legal career could be over before it has started!

U is for... Understanding

Studying the law isn't like GCSEs and A levels, much of which you could have done well in without having a deep understanding of the knowledge you acquired. Learning the law requires not only a capacity to accumulate and store knowledge, but an ability to appreciate the subtleties of each variation of each fact pattern and the different consequences even a small change in the those facts may bring about. You must continually test your understanding – reading something and thinking you 'get it' is not the same as coming back to the topic 24 hours later and writing a summary of the major points from the top of your head. The latter is a much better test not only of what you have retained, but also what you have understood.

V is for... Variation

Don't just rely on tutorials for someone else's point of view. While not disrupting your routine, it is important that you introduce variation into the way you study. Try things out. You may have got yourself into a solitary routine whereby you do all or most of your studying on your own. As effective as this may be, you will appreciate that the working world will require more interaction with others, so try to build in the occasional study-buddy session to consolidate an area of the course. However well you may be getting on working on your own, hearing someone else's perspective can give your approach to that subject a whole new dimension. Also, instead of learning 'yet another list of bullet points', is there a different way you can list them in order to commit them to memory? Perhaps a list of thumbnail picture prompts, a diagram or a flowchart would make the information easier to remember?

W is for... 'What if?'

After having analysed one set of facts, your law tutors will suggest a slightly different set of facts to test whether the same arguments still apply and if you would still reach the same conclusion. You should employ 'what if' scenarios to your studies as well, because that will help you explore the issues in much greater depth and give you a deeper level of understanding. Don't be afraid to ask your tutor 'what if' questions; it usually demonstrates you are thinking about the subject intelligently, and may give you some guidance as to how to approach the next 'what if' question.

X is for... eXtra reading

Do it! Everyone will (or at least) should be completing all the 'required' reading. There will also be additional reading which is recommended but 'not essential'. Sometimes, only a minority of students will take on such reading, but it will add depth to your understanding and if you can intelligently reference the reading in an exam, it will make your answer stand out, and should enhance your mark. However, don't attempt this extra reading until you have mastered the basics of the concepts which it covers. There is a danger of 'reading everything' and 'understanding nothing'. It is recommended that you build up your additional reading when you recognise that you are 'getting' the subject.

Y is for... Yesterday

As part of your consolidation strategy, continually ask yourself: '*what did I learn yesterday?*' Try to avoid the cycle of preparing for a session yesterday, attending the session the today, and forgetting it tomorrow. So what can you do? Try using what would otherwise be 'dead time' (ie travel time, time in the gym, or possibly even last thing at night) to go over in your head the main concepts and cases which you learned yesterday, without any books or notes. This is a good way of seeing how much of the important material you have absorbed in the last day or two and how much you actually understood. If (as there will be) there are gaps in your understanding or memory of the main concepts, make a point of quickly reminding yourself what they were when you next open your books. Regular repetition in this way will help you commit the important principles to your long-term memory.

Z is for... Zzzz!

Sleep! Get some sleep! Working regularly until 1.00am as a law student or occasionally slogging through the night is sometimes seen as a 'badge of honour', or a sign that you are diligent and hard-working. It's neither of these. Working until 'silly o'clock' is more a sign that you haven't planned your time properly. No student should sacrifice a night's sleep to hand in a piece of work at 9.00 am the following morning. Sometimes the work may be good, but invariably it will be below the standard you should be capable of producing during 'normal' hours. You may have achieved your target of handing in the work on time, but at what cost? The knock-on effect of a lost or short night's sleep will probably mean the next day or two is a 'write-off' in terms of good study and you probably won't feel like going out either. So what's the point? Get organised! Get the work done, have some fun and then get a full night's sleep.

Chapter summary

Being a law student is hard work. There will be the 'dull bits', but you should find more than enough stimulating content elsewhere to keep you going. Different modules will bring about different challenges, particularly in the way that you approach them. Some subjects will come more naturally to the 'arty' student, whereas those from a scientific background will appreciate the logic and methodical approach which modules like Land and Contract Law require. As you're studying, do think about what it is you enjoy (or don't enjoy!) about a subject and compare that experience to other modules. This will help you formulate ideas as to what practice areas may ultimately appeal to you and whether or not you wish to become a solicitor or barrister.

Key points

- Organise your notes and materials. It's good practice for practice!
- Being part of a study groups enhances and provides variation to your learning.
- Consolidate your learning as you go along – don't leave it until the revision period.
- Balance your study and leisure time.

Useful resources

McBride NJ (2010) *Letters to a Law Student: a guide to studying law at university* 2nd edition. Harlow: Longman.

Martin, E (2013) *A Dictionary of Law (Oxford Paperback Reference)* 7th edition. Oxford: OUP

Salomon v A Salomon & Co Ltd. [1897] AC 22

Becoming a solicitor…

BPP
LEARNING MEDIA

Chapter 7

Becoming a solicitor: the Legal Practice Course

With contributions from
Abi Flack and Keri Goddard

BPP
LEARNING MEDIA

Introduction

The traditional route to qualifying as a solicitor is set out in Figure 7.1, which assumes you are a full-time student throughout before you start your training contract. However, as you will see, the LPC (like a law degree and the GDL) can be studied in a variety of ways over many different timescales.

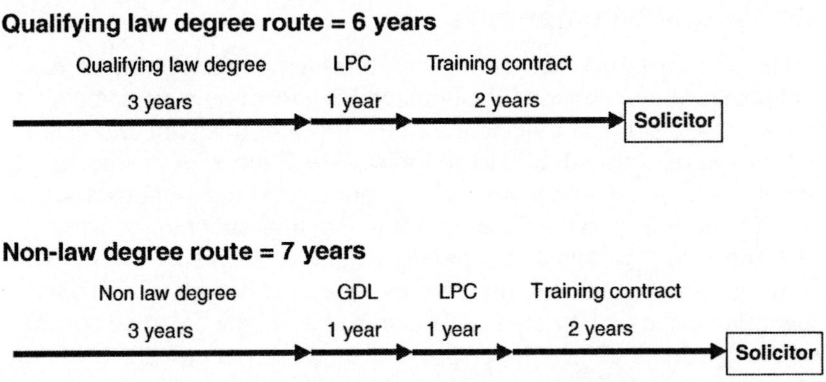

Figure 7.1: The traditional route to qualifying as a solicitor

After having completed a Qualifying Law Degree ('QLD') or the Graduate Diploma in Law ('GDL'), if you want to practise as a solicitor, you will need to:

1. Study and pass the Legal Practice Course ('LPC'); and
2. Complete a training contract.

Traditionally, it has taken six years from commencing a QLD to qualify as a solicitor. Non-law graduates have, traditionally, taken an additional year to qualify, because they need to pass the GDL before starting their LPC.

Getting onto the Legal Practice Course

Before you commence your study of the LPC, you must have:

1. Completed the academic stage of training (or be exempt from it).
2. Applied for student membership of the Solicitors Regulation Authority ('SRA').
3. Obtained a place on the course with an LPC provider.
4. (Overseas students only) Obtained a Tier 4 visa/entry clearance into the UK.

Completion of the academic stage of training

In order to have completed the academic stage of training you need to have either passed:

- A QLD; or
- A non-law degree in another subject (usually with a lower second class degree (2:2) or higher) and the Graduate Diploma in Law.

SRA student membership

Before you start the LPC, you must enrol as a student with the SRA and obtain written confirmation from the SRA that you have completed the academic stage of training. Your LPC provider does not organise this for you. You are advised to sort this out with the SRA as early as possible, especially if you are starting your LPC in the months of August or September. This is because the volume of applications which the SRA receives at this time of year could mean you are subjected to unnecessary stress as the deadline for your LPC provider to have this confirmation fast approaches. This deadline is strictly enforced so you must adhere to it or face the prospect of the SRA not permitting you to continue on your LPC.

Obtaining a place on the LPC

All applications for full-time places are made through the Central Applications Board, known as 'Lawcabs', in the year before you start your LPC. Many places are filled just before a course begins, although some providers still accept students in the early weeks of the LPC.

Overseas students

The UK government has a list of institutions which it trusts to admit students from overseas according to the UK Border Agency's points-based system. As a non-EU overseas student, you should look for a trusted university which is a 'Higher Education Institution with Highly Trusted Sponsor Status'.

In order to get a Tier 4 visa/entry clearance into the UK as a student, you have to enrol on a full-time course at a university or other educational institution which is on the register of sponsors who will sponsor you. You would also need to score enough points to be accepted as an international student in the UK. There are complicated provisions relating to the recognition of overseas degrees which are outside the scope of this title. If you hold an overseas degree, you should make enquires of the SRA to determine what (if any) further requirements you need to satisfy before commencing the GDL or the LPC.

In addition, if you are an overseas student whose first language is not English, you will also need to have attained an International English Language Testing System ('IELTS ') score of 6.5 or above.

Legal Practice Course: modes of study

You may wish to investigate the various modes of study which are available. For example, if you think that you will need to work part-time while studying, investigate the range of part-time LPCs which providers offer. Generally, the larger the provider the more likely it is that you will be able to tailor how you study the LPC to meet you personal needs. For example, you may be able to request that your timetabled sessions are on just two or three days during the week, or are more spread out.

You will find below some of the ways you can study the LPC, but you should research which of these are offered by your preferred provider.

Full-time LPC: one year

This is the most popular LPC and can be completed in just less than 12 months. It commences in September of each year with most providers, but look out for start times at other points in the year – eg both BPP University College and The University of Law also run full-time LPCs with start dates at the beginning of the calendar year, as well as the beginning of the conventional academic year.

Accelerated/Fast-Track LPC: around seven months

Students with leading LPC providers can now complete the LPC in around seven months rather than the traditional one-year course. Most of these courses are available for sponsored students who have training contracts with leading law firms, but there are examples (eg the Fast-Track LPC at BPP) which enable students without training contracts to complete the LPC in seven months.

Top tip

The LPC is an incredibly intensive course. Most students find the volume of work (rather than the general level of difficulty) a challenge on the 12-month course, so the seven month course is only recommended for students with a 2:1 degree or better.

Integrated LPC and training contract

Since its inception, completion of the LPC has always preceded the commencement of a training contract. However, with the approval of the SRA, BPP is now running an integrated LPC and training contract for the trainees of leading law firm, Eversheds. Students study Part 1 of their LPC in six months (ie as 'normal'). However, rather than proceeding with Stage 2 in isolation, they then start their two-year training contracts during which they complete Stage 2 of the LPC. Integrated LPCs and training contracts are likely to become increasingly popular, particularly for top law firms, not least because of the benefit of trainees studying an elective module while working in the same area in practice.

Part-time LPC: 15 months to two years

There are a range of part-time modes available across LPC providers, but, again, the larger providers provide the most options. In addition, students are now permitted to switch between providers for Stage 1 and Stage 2 of their LPC. The attendance requirements for face-to-face teaching are typically as follows:

- Part-time day: one or two days per week
- Part-time Saturday: approximately every other Saturday.
- Part-time weekend: Saturday and Sundays – approximately one weekend per month
- Part-time evening: two evenings per week

Supervised self-study LPC - limited face-to-face teaching, significant online study: typically two years

The SRA has not yet validated a purely online LPC, because of the value attributed to face-to-face teaching. However, a small number of LPC providers offer the opportunity to study a large proportion of the LPC online. While you receive less face-to-face teaching, you are required to complete various interactive tasks, activities and tests online. Enhanced tutor support is available to students on such LPCs. This mode of study is suitable if you cannot or do not wish to regularly travel to an LPC provider at weekends or in the evenings and wish to undertake the majority of the work as self-study. The flexibility of this mode is its obvious attraction, but the limited face-to-face teaching and the lack of regular contact with fellow LPC students will not suit most students' learning styles. But to others, who are time-poor, it is the only option.

Exercise 7.1 – Do you have time to work and study on the LPC part-time or full-time?

If you are working or have other substantial commitments (such as childcare), before you commit to studying on the LPC, work out a weekly budget as to how you would allocate your time each week. One way to do this is to keep a diary of how you currently spend your time over a typical week and then see if you can factor in 20 hours of study/classes for the part-time LPC or 40 hours for the full-time LPC. Be honest with yourself: it is better to over-estimate timings than to enrol on a course which is not compatible with your lifestyle and personal circumstances.

LPC:	20 hours (part-time LPC) / 40 hours (full-time LPC)
Work:	
Travel:	
Eating/socialising:	
Sleep:	
Bathing:	
Childcare/parental responsibilities:	
Shopping:	
Gym/sport/clubs:	
TV/Other leisure:	
Unallocated/spare time:	
Total hours in the week:	**168 hours**

In recent years, two-year law degrees and 'accelerated'/'fast-track' LPCs have reduced the time in which it possible to qualify as a solicitor. These courses are, not surprisingly, incredibly intense, but are nonetheless becoming more popular because being a student for a shorter period of time will save you money, and you can start working much earlier.

If you are considering any of the 'quicker' LPC options (which includes those students who apply to large law firms which will require them to take that route if their application is successful), you should carefully weigh up the benefits of a shorter period of study against the greater pressure you will be under, which may mean you miss out on much of the 'student experience'. In addition, these intense courses are unlikely to give you much time to commit to a part-time job if you need an income while you study. Having said that, most students on a one-year LPC admit to being time-poor, so don't think doing the 12-month course provides you with loads of free time. It doesn't! Most students still report that the workload is heavy – considerably more so than their undergraduate studies.

It is not essential to study Stage 2 of the LPC immediately after Stage 1. It is possible to complete Stage 1 and then return to study Stage 2 at a later date, and not necessarily at the same provider with whom you studied Stage 1. Generally, students have five years to complete the LPC. However, you should always check the current rules and regulations set by the SRA, as they will change from time to time.

Legal Practice Course – content

The LPC is a practice-based course on which students study various compulsory subjects and skills and select three elective subjects with a view to equipping them with the tools that they need to provide effective legal advice to clients. Students who study the LPC find it very different to their undergraduate studies because the focus is very much on the practical skills required to be a good lawyer rather than an in depth analysis of the law itself which you will have already done as part of your law degree or the GDL.

At the end of your LPC, if you pass, you will receive a transcript of all your grades. LPC providers will, typically, have a grading system in order to distinguish between students who pass. In descending order, these grades are:

- Distinction
- Commendation
- Pass

For a Distinction, you will normally be expected to have passed every subject at the first attempt and have averaged 70% or more across the exams in the core practice areas and electives.

LPC Stage 1

All LPC providers are required to cover:

- The three core practice areas (the 'CPAs'):
  - Business Law and Practice
  - Property Law and Practice
  - Civil and Criminal Litigation
- Skills
  - Advocacy
  - Interviewing and Advising
  - Practical Legal Research ('PLR')
  - Legal Writing
  - Drafting
- Pervasives
  - Professional Conduct and Regulation
  - Tax, Wills and Probate
  - Business Awareness
  - Commercial Awareness

Business Law and Practice ('BLP')

In BLP, you will examine the law that regulates how businesses are run, including the study of different types of business media, such as sole traders, partnerships, limited liability partnerships and limited companies, as well as the life cycle of a company. This module is the largest of all the CPAs in terms of subject coverage and hours of teaching. Consequently, keeping on top of the material as you go along is essential.

Property Law and Practice ('PLP')

This is a module which examines how the buying and selling of freehold and leasehold property works in practice. Many providers cover leasehold property in more detail than the SRA requires, particularly the larger providers. Depending on your choice of LPC provider, PLP may have more of a commercial property emphasis and less of a focus on residential conveyancing.

Exercise 7.2

To perform well on the LPC, you need to think logically, commercially and practically. Here is a simple practical problem in a Property Law context which students would need to solve on the LPC.

Your client wishes to buy 12 Lowham High Street (the 'Property') which is shaded grey on the plan below. Your client intends building a supermarket on the Property. Looking at the plan, what potential problems might your client have?

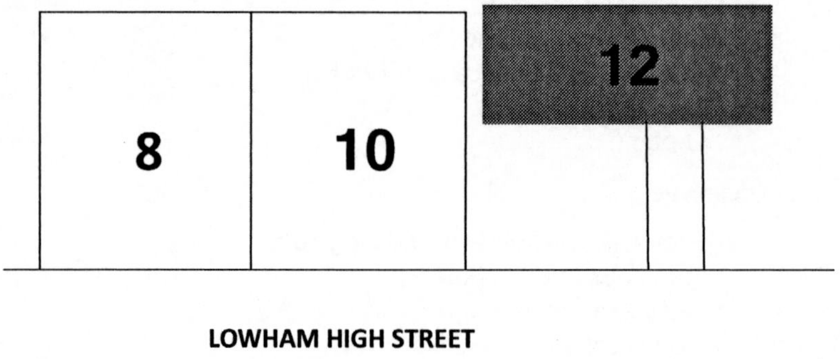

Answer to Exercise 7.2:

Unlike the properties at 8 and 10 Lowham High Road, No. 12 does not abut Lowham High Street. Does it matter? It might do! The owners of No. 8 and No. 10 are able to access their properties directly from main road. However, as No. 12 is set back from the main road and can only be accessed by the connecting road/pathway, you have to ask whether the owners of No.12 have a right of way over that road/pathway to get to No. 12 from the main road. If there is a suitable right of way, is it wide and strong enough to drive vehicles, like delivery lorries down? Who is responsible for maintaining the road/pathway which connects the Property to Lowham High Street? So, you will see that a typical LPC problem can involve practical, legal and commercial issues.

Civil Litigation and Criminal Litigation

Civil Litigation and Criminal Litigation are separate subjects, but they are treated as one module. You will spend around twice as much of your time in class on Civil than you will on Criminal Litigation. You will cover the process of civil claims and criminal prosecutions through the courts. Having a strong grasp of procedure and being able to apply it to the facts of a scenario is essential to doing well in both Civil and Criminal Litigation, which are often taught by separate tutors on the LPC.

Skills and pervasive subjects

Students need to be assessed as being competent in each of the skills which were listed above. To some students, running an interview with a client and providing instant advice with a list of options sounds daunting. Consequently, a significant proportion of students approach the *Interviewing and Advising* assessment with a certain amount of fear. This assessment is given added authenticity in several law schools because the clients are played by actors. The *Advocacy* assessment has a similar feel to it, as students' oral skills are once again tested, but this time in the context of a contested hearing. The vast majority of students get through these two oral assessments first time, but learn a considerable amount about their presentation skills, to which tutors can add enormous value by giving constructive feedback when the skills are practised in class.

Your legal research skills are tested in *PLR* when you will be expected to investigate a relatively obscure area of the law and provide a research note. *Legal Writing* is a test of your ability to explain complex issues in a clear, concise and client-friendly manner. For Legal Writing, you are not so much marked on the content, but how you have produced the piece of writing – in terms of how it looks, the language you use and how clearly you have expressed yourself.

Drafting is a pervasive subject as well as a skill. By being 'pervasive', we mean it crops up more or less everywhere, particularly in the CPAs. For example, you may be asked to draft, amend or critique Particulars of Claim in a Civil Litigation exam or a draft contract in a Property exam. On some LPC courses, Drafting is separately assessed as a skill, and in others it is assessed in other exams, like the CPAs – or a mixture of the two. Students often underestimate the skill of drafting, because they have been writing for last 20 or so years, so 'how hard can it be?' Quite difficult, actually! It's an acquired skill! You will be introduced to defined terms and how to use them when drafting, how to draft legal documents based on the ABC principles: ie to draft with:

- Accuracy
- Brevity
- Clarity

Like Drafting, *Professional Conduct and Regulation ('PCR')* can be separately assessed and/or examined in the CPAs. You will be given problems to solve which involve ethical dilemmas, such as conflicts of interests, as well as how issues of money laundering and the regulation of financial services affects solicitors in practice. *Solicitors Accounts* falls technically under PCR, but is really a standalone module which is separately assessed. The Solicitors Accounts module does scare many LPC students, particularly those who made a conscious decision not to become an accountant, but the reality is, although you will use a calculator, there is no real maths involved; if you simply learn the principles of double-entry book-keeping and can distinguish credits from debits and the firm's money from client money, you're half-way there. Practice does make perfect: it is one of those rare modules in which it's realistically possible to get 100%.

Most of the other pervasive areas listed above are areas of law and practice which are commonly embedded in other subjects across the LPC, most of which are not separately assessed. For example, commercial awareness is integral to many problems which students are set in their LPC assessments, because the facts are often based on a business scenario, which requires you to think practically and commercially, and not solely on the legal issues.

LPC Stage 2

In Stage 2 of the LPC, you will study three subjects, all of which you can choose ('electives'), although some sponsored students are required by their firms to select at least one specific elective – if not all three. Not all LPC providers provide the same elective subjects and you should therefore make sure you base part of your decision to select a particular LPC on what subjects are offered by the provider at the location you have applied to. In the first instance, you should endeavour to choose electives which match the area of practice in which you would like to qualify or the areas of practice that are covered by the type of firms you are applying to for a training contract.

While you are considering which LPC provider to apply to, it is important to check the list of elective choices offered in order to see if the areas of law that you are interested in are covered. Some electives are only delivered by one or two LPC providers. For example, Manchester Metropolitan University offers an elective in Housing Law and Welfare Benefits, Bristol Law School (part of the University of the West of England) offers Charity Law and BPP University College offers Insurance Law. These are subjects which few (if any) other providers deliver. While the availability of an 'unusual' elective in a subject which you are interested in may be a factor in choosing where to study for your LPC, it certainly should not be the only factor; choosing (or not choosing) a 'niche' elective is unlikely to make or break a training contract application.

Here is a non-exhaustive list of popular LPC electives. Please note that not all of these are taught by every LPC provider:

Advanced Commercial Litigation

This elective builds on the core practice area of civil litigation and is extremely useful if at this stage you have aspirations of becoming a litigator.

Advanced Commercial Property

Similarly, this elective carries on from Property Law and Practice which is studied in Stage 1 and usually focuses in more detail than PLP on commercial deals, property development and a more detailed analysis of how to negotiate lease clauses.

Advanced Criminal Litigation

This follows on from Criminal Litigation studied in Stage 1 and is suitable for students who are considering joining a law firm with a Criminal Law practice.

Intellectual Property

This elective covers intellectual property rights (eg copyright and patents). This subject may be delivered as part of a module which includes other commercial issues such as sale of goods, competition law and distribution.

Corporate Finance

This deals with the law and regulation of public companies regarding the raising of funds by way of debt and equity funding (eg loans and share issues).

Debt Finance/Capital Markets/Banking

'Debt' covers the raising of funds by companies through banks and bond issues. Students become aware of standard clauses in loan agreements and debentures, and learn how to negotiate them in practice.

Employment Law

This concerns the law that regulates the relationship between an employer and an employee, and includes the law relating to unfair dismissal and redundancy, discrimination, and employment tribunal procedure.

Equity Finance

Equity Finance deals with the law and regulation of public companies (ie those listed on the London Stock Exchange and on AIM), as well as the raising of funds though the public market and takeovers.

Family Law

This focuses on the law and procedure which relates to when a couple separates, including what happens when there are children involved. This elective may also look at civil partnerships, public and private children law, domestic abuse and the position of cohabitees.

Immigration Law

This is the study of the law and regulation which governs immigration in this country. The module typically covers applications for visas, British citizenship and political asylum, focusing on the procedures involved and the evidence required for a successful application.

Media and Entertainment Law

This elective covers the key rights and common agreements that a solicitor would expect to come across in a number of media and entertainment industries including music, film, television, advertising and sport.

Personal Injury and Clinical Negligence

'PICN' looks at how a third party can be held liable for injuries suffered by another person including where injury has been suffered, for example, as a result of negligent medical care.

Private Acquisitions/Mergers and Acquisitions

'PA' deals with the law and regulation in relation to the sale and purchase of private companies (eg those companies that are not listed on the stock exchange) and commercial agency. Some courses may deal with this in an international context.

Private Client (Wills, Probate and Estate Planning)

This elective concerns the law of trusts, wills and probate, what happens to an individual's estate when he or she dies, and the planning which can be carried out in order to make an individual's will as tax efficient as possible.

My fascination with law goes right back to when I was doing my A Levels – anything I studied which had a legal aspect captivated me. I always wanted a career that would present me with options and opportunities, as well as being intellectually demanding and challenging. Law certainly seems to fit the bill. During my law degree I found the Commercial Law based subjects fascinating, particularly the way in which the law seems to shape all kinds of business activities, which are inherently subject to some form of regulation or statutory control. My choice of corporate-focused electives on the LPC also reflects my long-term desire to join a City law firm.

Harriet Raybould, LLB graduate and LPC student

Choosing your Legal Practice Course

The best way to start is to look at the websites of LPC providers, a list of which is provided on the SRA's website. The content of LPCs can vary from provider to provider, and some providers offer a choice of emphasis in terms of the content of your LPC, depending on whether you are looking to follow a corporate or 'high street' route. So, it is important for you to identify whether you see yourself as a corporate animal, working in a niche area, the 'local' solicitor, or, as many do at this stage, a 'don't know'. Fortunately, most LPCs will cater for the latter group, because their content is broad and varied in terms of the types of case studies and areas you deal with. In reality, most LPCs will give you the ability to head off to the City, the High Street (or somewhere in between).

Top tip

If you do choose an LPC which is marketed as a specialist 'Corporate' or 'High Street' LPC, be certain that it is the direction you wish to follow in practice. If you are in any doubt, choose one of the many with less of an emphasis one way or the other.

Most LPC providers teach by way of a combination of:

- Live lectures
- Online lectures
- Face-to-face teaching in small group sessions comprising around 18 to 21 students.

Some institutions are validated to deliver an LPC which is, for the most part, taught online. Before you choose your provider you should think carefully about the kind of learning environment which best suits you.

There are over 40 institutions which are authorised to provide the LPC across England and Wales. With so many to choose from, you need to make sure you are choosing the right course for you. The largest providers are:

- BPP University College
- The University of Law

BPP University College and The University of Law both have multiple sites across England. Consequently, for most students, it is possible to study for the LPC with either of the two biggest providers while still living 'at home'.

Where you live is just one factor – there are many others you should consider when you are choosing your LPC. To help set you on the right track towards making this important decision, students should carefully consider the following.

Grading of LPC providers

The SRA has a published rating or grading system. Each university or law school is subject to inspection by SRA-appointed assessors who check that the required standards are being maintained in the teaching of the LPC. In addition to this, every mode of the LPC delivered in every institution (ie each format of the course, for example full-time and part-time) must be separately validated by the SRA.

The SRA uses three levels to grade the quality of an institution:

1. *Commendable Practice* – there is significant evidence of best practice
2. *Confidence in the provision* – appropriate standards are maintained; or
3. *Failure to meet the required level of provision* – appropriate standards are not being met.

Although standards within an institution can change (and vary), the SRA ratings are one of the best ways of checking you really are getting the best quality teaching from an LPC provider. Whichever provider you choose, you want to be certain that you are going to receive teaching of the highest standard. One of the best ways to do this is to talk to current and past students and tutors at open days and law fairs and to check which law firms send their trainees to which providers. You can always request that the admissions team at any LPC provider asks an LPC tutor to call you to discuss the course. You can also find out about each provider from the Junior Lawyers Division of the Law Society.

Funding your LPC

The cost of the LPC varies from around £6,000 to £14,000, depending on the provider and their location.

Top tip

When comparing course fees, make sure you are comparing 'like with like'. In particular, are all materials and text books included in the course fees? Do you get photocopying credits? Do you have to pay for re-sits? But it is short-sighted to chose your LPC on tuition fees alone; other factors like the quality of teaching (ie how well the course will prepare you for practice) will vary, and (rightly or wrongly) some employers will look more favourably on students who have taken their LPC at one of the leading providers.

If you are lucky enough to have a training contract with one of the top 50 law firms before you start your LPC, you will usually be required to study your LPC at a particular law school, because most top law firms have exclusive arrangements with one of the largest LPC providers. Top law firms will usually pay the LPC course fees of its future trainees as well as a reasonable amount in maintenance costs, ranging between £5,000 and £7,500. Medium-sized firms may pay a contribution towards your LPC fees or offer a loan, but little or no maintenance, although some will pay both. In general, smaller firms provide less assistance for their future trainees' LPC fees and living costs. Indeed most small to medium firms provide no financial assistance all. Nevertheless, in the current economic climate, it is worthwhile remembering that it is a tremendous achievement to possess any offer of a training contract before you start your LPC, even if you have to self-finance part or all of your LPC fees and living costs.

Those with training contracts at larger firms don't have it all their own way: most large law firms who invest between £15,000 and £20,000 in each future trainee (at this stage alone) will monitor their progress and general performance during the LPC. Students with training contracts with some (but not all) larger firms who 'under-perform' may find that their training contract is at risk unless there are mitigating circumstances. Most sponsored students should be capable of achieving a commendation (if not a distinction) on the LPC, but few firms will go on record to say that a training contract may be at risk if their student 'merely' passes the course.

A few LPC providers offer scholarships, although there are only a handful of fully-funded scholarship places across all LPC providers. Otherwise, your options are to:

- Arrange a loan. Your LPC provider will be able to refer you to a low cost loan provider which specialises in loans to LPC students.
- Work part-time during your full-time LPC (which is not recommended because the one year full-time course is intense).
- Study the LPC part-time over two years while you work full-time.

Timing

The LPC has, historically, been a full-time one-year course, which is still the most popular option. However, there are many other routes you can take to qualification which include:

- An 'accelerated' or 'fast-track' LPC (which students with leading LPC providers can now complete in around seven months rather than the traditional year's course).
- An integrated LPC and training contract. At the time of going to print, such opportunities are limited to specific arrangements between providers and specific law firms which have been sanctioned by the SRA (eg BPP's arrangement with Eversheds) but this option is likely to become more popular.
- Part-time, which can take you up to twice as long to qualify.

Practical experience of LPC lecturers and tutors

Another way to assess the teaching on any particular LPC is to look at the lecturers/tutors who will be delivering the course. The LPC is a practice-based course which aims to provide you with the skills that you need to succeed as a practising solicitor. At some LPC providers (including the larger ones), all lecturers and tutors are either qualified solicitors or barristers who have spent time in practice, several of whom have been partners in large law firms. In contrast, some LPC providers have a higher proportion of academic lawyers with less experience of life in legal practice. Academic lawyers can do a perfectly good job of teaching the LPC, but they may, at times, not give you the commercial and practical edge which an experienced practitioner has to offer.

Supporting your learning

When you are looking into LPC providers, you should investigate how your studies will be supported. Check whether you will you have access to:

- A personal tutor
- A mentoring programme designed to help you to get the most out of your studies
- Revision packs
- Past papers
- Mock examinations
- Consolidation activities
- Regular feedback from your tutors as to how you are progressing
- A well-organised student intranet

If you have specific learning support requirements (eg you may be hearing-impaired, blind or partially-sighted, or have dyslexia, dyspraxia or some other condition which may make part or all of your studies or your exams even more challenging than they will be already), do enquire how your needs will be supported. Will you be given extra time in your assessments?

Students are sometimes reluctant to discuss their learning support needs because they feel it will count against them in some way, or they don't wish to be treated any differently than anyone else. This is simply not the case: educational institutions have an obligation to provide equal opportunities for persons with disabilities and learning support needs so that there is equality of opportunity. You have a responsibility to yourself to maximise your potential, so if you think help may be available to you, it would be foolish not to look into it or refuse what is offered to you.

Links with law firms

You have already read that almost all of the top law firms have exclusive arrangements with one of the leading LPC providers. If you are offered a training contract with a firm which has such an exclusive arrangement, you will be told where you will need to study the LPC. Exclusive relationships are a good indicator of the quality of a provider, its teaching and materials, because successful law firms have decided that that is the standard they want for their future employees. After all, each year, those firms are investing million of pounds in their future trainees' education. But just because the largest LPC providers have arrangements with top law firms, it does not mean that they are every student's best option.

It isn't just the largest LPC providers in London who have links with law firms; even the smallest LPC providers will have links with local firms who attend events and speak to LPC students, sometimes actively recruiting the attendees for training contracts. And, of course, if you study in one of the regional centres of the larger LPC providers, you will also have the opportunity of meeting local practitioners. The types of links which law firms have with law schools varies widely; representatives of the profession may sit on an advisory board which helps to design and shape an LPC course and there are also a number of practitioner/student mentoring schemes as well.

How you are assessed

Whichever provider you choose, you will be assessed by way of written and oral examinations. Providers have different rules in terms of what materials and books you are permitted to take into your assessments and how you may annotate them. These rules can vary year on year and so you should always check the providers' websites for the up to date position.

A great deal of discussion takes places on internet discussion boards every year over the fact that you can take any materials into the exams at one institution and the policy is more restricted at others. The 'advantage' of one approach rather than the other is hugely over-stated by students, and is, in reality, negligible, if it exists at all. The LPC is a test of how students *apply* the law to given scenarios, which requires practical skills which no textbook or set of notes is going to help you with in the exam. The reality is that even in the institutions which limit permitted exam materials to statute books only, students who prepare well will highlight, flag and underline their statute books (where permitted) in all the 'key' places, which can act as trigger-points in the exam, if needed.

Timetable flexibility

Some LPC providers only offer a limited way to study, by way of a rigid daily timetable of a single one-hour lecture followed by a single one and a half or two-hour class each day. Other institutions offer the opportunity to study two, three, four or five days per week, some with live lectures and others with lectures that can be watched online. Some have a combination of live and online lecture delivery.

Top tip

If you get the opportunity to choose to attend a full-time LPC on only two or three days per week, don't make the mistake of thinking you can hold down a job for the other two or three days. Full-time courses are billed as being 'full-time' for a reason – when you're not in class or a lecture theatre, you are expected to be online or dipping in and out of your books and notes. The bottom line is you need to spend at least 40 hours per week on the full-time LPC. Those who do not underperform, and many end up failing the course.

Upgrading your LPC

Studying for the LPC at some LPC providers will give you credits towards a Master's Degree. Many students are now taking advantage of this option, particularly those who don't start a training contract immediately after they complete their LPC. There is some debate as to how valuable such an additional qualification is, particularly because more students are now staying on to complete their Master's to improve their CV. But that should not be your prime motivation. To study for a Master's you should have a passion for the areas you wish to research/study, ideally in a field which you see yourself practising in.

Careers support

The best LPC providers have dedicated careers teams to support students in their quest to secure a training contract. Many students arrive on the LPC without a training contract and acquire one while they are studying the LPC with the help of the careers team. You should check the websites of all LPC providers that you are considering applying to in order to see whether the LPC provider has any links with law firms, which can be key to finding a training contract, and also to see what careers advice is provided to students. A good careers service will, for example, provide advice in relation to CV drafting and mock training contract interviews shortly before the real thing.

Size of LPC provider

Size isn't everything! Students at smaller providers report a more personal approach, which they also report at the smaller centres of the larger providers outside London. However, the more student places an LPC provider has, the greater the investment there is likely to be in IT resources and careers support.

Information technology

Institutions vary in terms of the IT resources that they offer. Some offer online lectures only while others live delivery only. Some provide a combination of the two and leave it to individual students to decide which method of study is best for them. Online facilities can include MP3 and MP4 recordings which you can download and listen/watch in your own time without needing WiFi access. Most providers will have a virtual learning environment ('VLE') but the extent of what is on offer does vary considerably. When researching your choice of LPC, find out which of the following are on the provider's VLE:

- PDF copies of course materials
- Past papers and revision materials
- Online lecture recordings and slides
- Online/catch-up sessions
- Interactive quizzes
- Virtual classrooms

Case study

Will's first language is Chinese, and although his English is competent, he still finds it challenging to concentrate for the whole length of a live lecture, which can last up to an hour and a half. In some lectures, Will finds it extremely difficult to focus when his desire to take an afternoon nap coincides with the less interesting contents!

He appreciates his LPC provider's online lectures, which are audio recordings with slides that he can access via the VLE. Will wishes lectures had been delivered this way on his degree course, because he can now stop the recording any time he likes and go over a point he doesn't understand before resuming the lecture. His provider also makes downloadable MP3 and MP4 versions of the lectures available so Will can listen and watch them 'on the move' whenever and wherever he likes.

I studied for my LLB and LPC at the same provider, which has a fantastic virtual learning environment (VLE) consisting of all the materials relevant to your time on its courses, which are easily accessible on a single online database. The VLE also deals with a whole range of ancillary matters including careers support, and pro bono projects, as well as how to get involved with all the clubs and societies on offer. Starting off as an undergraduate student, the VLE allowed me to enrol onto pro bono projects quickly and easily.

Perhaps the most useful feature of my provider's VLE is the fact that any information you require can be available at the click of a button. So, if for any reason, you have missed a session, you can catch up in the comfort of your own home by listening to recorded online lectures and online sessions, working through suggested solutions to consolidate your understanding of the topics and going through short form and multiple-choice questions to ensure that you are up to date for the next class.

The VLE makes life at my law school a lot easier, allowing me to focus my time and efforts on the things that matter.

Manjeet Kaur Singh, LLB graduate and LPC student, BPP University College

Pro bono work

'Pro bono publico' means 'for the public good'. In a legal context, the abbreviated term 'pro bono' means providing legal services for no fee (or at a significantly reduced fee) to members of the public who, ordinarily, cannot afford to pay. Many students want to be involved in 'pro bono' work during their LPC as it is a valuable way to gain experience and boosts their CV. If you are interested in pro bono work you should check if there is a pro bono unit attached to the law school that you are thinking of attending. Students involved in pro bono often help out with local authority housing, welfare benefits and employment problems. As interesting and satisfying as pro bono work is, remember you are still a law student, and so your priority must be to get the highest marks which you are capable of in your studies. So, do take the opportunity of doing pro bono work – it is good for you and good for others, but remember, if you want to practise as a solicitor, you have to pass the LPC first! It's easy to get distracted by the lures of 'the next client', but there will be plenty of time for that – after you qualify. It's just a question of getting the balance right.

Ready for practice

A good LPC will train students to apply the law to practical legal problems in order to ensure that they are fit for practice on the first day of their training contract. Good LPC providers make the scenarios practical, varied and student-centred, bringing the subjects to life by the use of realistic case-studies. LPC graduates' views as to whether they consider themselves ready for practice will vary. Some students will say they were just taught to pass the exam, whereas others will be given the opportunity to develop their learning and experience considerably beyond the LPC materials. Look out for optional non-examinable modules which some providers run.

How to approach studying the LPC

Whatever mode of study you choose for your LPC, you will need to be dedicated to succeed and you will need to ensure that you can set aside the right amount of time each week in order to attend all of your live timetabled sessions (and any online sessions) and complete your preparation for these sessions. In particular, if you are working while studying, you will also need to make sure that you have sufficient revision time set aside. LPC students, particularly those who work part-time, need to use the same organisation and time management skills which they are expected to employ in practice.

If you do have concerns about the course, your classmates, your future, or perhaps outside issues which may be adversely affecting your ability to study, make use of the support which may be available from:

- Your personal tutor
- Your programme leader
- Student support services
- Your LPC provider's mentoring scheme (if one is available)

Top tip

Students who struggle on the LPC tend to do so because they:

- Don't seek assistance from tutors at the earliest opportunity
- Don't get to grips early enough with the practical rather than academic nature of the course
- Do not organise their time effectively
- Don't prepare for and attend all their classes
- Think they can cram everything a few days before the relevant exam

Students who perform well on the LPC do so because they:

- Leave sufficient time to prepare well for sessions
- Engage fully with the material being covered
- Are dedicated and work hard
- Make the most of the resources on offer
- Trust their tutors to lead them through the course and then follow the suggested study plans and guidelines

Chapter summary

The LPC is a demanding but manageable course if you approach it diligently.

Choose your LPC carefully:

- Research the providers
- Prepare a shortlist, based on your own circumstances and preferences weighing up the factors discussed in this chapter.
- Compare what each of them has to offer in the areas you consider are most important to you.
- Then (and only then) make your application.
- Make use of your LPC provider's careers and mentoring facilities, particularly if you don't yet have a training contract. You are paying for these services! They may make the difference between leaving the law school with or without a training contract.

Key points

- The course content varies between providers.
- Make sure your choice of electives is consistent with your desired career path, or at least keeps as many options open as possible.
- Combining outside work and/or family commitments with the LPC requires commitment and robust time management.

Useful resources

www.lawcabs.ac.uk

www.sra.org.uk/students

www.bpp.com

www.law.ac.uk/home

www.juniorlawyers.lawsociety.org.uk

Chapter 8

Becoming a solicitor – applying for a training contract

BPP
LEARNING MEDIA

Introduction

The aim of this chapter is twofold:

1. To make sure you still want to become a solicitor; and
2. If you do, how to maximise your chances of securing a training contract.

A training contract traditionally lasts for two years and is the final stage of a solicitor's training following:

- The academic stage – a law degree or the GDL
- The vocational stage – the LPC

The vast majority of trainees complete their training contracts at law firms (which is where we will focus in this chapter), but there are also opportunities to do so in the public sector, such as with local authorities and the Government Legal Service. A small number of training contracts are also offered each year in the private sector (ie in the legal departments of some large companies).

The University of Law (previously The College of Law) polled almost 2,000 of its full-time graduates who passed the LPC in July 2010. At first reading, the headline *'84% of the University of Law's 2010 graduates have secured work in the legal profession'* (University of Law, 2012) looks impressive when you consider the prevailing economic climate. However, when you look below the headline, less than two thirds (62%) had secured a training contract, a significant number of which were in place before the students arrived at the University. Twenty-two per cent of the students polled were working as paralegals – doing a similar job to that of a trainee solicitor, but without the opportunity of qualifying after two years.

So, with a significant proportion of LPC graduates failing to secure training contracts, you need to have a co-ordinated strategy to pursue your goal. Unless you are truly exceptional, a training contract will not fall into your lap: you have to work hard to get one, and if you're not prepared to put that work in, you need to ask yourself why you bothered to study on the LPC in the first place!

'Seats'

You will spend your training contract in a variety of departments, typically for three, six or eight months at a time. Traditionally, firms provided four six-month placements, but nowadays, some trainees get as many as six seats. Your training contract must ensure a split between contentious and non-contentious work during the two years. In other words, you must have some litigation experience – ie any form of dispute resolution – anything which could end up in a court or tribunal. This includes all forms of litigation (ie not just Criminal and Civil Litigation), but also specialist areas such as Employment and Family Law work, as long as it is not purely advisory. Sometimes your firm will ask for your department preferences, and while you are rarely given any guarantees, most large firms endeavour to accommodate your first preference.

Large law firms provide a vast range of legal services, and within each of their many departments, there is a huge variety of work. Consequently, the experience gained by two trainees at the same large law firm is likely to be completely different, even if they work in the same department. This is not to say that the work isn't planned or structured – far from it! Large firms take great care in planning and monitoring the progress of their trainees, which is quite a job when you consider that some of them take on over 100 new trainees each year!

In smaller firms, there is a little more consistency and predictability to the type of work trainees will do. Sometimes you may be asked which litigation seat you would prefer, but at other firms with more of a litigation bias, you may get the opportunity of two or three litigation seats.

In each seat, you will be assigned a supervisor with whom you will often share an office. Your supervisor will usually be at least two or three years qualified, and is likely to be a partner in a smaller firm. Most of your work in each seat will come via your supervisor, so it's important you try to strike up a good relationship. You don't have to escort them to their life-drawing class every Thursday evening, but at least feign a little interest in their kids or pets: if asked, lawyers (like anyone else) can't resist the temptation of updating you about the little things in their lives – not least because it reminds them why they're working so hard!

During your two years, you should receive regular feedback on your work both informally (possibly in weekly or monthly reviews from your supervisor), but also, more formally through your firm's appraisal system. The SRA requires trainees to have three formal appraisals during their training contracts – one part-way through each year and a further one at the end of the contract. The SRA suggests that your performance should be reviewed in every seat or every six months.

Although you and your fellow trainees will form what is a vital mutual support network, there is no getting away from it: at the end of your two-year training contract, it is very unlikely that there will be a job for every one of you. Your performance will, inevitably, be compared to that of others. So, as well as being a training contract, treat those two years as an extended job interview! Working hard and catching the eye of more senior colleagues with the quality of your work, your personality and professionalism, even if you're not enjoying that particular department, should be your goal in each seat. Word spreads fast as to the competence (or otherwise) of trainees, which can be vital if you want to be offered a job at the firm on qualification. The prospect of being judged, almost on a daily basis, may sound daunting at first, but you soon end up putting such thoughts to the back of your mind – not least because your diary is packed, the phone is ringing and your inbox is full!

Your best bet for a job on qualification, particularly in the current climate, is with the firm you train with. In addition, your CV will look better if you do stay on after your training contract – even if it is just for a couple of years. Your first employer's vote of confidence will count in your favour if and when you decide to move on later in your career. However, it's not fatal if you decide to move on – many do, and for the better!

Vacation schemes ('Vac Schemes')

In the same way that mini-pupillages are excellent ways for aspiring barristers to work out which area they may wish to specialise in, Vac Schemes are also an invaluable resource for any would-be solicitor who is looking to work in a top-100 law firm. Most schemes run during the summer but some firms also run them in late December/early January, Easter and in the spring. Most schemes are in London and last one, two or three weeks. Financial help is available – most large firms will pay £200 to £400 per week. It won't make much of a dent in your student overdraft, and you won't be dining at the Ivy yet, but it should just about cover your accommodation, travel and food.

Law firms are acutely aware that the best candidates won't be able to see everyone, so they tour the top universities to market their Vac Schemes in an attempt to attract as many high calibre applicants as possible.

You need to keep a close eye on the deadline dates for when Vac Scheme applications need to be submitted, because they vary from firm to firm. The last date to apply for a place on most summer Vac Schemes is the January prior to the summer placement, although one or two are even earlier. Get your applications in early – it is becoming increasingly competitive to get a place on a Vac Scheme, and places fill up very quickly.

On a Vac Scheme, you are likely to experience some or all of the following:

- Talks with partners, associates and trainees, explaining the firm's key practice areas, and what it's like working in those fields.
- Shadowing a working solicitor.
- Being advised as to the structure of the firm's training contract.
- Being shown that there is a social side to the firm – firms are keen to show their future trainees that life isn't just 'work, work, work!'

A minority of firms treat Vac Schemes as the first part of the recruitment process and set you tasks to undertake, often to be achieved within a tight timescale to see how you respond under pressure.

Treat a Vac Scheme like a first date for someone who is looking for a 'serious relationship'. Firms are trying to look their best in order to attract the best candidates to apply to them for training contracts, but they are also looking out for students whose personality and potential make them possible partners of the future.

You will see all sorts during a Vac Scheme – both in terms of the people who work for the firm and your fellow students. There can be as many as 80 or 90 (but more typically 30 or 40) placements on the Vac Schemes of larger firms, so you will come across a hearty mix of personalities. Let the cocky alpha-males who think 'loudest is best' do their thing – but if you think that may be you, think before you engage your mouth. Enthusiasm is a fantastic asset if it's not overbearing, but if you dominate discussions or group work, you are unlikely to be doing yourself any favours: team-working skills and self-awareness are two of the criteria which firms are looking out for. On the other hand, if your eyes don't leave your shoelaces for two weeks or your mouth only opens when you nibble on the corner of a gravlax canapé, no one will notice you've even been there.

Make an impression. But make the right impression. Good and bad first impressions will be noted not just by you but also by the firms; an eloquent contribution to a debate is just as important for the firms to record as someone who has taken on board too much alcohol at an evening event. At this stage, 'it's folly to get jolly on the Bolly!' Getting drunk on a first date may be fun while it lasts, but you'll probably wake up in the morning and regret it because you've blown your long-term prospects. There will be plenty of time for partying after your multi-million dollar deals close while you are on secondment at your firm's Hong Kong office. But you've got to get there first.

In order to secure a Vac Scheme placement, I applied to four firms that I had a particular interest in using cvmailUK.com. Of the four firms I applied to, one of them, a mid-tier London City firm, invited me to an assessment day. This included an individual activity and an interview with an associate, following which I gained a place on the firm's Vac Scheme.

The Vac Scheme lasted two weeks, with each week being spent in a different department. There were many assessments throughout, and at the end of the two weeks, there was a partner interview.

Unfortunately I did not get the training contract at the end of the Vac Scheme. However, the experience of working in a law firm, and completing the assessments was extremely useful, and made applying to other firms much easier. The experience ultimately helped me to secure a training contract at another firm.

Alexa Cohen, LPC student

Case study

Michael gained a place on a Vac Scheme for a week at a City firm through a family contact. He got a real insight into what a lawyer actually does and life in the City, working in a litigation department, conducting legal research, scheduling case correspondence as well as assisting with general office administration.

Observing that the fee earners were already there when he arrived in the morning and that they were still in the office when he left in the evening, Michael learned that practising lawyers have to work 'as long as it takes' to get the job done.

Top tip

Keep a contemporaneous record of absolutely everything you did, saw and felt during a Vac Scheme, because it will be important ammunition for training contract applications and interviews.

- Who did you speak to?
- What tips did they give you?
- What events did you attend?
- What tasks were you set?
- What did you learn about the practice areas you observed?
- What did you learn about what a solicitor does?
- What did you like about the place, the work, the people?
- What didn't you like?
- What surprised you?

Applying for a training contract: getting started

Where on earth do you start? Almost certainly England or Wales, unless you're mad or keen enough to want to qualify in another jurisdiction: maybe the lure of a penthouse in Manhattan is too great a temptation and you fancy a shot at the New York bar exams. But to most, by the time you've completed your LPC the last thing on most students' minds is the prospect of another period of intense study followed by a healthy diet of revision and exams. To most, the New York bar can wait until your stag or hen party.

With over 10,000 firms in England and Wales, how do you know which one to get hitched to? Again, it's just like dating – by finding out what and who you like. The only way you can do that is by switching on your laptop or tablet and donning that sharp suit which has been staring at you in the wardrobe. Go on some dates, meet a wide cross-section of legal people, but find out who they are before you meet them, so you don't end up wasting your time or theirs. In particular:

1. Research of the legal services market in the sectors which interest you; and
2. Meet people who are currently practising in those areas – trainees, qualified solicitors and partners. And don't forget the clients either. For example, if you have a yearning to be a music lawyer, get some work experience at a record company or a music publisher.

Narrow your focus

You may already have an idea which branch of the law interests you most. It may be that once your childhood dream of being a Premiership footballer was shattered (after you failed to hold down a place in your local under 12s third team), you've had your eyes set on the 'next best thing' – becoming a sports lawyer: negotiating personal endorsements, advertising contracts or media sports rights. Or maybe you haven't a clue as to your ultimate destination, other than the fact that the corporate/commercial world is (or is not) where you see yourself heading.

Parental and family guidance can be helpful, particularly if they have knowledge of the legal services industry. But be prepared to turn round to them and say 'no' if you feel they are pushing you into the small family firm when you have realistic ambitions of something bigger, or just something different. Equally, stand up for yourself if everyone is pointing you in the direction of the City, when deep down you know you're not a corporate animal. These can be difficult conversations, particularly if a parent plays the 'I've bankrolled you for 20 years' card. Express your gratitude and appreciation for everything they've done, but respectfully remind them that it's your career, not theirs. Having said all that, sometimes parents, friends and teachers are better judges of your talents than you: keep an open mind to the advice they give you, process that advice properly and carefully select what to accept and reject.

When narrowing your focus, there are three main considerations:

- What type of law firm/organisation do you see yourself working for?
- Which practice areas interest you?
- Where in the country do you want to work?

The first two considerations should be your priorities, and once you know what they are, consider what geographical options or limitations (if any) you have. For the purpose of this discussion, we will focus on training contracts at law firms, although it is worth checking with local authorities, the GLS and in industry to see what other training opportunities may interest you.

What type of law firm is right for me?

The profession ranges from small High Street practitioners to the global powerhouses which populate part of the skyline of most major cities in the UK and overseas. The range of law firms is immense and it is, to a certain extent, artificial to pigeon-hole them into categories. However, since some readers of this publication may have little knowledge of what's out there, we think it would be helpful to provide some guidance – subject to the caveat that, in reality there are many more categories and sub-categories of law firm.

High Street firms

Most High Street firms are 'general practices' – dealing with the everyday 'bread and butter' legal requirements of the general public: eg Wills and Probate, Conveyancing, Family Law, Personal Injury and Crime. Most will also have some form of commercial or corporate department catering for the needs of small to medium-sized businesses as well. As a trainee in such a firm, you are likely to get a high level of responsibility early on – many report exchanging contracts or attending directions hearings at court in the early weeks of their first seat. But you're equally likely to be given low-grade work and end up doing something menial like photocopying or preparation of bundles for court, which you may feel is 'beneath you'. Treat each experience as a 'positive': knowing how the support staff go about their day-to-day work gives you an insight into their world, so if you later become the partner responsible for hiring such staff, you'll have more of an idea as to what their job entails.

If you're looking to become a partner in a small firm within a few years of qualification, you may have a chance if your billing is high and you are bringing in work to the firm. Small firms need to find a way of encouraging you to stay, rather than to move on with your 'following' (ie your own personal clients). The prospect of a partnership is often used as an incentive to work hard. If you are successful in achieving that goal, having committed yourself to the firm, it becomes more difficult (but far from impossible) to extricate yourself from the relationship (than if you are an assistant solicitor) if and when you wish to move on.

The advent of ABSs (or 'Tesco Law' as they have been branded) is proving a real risk to a sustained future for High Street firms. ABSs are 'Alternative Business Structures' – they are a different business model to that of conventional law firms, which, have, historically, been exclusively owned and run by qualified solicitors. The legalisation of ABSs means that non-lawyers, like large household names such as supermarkets, banks and insurance companies are now permitted to become providers of legal services, whereas they were previously prohibited from doing so. As a consequence, many High Street practices are likely to be taken over or driven out of business altogether. The 'Co-op', which was the first leading brand to come out of the ABS blocks has ambitious plans for 'Co-operative Legal Services'; it already employs several hundred lawyers and has ambitions to employ 3,000 by 2017. (The Co-operative Group, 2012)

To combat this threat, over 400 firms have formed an alliance under the 'Quality Solicitors' brand, which is intended to create clear legal water between the established members of the profession and ABSs. The High Street solicitor will survive, because there will still be a demand which is not solely driven by price, but, in the same way that the number of family-owned corner shops has reduced in recent years, many of their long-time legal neighbours will face a similar fate.

That said, small and High Street firms need trainees and are still recruiting. Most invite applications by way of a combination of letters, CVs and online application forms followed by an interview (or two) with a partner (or two). However, because of financial restraints, you will be lucky if your High Street training contract comes with any financial assistance during your LPC.

A typical High Street firm may offer six months in each of the following:

- *General Litigation.* You could be dealing with a miscellany of divorce, personal injury, employment and debt collection cases as well as more complex civil litigation. Yes, there will almost certainly be some photocopying and document bundling, but usually some low-grade advocacy and client contact as well. You may even get a few files of your own.
- *Corporate.* The sale and purchase of small businesses. On a sale, for example, you may be collating all the disclosure documents and taking instructions from clients in relation to enquiries about the business raised by the buyer.
- *Private Client.* Trainees in High Street firms often draft wills for clients after having taken their instructions. Trainees will often administer small estates as well.
- *Real Estate.* There will be plenty of residential conveyancing (subject to the state of the housing market). Under close supervision, you may be given your own sales and purchases to progress during your seat, which is normally long enough to see several transactions through from start to finish. Some High Street firms may give their trainees commercial landlord and tenant work as well.

Mid-size and Regional Commercial firms

'Mid-size' is a bit of a vague concept and so not everyone's view of what this means is the same. Some commentators put any firm which is outside the 'top ten' in this bracket, but that is misleading. Firms with nearer 100 partners will have much more in common with Large Commercial, City and International firms. So, for now, think of Mid-size firms as those with 20 to 100 partners who provide a full range of commercial and other legal services, some general (eg Commercial, Mergers & Acquisitions, Private client and Real Estate) but some specialist departments as well (eg Health & Safety, Information Technology and Intellectual Property). The larger they are, the more likely it is that the litigation departments will work independently in accordance with the type of litigation they practise (eg with separate commercial litigation, employment litigation and family litigation departments). Mid-size firms may be based from a single central office in London, another city or a large town, and/or they may have several offices in strategic locations as well.

These firms will not be involved in certain types of highly specialised corporate, financial services or banking work (unlike the big boys in the City), but Mid-size commercial firms will frequently undertake general work in each of those areas.

But don't think that if you can't get or don't want a training contract with a Large Commercial, City or International firm, you're playing in the lower leagues. Many Mid-size firms are the 'go to' experts in specialist areas such as Administrative law, Bankruptcy, Construction, Defamation ... the A-Z list is simply too long to mention. These firms may not have an international presence, but they will be 'big hitters' in their own right, and will often have an outstanding reputation in the market place in certain specialist areas. In particular, the largest Regional firms who have little or no London presence have, over the years, won and maintained highly lucrative clients who are based locally. As London-centric as the profession can undoubtedly be, there are many varied and rich pickings to be found outside the 'Smoke'. That's assuming you're not tempted by the prospect of being boxed in a tube twice a day attempting to read the Evening Standard from a distance of twenty millimetres because a tourist has had the audacity of joining your carriage with three enormous suitcases and all eight members of his family.

It is certainly a different experience to work at a Mid-size firm compared to a 'Magic Circle' firm in the City. Trainees and staff at the smaller mid-size firms appreciate being in an environment where 'everyone knows everyone', which is simply impossible in larger firms where you wouldn't recognise half of the partners if they crossed you in the street – and that's even if you, yourself, are a partner! That said, the larger firms do recognise that a corporate atmosphere has its disadvantages (as well as its many advantages), so there are always opportunities to network with a wide range of people both within your office and outside. The work-life balance of Mid-size firms is reportedly better than larger firms, but when a deal is on, you keep going until it closes, whichever side you're on.

The larger Mid-size firms will usually pay a contribution towards your LPC fees and some may pay a small living allowance on top, but you're unlikely to get much help from the bottom end other than the possibility of an interest-free loan.

The range of work which two trainees may undertake at the same Mid-size firm could be extremely varied. Here's an example of the areas one of them may get involved in:

- *Real Estate.* You may assist a fee earner on the acquisition of land for a developer client, possibly drafting a report on title for a straightforward registered commercial property. You may work mainly on Landlord and Tenant matters, dealing with the granting of licences (ie permissions) which your landlord clients may be prepared to give to tenants – eg for making alterations to leasehold premises. You may also act in a corporate support capacity – eg supporting colleagues in the Corporate Department: they may be involved in the acquisition of a company (eg a retail group) which owns a portfolio of properties and your team's job will be to investigate the titles of all properties in the portfolio and provide reports on title. It is likely that you, as the trainee on the deal, will be given the simplest titles to investigate.

- *Employment.* There is likely to be a specialist department which represents and gives advice to clients on employment matters. You may be drafting contracts of employment, advising HR directors of companies with regard to the appropriate redundancy or unfair dismissal procedures to adopt or representing a party in the Employment Tribunal. One of the common jobs undertaken by trainees is advising and/or drafting compromise agreements. These are standard 'full and final settlement' compensation agreements signed by an employer and employer when they agree to part company, often in a redundancy situation.
- *Medical/Healthcare.* This specialised area often crosses the boundaries of medical and legal ethics: the fact patterns and dilemmas can pull at the heart-strings like any episode of *Holby City* or *Casualty.* As well as dealing with medical negligence actions (eg in respect of botched operations, neglect and misdiagnoses) your department may get involved in matters of huge public interest, like, for example, representing a National Health Trust in respect of a patient's 'right to die' case. As a trainee, you will spend much of your time perusing medical records, drafting witness statements and attending court taking notes of the proceedings.
- *Private Client, Trusts and Tax Planning.* Regional and Mid-size law firms often act personally for the directors of their corporate and other high net-worth clients. Managing their wealth, helping to minimise their tax liabilities and settling assets on trusts for family members is par for the course. You may be involved in taking instructions and drafting some of these documents, but you could, equally, be drafting wills and administering estates.

Top tip

Personality and character play an important role in the selection process as well as academics at Mid-size firms. If you know who will be interviewing you, research them thoroughly and see if you have something in common with them. You may both be from the same part of country, have attended the same university or share a similar interest or achievement. The partner and associate profiles on law firms' websites will often give you something to go on. Such 'connections', however tenuous, are quite handy to casually drop in as you're walking into the interview room. But time your comment carefully so that it doesn't look too gratuitous or sycophantic.

Exercise 8.1

If you are thinking of applying to a particular Mid-size or Regional Commercial firm, work out who their main competitors are, and in particular, who the local ones are if they are a regional firm. There may be several competitors in different practice areas.

Once you've done your homework, write down on not more than a single side of paper or in 250 words what makes the firm you are applying to stand out?

Clue: Ignore the marketing spiel about being 'client-focused', 'excellent value for money', 'highly professional' – everyone claims to be all those things. What is the firm's USP(Unique selling point)? Is it location, history, the outstanding achievements of some of its partners in or outside the workplace? Then see if you can link that to your USP.

The recruitment policy of Mid-size firms varies enormously. Many still use the tried and tested method of a letter/application form plus CV followed by an interview, but the larger ones are becoming more sophisticated and are using many of methods now used by Large Commercial, City and International firms (see below).

Large Commercial, City and International firms

With over 1,000 training contracts on offer each year at Large Commercial, City and International firms, you would have thought that there's plenty to go round if you're a 'straight A' student with a 2:1. Alas not. The competition is fierce and if and when you get a training contract you will feel like Charlie Bucket having just received his Golden Ticket. Why? Here are just a few of the reasons:

- You'll get excellent training from people at the top of their game.
- The work will be diverse and challenging.
- You may get a seat in one of the firm's international offices, or in the legal department of a big client.
- You'll be regularly dealing with blue-chip companies and other household names such as those in industry, banking and finance.
- If you impress, you should have a wide range of options to qualify into if you wish to stay at the firm.
- It's a massive vote of confidence in you both as a person and as a future lawyer.
- You should get your Law School fees paid together with some living expenses. And the pay's not bad either for a trainee: most first year trainees at Large Commercial, City and International firms can expect to earn between £35,000 and £45,000 in their first year. The American firms tend to be the biggest payers, but, be warned, they are also, reputedly, the hardest task-masters.

Large Commercial, City and International firms go to extraordinary lengths and expense to ensure they recruit the 'best' people to train in their businesses. You may be the trainees of today, but you are the senior fee earners and partners of tomorrow, so there is an awful lot of that green and metal stuff riding on you. Consequently, the procedure by which these firms select their trainees varies widely, as they all have different views as to how to recruit 'the best of the best'. All will start the process off with Vac Schemes (see above), which you ought to secure a place on before you apply for a training contract: a training contract application to such a firm looks a little naked without the Vac Schemes of two or three major firms on your CV.

It is important to stress that these large firms are not 'all the same'. In several cases, the culture and ethos will be quite different, but you will also notice that different departments within the same firm sometimes have the feel of completely different firms. The long hours, the work ethic, the socialising (or lack of it) – that's why Vac Schemes are so useful: you can get an instinctive feel for the place by being that 'fly-on-the-wall' and talking to those who currently work there.

It is beyond the scope of this book to give full details of the range of work undertaken by City law firms, which merits a separate book in itself. You can easily research this yourself, but, by way of an example only, a trainee in a Large Commercial/City/International firm, may be required to spend time in:

- *Banking Litigation.* In the current economic climate, banks are counting their losses and looking at who they can blame (apart from themselves!) Sometimes it will be other banks, but they may also look to elsewhere to enforce guarantees and other forms of security in order to mitigate their losses. Your role in acting for either side is damage limitation – recoup as much as possible to reduce your client's losses (if you can't clear them completely). Or if you're acting for the defendants, you may be challenging the legality of the security or negotiating a settlement to minimise your client's ultimate exposure.
- *Corporate Reconstruction and Insolvency.* You may be acting for those who are charged with the responsibility of reconstructing a company in distress (such as an administrator) or the company itself. Strategic decisions need to be taken with regard to which parts of the business to sell, which to close and which to remain trading. You will be working on the team advising on the implications of each decision and helping to make them happen.
- *International Capital Markets.* You will get involved in the issue and sale of bonds on the international capital markets. This area is highly regulated and when you've not got your head in the Financial Services legislation or the latest Prospectus Rules, you will probably be checking the documents drafted by more senior colleagues to ensure that, for example, the contents of a prospectus are fully compliant with all relevant regulatory requirements.
- *Corporate (M & A).* Dealing with mergers and acquisitions of or by large companies is a popular seat. If you're lucky, you'll get to see a deal from start to finish, and you, as a trainee, will usually be there at 'silly o'clock' when the deal closes, having run around half the night making slight amendments to documents and ensuring those which are required for closing have been duly executed by all parties and are in the agreed form. You will have built up a checklist during the transaction of all the documents involved and the purpose they serve in the context of the deal, and it may be down to you to ensure that everything is properly collated into the 'bible' of documents after closing – so that your firm has a full record of all the signed documents in the deal.

It shouldn't be the bright lights of the City, the weight of the pay packet or the prestige which attracts you to these firms. The only thing which should attract you is the type of work and prospect of working in a hugely challenging environment. You must also have a general interest or at the very least be curious about the commercial and financial world.

While they don't expect you to have an MBA in commerce, if you show up to an assessment centre during the recruitment process unable to undertake a simple currency conversion or you're not able to explain the criteria involved in a bank's risk-assessment before lending to a business, you're in the wrong place. The Large Commercial, City and International trainee recruitment programmes can test your commercial awareness, creativity, numeracy, literacy, analytical skills, critical reasoning, legal knowledge and common sense. They are unforgiving and will expose your weaknesses as well as allowing your strengths to shine.

The selection process

So you've met the Pope, the Dalai Lama and Nelson Mandela. You sang for the Queen when you were a child chorister and gained distinctions in all your ballet, tap and modern dance exams. You were head girl at school and won every prize going from the egg and spoon race to an impressive industry-sponsored award at law school which paid for your trip to South America where, single-handedly, you re-built the sanitation and communications infrastructure for an entire Amazonian village. You've got more A stars to your name than any top Hollywood agent, you rowed for Oxford ... and for Cambridge, and to top it all you're a balanced, well-rounded individual. Yes, you're fantastic. But they still want to meet you. Test you. Probe you. See you outside your comfort zone and work out whether you can cut it as a lawyer.

Don't worry! No one's that impressive! But a few candidates' CVs will be almost as unbelievable. The point is that an impressive CV may get you a place on the starting line, but it doesn't, ultimately, guarantee you a prize.

Law firms want to see that you are hungry to practise as a lawyer, not that you're just one of the many dazzling high-achievers in the beauty parade waiting for an invitation to join the party. Do you want it enough? And more importantly, do they want you?

Law firms all have different ideas of how to find the best trainees and they all go about the process slightly differently. The selection process to be a trainee may involve various combinations of the following:

- Assessment centre tests and practical exercises
- Critical reasoning tests
- Final selection day: involving tests, interviews and activities
- Interviews – often initially with the HR department (which can be by telephone as well as in person) and then one or more partners

- Online tests
- Open days
- Practical exercises
- Presentations
- Psychometric testing (eg verbal reasoning skills)
- Questionnaires
- Research tasks
- Role-play exercises (eg to test negotiation skills)
- Teamwork/group exercises
- Vac Scheme assessments
- Written tests

Top tips when giving a presentation

- Keep your slides simple and the text to a minimum. Remember, it's your presentation skills they're looking for, not an essay reproduced on a set of slides.
- Consider using simple animation features to bring the slides to life with one or two images. But don't overdo it! The last thing you want them to think is that you want to be Nick Park or Steven Spielberg.
- Don't spend hours on the slides – focus your time on your sales pitch.
- Rehearse your presentation with friends as your audience and ask them to interrupt your flow with a question, answer it and then get back on track. Ask for feedback at the end.
- Video yourself and watch it back, if you can bear it!

'Perfect' timeline to a training contract ('TC') for a student commencing an LLB in Oct 2014

	Jan	Apr	Jul	Oct
2014	• A levels	• A level exams	• Work experience	• Start Yr 1 LLB
2015	• Research firms	• LLB Yr 1 exams • Research firms	• Work experience • Research firms	• Research firms • Start Yr 2 LLB • Apply for Vac Schemes in 2016 • Attend Law Fairs
2016	• Research firms • Apply for TC	• Research firms • LLB Yr 2 exams • Vac Scheme • Apply for TC	• Research firms • Vac Scheme • Other work exp • Apply for TC	• Research firms • Start Yr 3 LLB • Apply for Vac* Schemes in 2017 • Apply for TC*
2017	• Research firms* • Apply for TC*	• Research firms* • LLB Yr 3 exams • Vac Scheme* • Apply for TC*	• Research firms* • Vac Scheme* • Other work exp • Apply for TC* • Start LPC (Sept)	• Research firms* • Apply for Vac Schemes in 2018* • Apply for TC*
2018	• Research firms* • Apply for TC*	• Research firms* • Complete LPC • Apply for TC*	• Research firms* • Vac Scheme* • Other work exp • Apply for TC*	• **START TC IF YOU HAVE ONE!**

* Action if you do not yet have a TC

Fig 8.1

When should I start to apply for a training contract?

In **Figure 8.1**, we have provided you with an illustration to show how a student starting a three-year LLB in October 2014 may go about securing a training contract with a Large Commercial/City/International firm. You will notice that the search for the right training contract for such a student is a continuous project which starts in your first year as an undergraduate and is never completed until you get the right offer.

Some of the biggest firms make offers as early as two years before the proposed start date of a training contract! Even if you set your sights on a different type of firm, use the prompts in **Figure 8.1** to plan your campaign. While smaller firms tend to recruit nearer to the start date of the training contract, most prefer to have recruited their trainees at least one year before their training contracts commence.

We have called Figure 8.1 the 'Perfect' timeline – ie one where the target is to secure a training contract which starts shortly after you complete the LPC. However, the reality is a significant proportion of LPC students won't be successful in achieving that goal: the search for a training contract often goes well beyond completion of a student's LPC.

The focus of your first year as a law undergraduate should be on your degree, not least because, for most students, starting to think like a lawyer has to come before you actually start planning your career as one! Use your first year to seriously think about whether you want to become a solicitor, barrister or something else, and if you think you might want to become a solicitor, start thinking about what type of firm may suit you and which practice areas you may be interested in. Start to research the websites of a variety of law firms, which may help you start to formulate a plan of where you want to go.

Large law firms normally want to know every grade for every module you take in a law degree, so keep your eyes in your books, because tripping up in your first year (while still redeemable) isn't a great start, particularly if you're asked to disclose those grades on applications for Vac Schemes and training contracts.

You should be aiming to get some (more) work experience in the summer holidays of your first undergraduate year and once you start your second year, you should be applying for places on Vac Schemes which are taking place in the Easter and summer of the following year. Or, if your sights are set on a smaller firm, find out when they hold a trainee open day, go along to impress, take mental notes while you are there and write them up as soon as you get home. Also, during your second year, start to make a shortlist of the firms you will target for training contract applications. You will get an opportunity of meeting representatives from many of them on the autumn law fair circuit, so make sure you attend the law fair at your university and sponge whatever information you can get from them, particularly from any trainees who may be stationed on their stand.

Keep a close eye of the closing dates for both Vac Schemes and training contract applications and ensure that your applications are submitted well before the closing date. Places fill up fast – because of the volume of applications, expect firms to start processing the applications before the closing date.

Get used to rejection

Broadly speaking, around 10% of applicants get interviewed. That's a lot of CVs with 2:1s in the 'reject' pile. If you draw blanks with your applications for Vac Scheme placements or training contracts, you may, if you're very lucky get some feedback as to why your application was unsuccessful. But most of the time, you'll have to go over your application and CV and ask yourself, what went wrong? Sometimes, it will be hard to assess, but you may, three months on, spot a typographical error, a spelling mistake, or an errant apostrophe. Perhaps the bad day you had in your Contract exam isn't doing you any favours. That may be all it takes to make the rejection pile, despite your otherwise glowing academic record. But don't give up, particularly if colleagues of yours with similar CVs are getting placements or offers. A reason for rejection by firm X may not be a problem for firm Y.

Having your training contract application rejected is undeniably tough. It seems especially unfair to receive a generic email rejection having spent so much time and effort making sure that the application form was completed to the highest possible standard. I have, however, always prepared myself for getting rejected at least a few times, as this is almost inevitable given the number of applicants. It has therefore been fairly easy for me to move on and not to think about it too much after receiving those kinds of rejections before the interview stage.

Being rejected after an interview is a different story. Going through the full application and assessment process has given me invaluable experience and has made me a lot more prepared for future interviews. My rejection after interview involved some feedback pointing out my mistakes and weaknesses and will definitely change the way I present my applications in future. Even though it is much harder to face, as you've invested more time, hope and emotion in the process, I think that this kind of rejection has actually been a great help in perfecting my interview technique. The result: when I complete my next application, I will do so to an even higher standard.

Zane Vitola, LPC student

Chapter summary

You need to start planning your campaign for a training contract in the first year of your law degree (or year two of your non-law degree). Research which areas of the law interest you and what type of firm you see yourself practising in. The race for a training contract is hugely competitive, but there will be many winners, even if some of them have to run several more laps than others. You can't run a decent marathon without any training – and in this marathon, good training will not only be your diligent study of the law, but also the quality of your research into the legal services market.

Key points

The secret to getting a training contract are the three 'P's:

- Planning – do your research and work out your strategy.
- Patience – it's not going to happen overnight; this is an ongoing project so be prepared for the 'long-haul'.
- Perseverance – when you get knock-backs, pick yourself off the floor and start again.

Useful resources

www.sra.org.uk

www.chambersandpartners.com

www.lawcareers.net

www.cps.gov.uk

www.gls.gov.uk

www.prospects.ac.uk

www.targetjobslaw.co.uk

www.rollonfriday.co.uk

Chambers Student Guide 2013: The student's guide to becoming a lawyer, Chambers and Partners Publishing, London 2013

Training Contract & Pupillage Handbook 2013. 16th edition. London: Globe Business for the Law society. For more information go to www.tcph.co.uk

References

University of Law (2012) University News. [Online] Available at: http://www.law.ac.uk/about/news/news-2011/25-May-2011--84--college-of-law%E2%80%99s-2010-Lpc-graduates-have-secured-work-in-legal-profession-survey-reveals/ [Accessed December 2012]

The Co-operative Group (2012) The Co-operative announces plans for 3,000 jobs in Legal Services. [Online] Available at: http://www.co-operative.coop/corporate/press/press-releases/headline-news/the-co-operative-announces-plans-for-3000-jobs-in-legal-services/ [Accessed December 2012]

A day in the life of a trainee solicitor

Type of law firm: Magic Circle **Department: Litigation**

Time	Wednesday
9:00am	'Although we do not generally need to be in the office before 9.30am, I like to read my emails on my BlackBerry on my way in. That way I am ready to begin my work as soon as I get in. Most days I receive various 'know-how' emails from my firm's information team updating me on developments in the law and practice of the department I am sitting in. Reading today's email, I notice that a professor has just written an article on a High Court case I had been working on a few weeks ago. This had been my first opportunity to work on a big trial and it is pretty exciting to see that the professor considers it important enough to write about. Though my working hours during the trial were long, the buzz of the court room coupled with the cut-and-thrust of our run-ins with the other side's lawyers kept me going throughout. As you may have guessed, I am currently sitting in my firm's litigation department and this is the first seat of my training contract. There are about 50 qualified lawyers in my department and 20 other trainees. Though this sounds like a lot, over the course of six months you end up working with most of these people and by the end it can feel like quite a close team. I will rotate department every six or three months over the next two years, meaning that I'll have the chance to sample at least four distinct areas of law before I qualify. My firm tends to have good retention rates and a lot of qualifiers get placed in their preferred department. Still, it is important to make sure you've gained lots of experience in each department so that you can make a more informed decision about where you want to end up.

Time	Wednesday
9:25am	All the trainees in my firm share an office with their 'supervisor', who will either be an associate or a partner. My supervisor 'Michael' is a mid-level associate (it is only three years since he qualified) and we get on really well. Michael sets me the vast majority of my work, though at times I do work for others in my department, and more generally he tries to make sure I'm getting as much experience and development as possible.
9:30am	Most mornings Michael and I spend the first few minutes discussing anything from what we saw on television the night before to our plans for the weekend. However today we have to cut things short as we receive an email from Jessica, one of the partners in our department, asking us to find out whether the judgment given yesterday in a big Supreme Court case will have an impact on one of our clients. I easily find the judgment online, but it is over 100 pages long! Michael and I both read it over the next hour and then discuss together what the impact might be. We agree that the judgment helps our client's case and I draft an email for Michael to send to Jessica setting out precisely why.
11:30am	Later in the morning I'm booked in to attend a training session. I generally have three to four training sessions per week, which can include department-specific training (eg on witness statements), trainee-to-trainee training (where we take turns to present a legal topic to the other trainees), general corporate training (eg on share purchase agreements), firm-wide training (on recent work that my firm has done) and professional skills training (eg on confidence and communication). Today's training is one of a series on learning about how the City of London works, with this morning's session looking at 'futures'. A 'future' is a promise to buy or sell something in the future at a price set now – eg a buyer promises to buy 100 tonnes of coffee beans from the seller at £2,000/tonne in 12 months' time. I've never really understood these too well and luckily haven't come across them so far. However, my next seat will be in the corporate department and so I'm glad to have the chance to ask any questions now. Our speaker guides us expertly through this tricky area and by the end I feel a lot more confident (though I still hope that I never have to deal with them in practice!).

Time	Wednesday
12:30pm	At 12.30pm the class ends and we descend on our firm's canteen. Nearly all the firm's staff eat there every day, making it really sociable and a great place for us to swap stories. The trainees at my firm all went to the same law school and several ended up being in the same class, meaning that many of us have been friends for one to two years before even starting the job!
1:30pm	Trainees in litigation at my firm tend to spend their time doing one of three tasks: (i) reviewing documents to see if they aid or weaken a case; (ii) preparing folders of documents for trial; or (iii) researching obscure bits of law. It seems this afternoon I'll be doing the third as on my return from lunch Michael asks me to write a research note. We won a trial a year ago and the judge ordered that the other side pay our costs. However, we have not yet received a penny and Michael wants to know how we can force the other side to pay. It only takes a quick word search on one of the online legal databases for me to find an article summarising the law in this area. I then check all the references to the law to verify that the article is correct and its analysis up-to-date. My research complete, I type up my findings in my firm's 'house style', taking time to check all my commas, semi-colons and line spacings before printing it off and presenting it to Michael. The first time I was asked to write a research note I felt panicked, but once you've done a few you learn the best places to look to find the answers and rarely find yourself utterly lost.

Time	Wednesday
4:30pm	Michael receives an email indicating that a dispute we thought had finished two years ago is now coming back to life. He asks me to dig out a private investigator's report previously prepared on a matter at the heart of the dispute. One problem though: he can't remember when it was written or who wrote it! There are tens of thousands of emails and documents in the relevant folder and it would take me several days to read through them all. I need to narrow down the selection by using some appropriate search terms. Searching for "private investigator" brings up nothing, while searching for "report" brings up over 3,000 hits! In a moment of inspiration I decide to search for "Miss Marple" on the assumption that a lawyer at some point would have made a lame joke about a 'P.I.' and, would you believe, the one result that appears is precisely the one I'm looking for!
5:00pm	We are due to go to court tomorrow morning for a brief hearing to decide on some administrative matters for an upcoming trial (eg what the deadlines should be for exchanging certain documents with the other side's lawyers). My job is to make sure that we bring to court everything that we might need. I prepare 'clips' of our correspondence with the other side, make copies of the various documents we have submitted to the court so far, and collect together as much stationery as I can carry (I forgot to bring the hole-punch last time and the judge got so angry we almost lost the case!) Tomorrow, I'll be sitting at the back of the court room next to Linda, the General Counsel (the most senior lawyer) of our client (a big multinational company). In addition to taking an attendance note of the hearing, I am to answer any questions that Linda might have and provide her with any papers she might request. I take a few minutes to make sure I know where to find all the documents so that I can help Linda as quickly as possible.

Time	Wednesday
6:15pm	Having finished my day's work, I leave for home. I generally leave at 6.00pm. However, if I have a lot of work on, I can leave at 11.00pm or even later. During my big trial a few weeks ago, I left at midnight every workday for three weeks (and worked for a few hours each weekend!) You have to accept in this job that from time to time you will work long hours and potentially miss social engagements, but in return you do get to work on some of the most high-profile cases at which millions and sometimes billions of pounds are at stake. Working here, you get to operate at the cutting edge of the law, often developing and trying out things that have simply never been attempted before, which, though admittedly challenging, is hugely rewarding and exhilarating!'

A day in the life of a trainee solicitor

Type of law firm: Small **Department: Litigation**

Time	Monday
8:30am	'I arrive at the office and immediately head to the basement to help the post room manager, Mike, open the post. Sara, the firm's other trainee is already there. She's two months into her final seat of her training contract, a year ahead of me. She will qualify in four months' time and has been offered a job in the firm's Wills and Probate department, which she has accepted already. I'm trying to make a good impression in the firm's busy litigation department, as that's where I see myself going in a little over a year's time ... if they'll have me! The managing partner, Annie, is also in the post room casting a very quick eye over all the correspondence. I'm still not used to calling her "Annie". She looks, sounds and reminds me of my old head teacher, who would have had a thing or two to say if I'd called her Margaret! Annie tells us she was in Tuscany over the weekend. I just about made it to Tesco. Annie disappears with her post, leaving Mike, Sara and I to sort the rest into separate piles for each fee earner. Sara and I take each of our department's post to our respective department heads, and the office junior (who is training to become a legal secretary) is responsible for distributing the remainder. I often joke with Sara that we didn't earn our 2:1s and go to law school to end up paper-pushing, but Sara reminds me that, being trainees, we get to experience all aspects of the firm's business – even the boring administrative stuff. She's right of course. I secretly make a bet with myself that she'll 'make partner' in less than five years. I share an office with the head of litigation, Dilip. Or rather, I sit with him. He's on the phone advising a client about an employment law issue, and without disrupting the flow of the conversation, he gestures with his outstretched hand for me to leave the post on his desk. I do so, and then log on, checking my e-diary for the day and my work emails.

Time	Monday
9:30am	I'm due in court at 10.30am on one of Dilip's cases. It's an application by the other side's solicitors for an extension of time to serve their client's defence. So this will just be a short interim hearing about timing – not the trial itself. Dilip's client, the claimant, who is suing for the non-payment of goods delivered to the defendant, previously agreed to a 21-day extension, which expires at the end of this week. The Defendant is now applying for a further 28-day extension to serve its defence, which I'm instructed to oppose. Dilip has told me that the court will almost certainly grant the Defendant a short extension. I prepared for the hearing on Friday and review my notes. When Dilip finishes his call, I briefly rehearse my arguments with him before taking the ten-minute walk to the county court, where I report to the usher. My opponent has not yet arrived, but I see we are second in the Deputy District Judge's 10.00am list. We are listed for 15 minutes.
10:00am	At 9.58am, my opponent clatters into the waiting room, clearly stressed and sweating profusely. I know he is my opponent before he quizzically exhales my firm's name to the waiting room. Dilip's description of Sid Shore is remarkably accurate. It's a good job Sid doesn't know the limit of my experience: I've only done three previous hearings, but as the first two were at law school and the other 'real' application was unopposed, this is my first contested application. So, yes, I'm apprehensive!

Time	Monday
11:00am	We don't appear before the DDJ until just after 11.00am, because she is required to hear an emergency application. This gives me a little while to assess my opponent. Dilip told me earlier not to give much away before the hearing, but there's little chance of that as sweaty Sid spends most of the waiting time talking into his mobile in a private room off the lobby area. The hearing: Sid looks disorganised as he shuffles through his papers after each of the DDJ's questions, clearly testing the DDJ's patience. I haven't even said anything yet and I feel like I'm winning! I stutter a little in response to the DDJ's questions, but despite being nervous, I manage to put forward my client's well-rehearsed arguments. I even go off-script and "submit" to the court (because advocates don't "think" or "feel", they "submit") that the Defendant's delay was "partly due to the fact that my friend has not got his act together". Yes, somewhat perversely, you refer to the solicitor on the other side as your "friend". The DDJ agrees and only permits a seven day extension of time, awarding my client the costs of the application. Sweaty Sid bumbles off after the hearing without saying a word and I make a mental note not to turn into him.
11:30am	Dilip is delighted with the result. It's early days in my training contract, but I let him know that I really enjoyed the experience. I hope he gets the hint and remembers this in a year's time when I'm looking to secure a job towards the end of my training contract. I want to update my Facebook profile and email my friends and family to let them know I feel like I'm a real hot-shot lawyer now (even though the hearing wasn't that much of a big deal), but Dilip doesn't let me enjoy the moment. Once I record the time I was engaged at the hearing on the firm's time-recording system, Dilip instructs me to devote the next few hours to preparing and copying bundles for a brief to counsel, which I will walk round to chambers at the end of the day.

Time	Monday
3:00pm	Sarita, the other partner in the department, and Vernon, a two-year qualified solicitor, make up the rest of the qualified litigation staff. Unlike larger firms, no one is a specialist in any particular litigation field, such as employment law or personal injury cases. They all do 'a bit of everything', although Sarita is normally keen to deal with any family law matters. I spend two hours taking notes in a conference with Sarita and a new divorce client, Vicky, whose wealthy husband (No. 2) is trying to kick her (and the kids from her first marriage) out of the matrimonial home, which is owned by husband (No. 2). It's messy and emotional but Sarita displays sufficient empathy for the client's problems to elicit the required information in order to come up with an action plan. Impressive. Not sure I'm quite there yet and perhaps matrimonial law isn't for me after all. I'm not sure I could spend the whole of my professional life helping my client to swim through a river of tears.
5:00pm	Towards the end of the afternoon, I sometimes help Mike with the outgoing post, which I do today, after which I drop off the brief to counsel, which I helped prepare the enclosures for earlier in the day.
6:00pm	Like most working days, I finish around 6.00pm, but Sara has warned me that I will, on occasions, have to work until 8.00 or 9.00pm helping one of the partners or Vernon, in the lead up to a trial. It usually involves a considerable amount of photocopying. Occasionally, I get to sit in on a late meeting or conference call, which is invaluable experience and should, hopefully, stand me in good stead on the way to becoming a litigator.'

Chapter 9

Becoming a barrister – the Bar Professional Training Course

BPP LEARNING MEDIA

Introduction

If you want to work in private practice as a barrister (ie at the 'independent bar'), you will need to:

1. Study and pass the BPTC.
2. Complete a one-year pupillage.
3. Find a tenancy after pupillage (usually in chambers with other barristers).

Traditionally, it has taken five years from commencing a QLD to qualifying as a barrister – at least for those who get there. Non-law graduates have, traditionally, taken an additional year to qualify, because they need to pass the GDL before starting their BPTC.

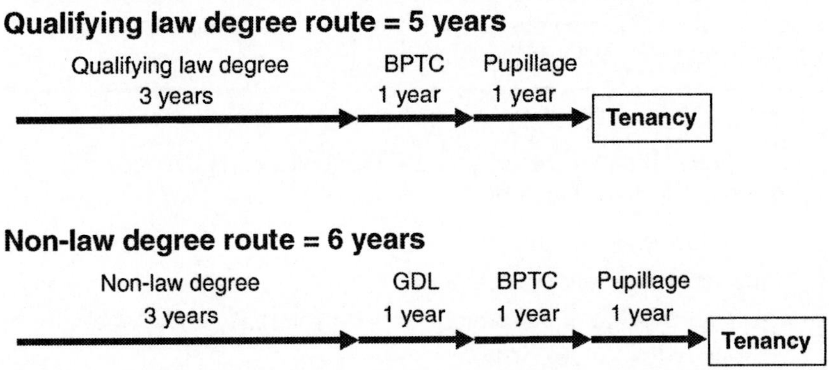

Figure 9.1: The traditional route to qualifying as a barrister at the independent bar

The reality is that many barristers who ultimately secure pupillage do not do so until a year or two after they have complete their BPTC, so the minimum timescale outlined in **Figure 9.1** will frequently not apply.

Getting onto the Bar Professional Training Course

If you wish to study the BPTC, you must have:

- Completed the academic stage of training (or be exempt from it)
- Applied for a place on a BPTC via the BSB (see **Figure 9.2** below)
- Passed the Bar Course Aptitude Test

- Joined one of the four Inns of Court by 31 May in the year you intend starting your BPTC
- (Overseas students only) obtained a Tier 4 visa/entry clearance into the UK.

Completion of the academic stage of training

In order to have completed the academic stage of training you need to have either passed:

- A QLD (with a minimum of a 2:2) **OR**
- A non-law degree and the GDL.

Application for a place on a BPTC

The Bar Standards Board ('BSB'), which is the governing body for the bar, says that around 3,000 candidates apply for approximately 1,800 places on the BPTC, so even if you can afford the fees of up to around £17,000, you may still not get a place.

Top tip

To maximise the chances of your BPTC application succeeding, providers will closely look at:

- Your academic record
- Your communication skills
- Your knowledge of the profession – do you really know what a career at the bar involves?
- Good references
- Your reasons for picking the provider

All applications for places on any BPTC must be made directly via the BSB. You cannot apply directly to the BPTC providers. There is a one-off application fee of £40 to pay to process your application, which can only be made online. You are asked to list your BPTC providers in order of preference, but only your top three will be considered in the first round of applications.

There are only nine BPTC providers, less than a quarter than those who provide the LPC. They all deliver a full-time course, although some also have a two-year part-time course. The providers are:

- BPP University College (London and Leeds centres and from September 2013, Manchester)[1]
- The University of Law (London and Birmingham centres)[1]
- Cardiff Law School

- City Law School[1]
- Kaplan Law School
- Manchester Metropolitan University[1]
- Nottingham Law School
- University of Northumbria (Newcastle)[1]
- University of the West of England (Bristol)[2]

---

1 Providers who offer a two year-part-time course as a well as a one-year full-time course.

2 Partial distance-learning and part-time BPTC offered

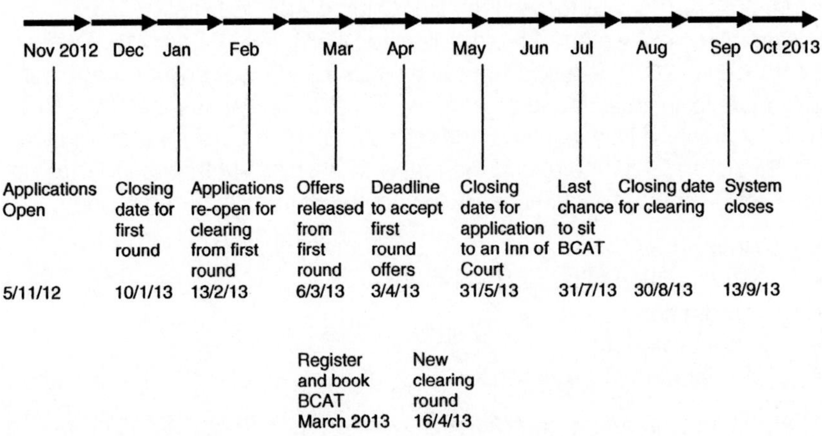

Figure 9.2: The BPTC application route: 2012-13

Some BPTC providers have introduced a '2:1 and over' admissions policy, because it is only in around 5% of cases that a successful applicant for pupillage has a 2:2 or worse; the very few with a 'Desmond' (2.2) who do now secure pupillage are only likely to do so if they have an extraordinary background, like a successful previous career, or proven business or advocacy skills.

The stark reality is that less than 25% of BPTC graduates ever secure pupillage, despite the majority of them having excellent academic records, so if you do have a 2:2, you should seriously consider whether the BPTC is for you.

Top tip

It is incredibly difficult to secure pupillage with a 2:2, so you should be realistic with your ambitions. If you have a 2:2 and you're dead-set on advocacy, you've got more of a chance getting there as a solicitor than as a barrister; it will still be an uphill battle to get a training contract with a 2:2, but if you do get there, and you're exceptionally good at advocacy, you can still acquire the Higher Rights of Audience qualification, which permits you to appear as an advocate in the higher courts.

Bar Course Aptitude Test

Students are required to pass the Bar Course Aptitude Test (BCAT) before they can be offered a place on the BPTC. The BCAT, which was introduced in 2013, is a one-hour test which can be sat between April and July at multiple locations across the world. The BSB states that the BCAT tests 'students' critical thinking and reasoning, the core skills required for the BPTC' and that 'the aim of the test is to ensure that those undertaking the BPTC have the required skills to succeed'. Areas covered include:

- Inference
- Recognition of assumptions
- Deduction
- Interpretation
- Evaluation of arguments

There is an example of the BCAT and other sample questions on the BSB's website, which you should complete shortly before you take the test in order to familiarise yourself with the format and content of the BCAT. Other than that, there is no significant preparation you can do. You find out the result of your test immediately afterwards at the test centre itself – you will be told whether you have passed, marginally failed or significantly failed.

The conclusion of the BSB's Aptitude Test Consultation was that 'by using a test universally we will be able systematically to identify students who are likely to fail the course and they will be prevented from undertaking it, thus saving them wasting their own time and money.' (Bar Standards Board, 2012) You are permitted to re-sit the BCAT, but not within 30 days of your last sit, and at a cost of £150 per test (£170 if you sit outside the EU), if you fail a couple of times, you may need to ask yourself whether the next test fee and the BPTC course fees could be better invested in your education elsewhere. More importantly, if you're struggling to pass the entrance test, you need to seriously question whether the bar is your best career option.

Exercise 9.1 – Example of the BCAT (Deduction)*

For the purpose of this exercise, treat the following two statements as absolute truths on the basis that there are 'Strong' law students and 'Weak' law students:

Statement 1: 'All students find some law exams challenging.'

Statement 2: 'Weak students fail challenging law exams.'

In the light of the above, which of the following conclusions **necessarily follow**:

1. Weak students fail all of their law exams.
2. Strong students sometimes find law exams challenging.
3. Strong students sometimes fail challenging law exams.
4. Some students find all law exams challenging.

*This exercise has been provided for illustrative purposes only. It is NOT one of the BSB's questions.

Answer to ***Exercise 9.1****:*

1. This conclusion does **not** necessarily follow. Weak students do not necessarily fail every law exam they sit, because they may not find every law exam challenging. Consequently, it is possible, on these statements, for a weak student to pass an exam which is not challenging.
2. This conclusion **does** necessarily follow, given the content of the first statement,
3. Although this is possible, the conclusion does **not** necessarily follow. The second statement only gives information about weak students; it gives no indication as to whether strong students also fail challenging exams.
4. While this conclusion is likely to be true, it doesn't necessarily follow from either statement.

The examples of BCAT questions on the BSB's website (accessed May 2013) are essentially tests in logic and critical thinking, for which you need good comprehension and reasoning skills to answer correctly.

Pilot tests run by the BSB prior to the introduction of the BCAT indicated a clear connection between low scores in such an aptitude test and failure on the BPTC. However, the test has not been welcomed universally, as it is unlikely that everyone who attains a low score on the BCAT would fail the BPTC. Consequently, as to whether there is any direct correlation between success in such a test and the BPTC, the 'jury is out'!

As soon as it was announced that there would be an aptitude test for the BPTC, I was keen to find out as much information as possible about the test. My research revealed that the BCAT would be based on the Watson-Glaser aptitude tests, so I searched for practice questions and mock exams. I found some useful resources, particularly from large law firms, who use similar tests when selecting prospective trainees and provide examples on their websites. Examples of questions also appear on the BSB's website.

The BCAT Practice test was the best preparation for the BCAT, as it was in exactly the same format and style as the real thing. I attempted the Practice test and passed – although with little feedback other than 'pass', I couldn't be sure if I'd passed convincingly or scraped through by the skin of my teeth.

I took the Practice test twice more in the weeks approaching my BCAT, just to check I hadn't fluked a pass and to make sure I was keeping on top of my 'revision'. Although the questions were the same, I felt confident that I was building on my 'revision' to better understand the questions and feel more confident in my answers.

On the day of my BCAT, I was very nervous but the test flew by, and I was very relieved to be told a couple of minutes afterwards that I'd passed. All of a sudden, my anxiety seemed such a waste of energy – but my preparation definitely wasn't! I was glad that I'd spent the time familiarising myself with the type of questions and the format of the test - it helped me stay calm when faced with the real thing and focus on the important aspects of the questions, rather than worrying that they were worded in a particular way that I was not accustomed to.

Cait McDonagh, prospective BPTC student

Application to one of the four Inns of Court

The four Inns of Court are:

- Gray's Inn
- Inner Temple
- Lincoln's Inn
- Middle Temple

All four are located within walking distance of the Royal Courts of Justice in London. To those outside the profession, the Inns have an air of mystique: they sound like secret societies Harry Potter would join to hone his magic skills. To those in the profession, they are the gateway to the bar, steeped in centuries of tradition (dating back to the 14th century), and unless you join one of them, you can't practise as a barrister in England and Wales.

The Inns provide aspiring barristers with a wealth of useful opportunities – not least funding (see below). Join as soon as you can because it's never too early to take advantage of their facilities or to rack-up your experience by:

- Participating in marshalling schemes (shadowing a judge)
- Being mentored by a practising barrister
- Joining a mooting and/or debating society
- Attending advocacy workshops
- Attending educational seminars and presentations on specialist areas of the law

So which Inn should you join? It doesn't really matter, but once you are a student member, you are required to attend 12 'qualifying sessions' in order to be called to the bar by the Inn. Yes, it is the Inns (and not the BSB) which hold the exclusive right to call you to the bar. The qualifying sessions used to be formal dinners (think Hogwarts, but without the magic) following which there was lots of legal chat. Nowadays, you can still attend dinners, but there are alternatives. For example, you can attend weekend brunches or 'whole weekend' events (which can amount to more than one qualifying session). Your 12th session will be your 'Call' ceremony, assuming you have passed the BPTC by then.

Overseas students

There are complicated provisions relating to the recognition of overseas degrees which are outside the scope of this title. If you hold an overseas degree, you should make enquires of the BSB to determine what (if any) further requirements you need to satisfy before commencing the BPTC.

In addition, if your first language is not English or Welsh, you will also need to have attained an International English Language Testing System ('IELTS ') score of 7.5 or above.

In order to get a Tier 4 visa/entry clearance into the UK as a student, you have to enrol on a full-time course at a university or other educational institution which is on the register of sponsors who will sponsor you. You would also need to score enough points to be accepted as an international student in the UK.

Bar Professional Training Course – content

The BPTC syllabus is made up of

- Skills
- Knowledge subjects centrally-assessed
- Two elective knowledge subjects

Skills

Advocacy

You will learn the core techniques involved in making applications and speeches in court, as well as the techniques involved in effectively examining and cross-examining a witness. Some BPTC providers design classrooms to look like courtrooms right down to the panelled walls, Royal coat of arms and the bench (table and chair for the judge) situated on a raised platform! Having advocacy classes in a mock courtroom is invaluable experience even though it can be more than a little scary the first time you do it, but you soon adjust to your surroundings.

Exercise 9.2

Effective questioning of witnesses and good listening lie at the heart of being a successful advocate. This exercise/role-play game is designed to make you aware of one aspect of advocacy and how you can develop this key barrister's skill.

You need two friends, 'A' and 'B', plus three pads of paper, three pens and a good assortment of coloured crayons or felt tips.

You are a barrister, in court, interviewing a witness, 'A', who saw someone, 'X', walking away from the 'scene of the crime'. 'B' is playing the part of the jury. The aim of the exercise is to get 'A' to give you an accurate description of X in a short period of time. Here are the rules:

1. 'A' draws a full length drawing of X, without showing it to anyone. The drawing should contain as much detail as possible about X's features – height, build, hair length, facial hair, glasses, clothing, jewellery, and so on. 'A' should use coloured crayons to help with the detail.
2. You have two minutes to get as accurate a description as possible of X from 'A' by asking a maximum of 10 questions, with no more than 10 words per question. To focus the questions (and the answers) 'A' can give no more than 10 words per answer. (Keep to the spirit of the word limit here: the idea is to make the exercise flow, so don't stop or challenge someone who uses a few more words – that's not really the point.)
3. After your two minutes of questioning, you have a further minute to sketch 'A''s description of X from what you remember.
4. 'B', who represents the jury, sketches the image which 'A' describes throughout the whole of the three minutes allocated to your questioning and drawing.
5. Compare the pictures which you, 'A' and 'B' have drawn. How effective was your questioning? How effective was your listening?
6. Get feedback on your questioning technique from 'A' and 'B'.
7. Reflect on your approach and work out what you would do differently next time.

Try the exercise again, but rotate the roles with 'A' and 'B' this time.

Did you manage to avoid leading questions (ie ones with a 'yes' or 'no' answer, or other monosyllabic answers)? How did you phrase the questions in order to elucidate as much information as possible from the witness? For example: 'Describe X's height and build' is a more effective question than 'Was X tall?' or 'Was X fat?'

Conference Skills

You will learn to conduct structured, effective and efficient conferences, so you can gather the required information in order to deliver the appropriate advice.

Resolution of Disputes Out of Court

You will cover the processes by which litigation can be resolved without trial, and look at the essential techniques by which such resolution can be achieved, such as negotiation.

Opinion Writing and Drafting

You will learn to accurately and appropriately draft:

- Written opinions in which the barrister advises on the merits of a case
- Statements for the court in which the essence of a case is set out

Knowledge subjects

The knowledge subjects are centrally examined by the BSB by way of short answer questions and multiple-choice questions.

Civil Litigation and Remedies

You will be taught the essential processes by which all cases will be dealt with in the civil courts of England and Wales.

Criminal Litigation and Sentencing

This module introduces you to the procedure adopted in criminal cases in the courts of England and Wales.

Professional Ethics

By the time you complete this module, you should understand the rules regarding the professional conduct of barristers and understand the standards of conduct required when going about your professional work.

Elective modules

You must choose to study two knowledge subjects. The range of options offered does vary slightly for each provider. Generally, the smaller providers are not able to offer as wide a range of options. Providers also have more discretion as to the method of assessment for elective modules, so this will vary more than the compulsory subjects.

Providers are likely to offer some or all of the following:

- Company Law
- Employment Law
- Family Law
- Advanced Criminal Litigation
- International Trade
- Personal Injury and Clinical Negligence
- Property and Chancery
- Intellectual Property
- Judicial Review

BPTC assessments

Whereas most of the subjects are assessed by way of written exams which usually last between two and four hours, Advocacy and Conference Skills are examined by way of 'live' assessments. For example, in Advocacy, you will be required to undertake all of the following in three short assessments of around 12 minutes each:

- Application to a judge
- Examination-in-chief (ie questioning your side's witness)
- Cross-examination (ie questioning the other side's witness)

In Advocacy assessments, it is common for actors to play the witnesses. Actors may also play the client in your Conference Skills assessment.

Students are only entitled to two sittings for each assessment. The first sitting will be during the academic year and the second sitting will be in late August or early September.

> *Students who have previously attained good results on their undergraduate degrees and GDLs often perform well because they are strong academically. However, in some of the oral skills very academic students can sometimes lack good delivery and common sense which means they do not do as well as might be expected. In these subjects, sometimes less academic students can perform well because they have good delivery and good people skills.*
>
> Anna Banfield,
> BPTC Joint Director of Programmes, BPP University College

The method of assessment of elective modules is left to the providers to determine based upon what they see as the most important skill for that particular area of law. Not all providers publish details of the method of assessing their elective modules, so it is not possible to provide a definitive list, but an example of the methods of assessment may be:

- **Written Legal Opinion**: Company Law, International Trade, Property and Chancery, Intellectual Property
- **Conference with client:** Family Law, Employment Law, Personal Injury and Clinical Negligence
- **Drafting grounds of appeal**: Judicial Review

Your BPTC mark

The BPTC is aimed to prepare barristers for a career at the bar. Consequently, there is a focus not only on areas of legal knowledge, but also the skills you need to employ to apply that knowledge in the courtroom, in the conference room and in chambers. In descending order, the pass grades are:

- Outstanding
- Very Competent
- Competent/Pass

For 'Outstanding' you need to pass all assessments at the first attempt and score an overall mark of 85% or above, or score 'Outstanding' in six individual modules. To be 'Very Competent', you must secure an 'Outstanding' or 'Very Competent' grade in eight of your modules, with a maximum of one re-sit. The other pass grade is 'Competent', for which students must achieve more than 60% in all assessments, subject to satisfying the relevant re-sit rules.

Choosing your Bar Professional Training Course

The best way to start is to look at the websites of BPTC providers. The content of BPTCs can vary from provider to provider but because of the number of centralised assessments, BPTCs from different providers tend to have more in common than the range of LPCs.

Most BPTC providers teach by way of a combination of:

- Lectures
- Independent learning sessions
- Face-to-face teaching in small group sessions. Class sizes vary between providers: BPP University College's class sizes are amongst the smallest – around 12, except for advocacy where there are four students per class.

Other factors to take into account when choosing your BPTC provider are similar to those covered in Chapter 7 for students considering their LPC provider, although prospective barristers should also note the following:

Funding your BPTC

For a one-year course, the fees are even steeper than the LPC; you won't get any change out of £10,000 and the larger providers are charging around £17,000 for their London 2012-13 full-time BPTC. There are a few scholarships across BPTC providers, but there is considerably more assistance from the Inns of Court, who collectively give away over £4m in assistance for BPTC students. For example, in 2013, the Honourable Society of the Inner Temple (as it's known in all its grandeur) has announced that it will give away £1,428,000 in awards to members who are:

- Taking the GDL
- Taking the BPTC
- Interns
- Pupils
- Members with a disability

Most of this these funds are reserved for students taking the BPTC.

You need to get your application in early for scholarship from one of the Inns: the deadline for BPTC scholarships from the Honourable Society of the Middle Temple for students starting the BPTC in the 2014-15 academic year is 1 November 2013. (Middle Temple, 2013)

Practical experience of BPTC lecturers and tutors

The BPTC is a practice-based course which aims to provide you with the skills you need in order to successfully practise at the bar. Consequently, most lecturers and tutors are qualified barristers or solicitors who have spent time in practice, the majority of whom as barristers, several of whom are still practising.

Pastoral support

It is worthwhile comparing providers' pastoral support, as it will differ. The support of a personal tutor will be provided in the first instance, but what else is on offer? Other members of faculty? Because of their size, university-based providers normally have a stronger 'in-house' infrastructure with established links with independent counselling services, to support BPTC students experiencing personal problems.

Class sizes

These will vary between providers. The 'knowledge' subjects and written skills are taught in larger groups than the oral skills. Small class sizes are extraordinarily helpful, particularly because of the personal attention you can receive in the development of your oral skills, where the added value is in the quantity and quality of personal feedback you will receive on each performance.

Careers support

Given the fact that such a small proportion of students secure pupillage, a well-resourced careers service could make a significant difference to your prospects. It is worthwhile researching your BPTC provider's careers service and support, which can vary considerably between providers. Is it a careers service dedicated to careers in the law, or is it a part of a university's general careers service? Providers outside London may have established links with local chambers, which may provide easier and more regular contact with current pupils and junior barristers, although, of course, the London-based providers all have their own links with the Inns, former students, pupils and practising barristers.

Dedicated careers departments will usually offer assistance with drafting CVs, completing application forms for pupillage and will arrange for practitioners to give talks to students. Some also offer students mock interviews at which a tutor with relevant expertise may play the role of the interviewer. It is also worthwhile checking whether your BPTC provider permits students to use their careers service as soon as they have accepted a place on the course: this can provide you with several additional months of careers support before you start the BPTC. It is also worth comparing how much (if any) additional careers support you will get after you complete your BPTC.

Pro bono and Free Representation Unit ('FRU')

Does your BPTC provider run a pro bono clinic or have links with FRU whereby BPTC students are given the opportunity of honing their advice and advocacy skills? Investigate what opportunities there are for you before, during and after you study for your BPTC, because as well as giving you practical experience, pro bono work and FRU make useful additions to your CV and give you first-hand knowledge of what it is like to be a practising lawyer, which you may wish to draw upon during an interview.

Chapter summary

The BPTC is a very competitive course to get onto and if you get through it, it is even more competitive to secure pupillage. If you are unconditionally confident in your academic ability and presentation skills and if you are prepared for the financial insecurity which being a barrister brings in the early years (with no guarantee that you will succeed), then go for it! If you have any doubts whatsoever, but still wish to practise as a lawyer, then maybe becoming a solicitor is a better option for you.

Key points

- The BPTC is an extremely demanding course
- It is only suitable for those who are 100% committed to becoming barristers.
- Getting a place on the BPTC does not guarantee you pupillage.
- Ensure your elective subjects 'fit' with the practice areas you see yourself specialising in.
- Work towards and target a BPTC grading of at least 'Very Competent' (if not 'Outstanding'). A bare pass is unlikely to secure you pupillage.

Useful resources

www.barstandardsboard.org.uk

www.graysinn.info

www.innertemple.org.uk

www.lincolnsinn.org.uk

www.middletemple.org.uk

www.bpp.com

www.law.ac.uk

References

Bar Standards Board (2012) Bar Course Aptitude Test. [Online] Available at: http://www.barstandardsboard.org.uk/qualifying-as-a-barrister/bar-professional-training-course/aptitude test/ [Accessed December 2012]

Bar Standards Board (2012) Bar Course Aptitude Test (BCAT) Consultaion. [Online] Available at: http://www.barstandardsboard.org.uk/about-bar-standards-board/consultations/open-consultations/bar-course-aptitude-test-(bcat)/ [Accessed, December 2012]

Middle Temple (2013) Education and Training. [Online] Available at: http://www.middletemple.org.uk/education-and-training/scholarships-and-prizes/bptc-and-gdl-scholarships/timetable/ [Accessed May 2013]

A day in the life of a BTPC student

Time	Thursday
11:05am	'I start the day with a Civil Litigation class – my least favourite subject! It's about the rules governing civil law. It's all necessary knowledge for me to have but it's still pretty dry stuff – how to fill in various forms, the procedures you have to follow to make various applications, how much time you have to complete each stage of the process (the legal system runs on deadlines). There are some slightly more interesting topics some weeks, but on the whole this is stuff you learn just because you have to. Could be worse – at least I'm planning to practise in civil law. Everyone on the course needs to take this module, so even if I only wanted to practise in criminal law, and never had to set foot in the civil courts, I'd still have to learn all the rules anyway. Did you notice the time – I didn't! The class started at 11am and I arrived late. The BSB is very hot on making sure students turn up on time and if you're late to a class three times or more in the year without a proper excuse, you'll be in serious trouble (and 'my train was late' doesn't count!). This is now the second time I've been late – and it's still only the first term. Much as I dislike the rule, punctuality is very important in practice – about the worst thing a barrister can do is miss a hearing because they turned up in court after it had been called – but as someone who likes a lie-in I do struggle with punctuality.
12 noon	The day balances out though – I have my favourite subject today too – Advocacy. I head to the library to read up on a case one of my classmates told me they thought was relevant to today's class. The library is excellently well-stocked with legal books and an enormous bank of computers with all the legal software you're ever likely to need. You can look for cases in books or online and, as with 99% of my colleagues, I look online. I don't think the case is that relevant but I make a note of the salient points just in case it arises.

Time	Thursday
3:00pm	Lecture on Negotiation. Being a barrister isn't just about winning in court – there's an increasing emphasis on trying to settle cases beforehand, so today we're learning how best to use arguments to persuade our opponents to settle for a lower sum than they want. My classmates are slightly restless though because immediately after the lecture is the session most of us look forward to ...
4:00pm	The Advocacy class. For almost everyone on the BTPC, this is the centre of our week. We spend much more time preparing for our Advocacy sessions than any of the other classes and as the class approaches, arguments even break out in the corridor about how to tackle the issue of the day. We love this kind of stuff – it's why 90% of us want to become barristers. In the second term we will practise questioning witnesses (in the actual exam, the witnesses are played by professional actors) but for now we are just making legal arguments (eg "this Defendant should be granted bail"). We are paired up with another student who acts as the barrister for the other side and our tutor acts as the Judge. We then have about ten minutes each to argue our case, respond to arguments made by our opponent and answer questions from the Judge. Then there is five minutes each for feedback. Most of our classes are held in groups of 12, but for Advocacy we are split into subgroups of six so we can get enough individual attention – it also makes it less intimidating to know there are only four spectators! I am paired against Selina – the first week we were paired together she did a much better job than me and I've been trying to get her back ever since. Today I think I do – we get a very detailed assessment sheet afterwards from our tutor with scores in five different categories and I come higher than her in all of them. I take great delight in pointing this out to her afterwards – in the nicest possible way!

Time	Thursday
6:00pm	Our classes are all video recorded so I take my DVD to the library to look over my performance. I can't help but notice my tutor is right – I gesticulate far too much when I talk. I wasn't aware I was doing it but I must make a conscious effort to cut down because it is distracting. Although it's six o'clock, the library is still full of students.
6:10pm	As it's the end of the week and we put a lot of effort into preparing for the Advocacy class, my group likes to unwind with a drink at a nearby hostelry. There are a few other BPTC groups nearby and we swap stories about mistakes we made in our Advocacy sessions. James joins us a bit later – he has been seeing our personal tutor to get advice about job applications. Of our class of twelve, ten of us applied for pupillage the previous year but only two got one. The rest of us know this is the most important year for applications. We also know, statistically speaking, that, at best, only one in three of us will succeed. James has the right idea and I know I need to arrange to get some advice from our tutor too. The tutors are very good about giving extra time. It's not like school – we are seen as clients because we pay all the fees privately and we tend to get treated as such.
6:45pm	The pub is right next door to the Free Representation Unit – a charity that helps people trying to sue their employers but who can't afford to pay lawyers to represent them. FRU recruits law students to represent the clients for free: the clients get free legal representation and we get to appear in real courts and tribunals representing real clients. A lot of people on my course have taken on a case – it's excellent experience that teaches you how the law operates in practice, gives you lengthy advocacy experience, and gives you something to talk about in interviews.

Time	Thursday
	I want to specialise in employment law and intend to pick it as an option in the summer term – there are ten optional modules at my BPTC provider and we have to pick two. The content varies considerably depending on what you do – the Advanced Criminal Litigation option has a strong emphasis on Advocacy for example while the judicial review option has none! I have chosen to represent a man who claims he was unfairly dismissed. The hearing is in two weeks' time, which suddenly seems very soon, and I am exchanging documents with the solicitors representing the other side (actual, real solicitors!). They have sent me a lot of documents in the post. I pick them up from my pigeon-hole but don't have time to read them now – I have to hurry to Middle Temple because I'm dining at my inn tonight.
7:30pm	Before you can start on the BTPC you need to join one of the four Inns of Court – ancient organisations, based in buildings that resemble Oxbridge colleges. Centuries ago they used to provide something akin to a university education but over time their function has diminished so that most people's connection with them now is just to apply to them for scholarships and to attend dinners. All barristers have to get 12 'points' in the year before they get called to the Bar (the ceremony where you graduate as a barrister). The points are accumulated by attending events (mainly dinners worth one point each). At first they were quite fun but the novelty wears off after the tenth one! Still, they're good value for money and it is a way of meeting people studying on the BTPC in other institutions. I compare notes with two students from another BPTC provider and talk about pupillage with someone who has just started. After the meal there is a short concert – very high standard and all included in the price!
10:00pm	On the Tube heading home I start reading over the documents sent by the other side in my Employment Tribunal case. I can see I'm going to have a lot of reading to do over the weekend!

Chapter 10

Becoming a barrister – applying for pupillage

BPP LEARNING MEDIA

Introduction

The aim of this chapter is twofold:

1. To make sure you still want to become a barrister; and
2. If you do, how to maximise your chances of securing pupillage.

The final stage in a barrister's training is 12-months' pupillage, which the pupil usually undertakes from chambers. Pupillage follows on from:

- The academic stage – a QLD or the GDL; and
- The vocational stage – the BPTC.

You can only start your pupillage once you have been called to the bar by your Inn of Court (see Chapter 9). The pupillage year is divided into two very distinct parts, the 'first six' and the 'second six' – each 'six' referring to the first/second six-month period.

The 'first six'

You spend the first six months in a non-practising role shadowing your pupil supervisor(s) (one or more qualified barristers at your chambers) to see 'how it's done'. You are not permitted to accept any client instructions during this period. You will accompany your pupil supervisor to court and conferences with instructing solicitors and their clients. You may also be asked to undertake legal research to assist in your supervisor's preparation for court and help produce legal opinions or draft pleadings. Get used to your work being 'cannibalised' by your pupil supervisor and passed off as their own – you will be paid a pupil's award by your chambers during pupillage, they have to get something for their money! Of course, as well as providing you with excellent training, pupillage is a glorified job interview. So, while it may initially be disappointing that your name doesn't go on your brilliant legal opinion, your hard work will be noticed and reported back to the pupillage committee. You will get feedback from your pupil supervisors all the time (both positive and constructive) – after all, they are not only looking for what you can do now, but how quickly you learn and respond to criticism.

The 'second six'

You will, subject to receiving permission from your pupil supervisor or head of chambers, spend the 'second six' practising law, taking on your own work, although in some big-hitting Commercial and Chancery sets your advocacy opportunities may be limited. Instead, you may continue to support your pupil supervisor(s) with their work, taking on the occasional brief of your own (eg winding-up proceedings) to keep up your advocacy skills.

Historically, pupils usually spent both 'sixes' at the same set, but these days it is quite common for pupils to spend their second six at different chambers.

If you're lucky enough to secure pupillage, your future is still far from assured. Chambers have no obligation to offer you a tenancy (ie a permanent base from which to practise after pupillage). Under half of pupils are offered a tenancy at a set where they did their pupillage, so the majority are forced to move on and look elsewhere. A small minority are permitted to 'squat' for a 'third six' which permits them to effectively extend their pupillage for a further six months, often because chambers want to take a further look at the pupil.

Mini-pupillage

One of the best ways to gather information so you can make an informed decision as to whether a particular set is 'right for you', is to apply for and undertake work experience in chambers, which is known as 'mini-pupillage'. Applications are normally invited in the previous December/January for the following summer, details of which you will find on chambers' websites. Applications are usually by way of a combination of CV plus a letter or application form. Many accept applications from undergraduates and students currently studying for/ about to study the BPTC.

Be prepared to do your homework for these applications like we recommend for full-blown pupillage applications in Chapter 11. Wherever possible, demonstrate your interest and enthusiasm for their area of law, as well as your talent for public speaking.

Mini-pupillage will give an invaluable insight into the workings and personalities of various chambers and you will quickly discover that they are not all 'the same' – even if they specialise in similar areas. If you apply for pupillage to a set where you have undertaken a 'mini', you have a handy reference point, upon which you can draw in your pupillage application. However, it is still useful to draw upon your 'mini' experiences when applying for pupillage to other sets who work in similar practice areas.

Don't be afraid to use other connections you may have to secure mini-pupillage, like friends or family, or by simply networking at your Inn of Court if you have already joined. It doesn't matter how you get the experience – just get it! Apart from anything else, when you do get the invitation to spend a few days at chambers, it is a great morale booster that someone sees potential in you.

As an aspiring barrister, you should aim to undertake at least two or three mini-pupillages during the summer holidays after the second and/or third year of your degree or the summer after you complete your GDL. You can be offered anything from a day to a week. Take what you can get, although you may find after two or three days you get a 'feel' for the place and have seen all you need to see at that stage.

There is no formal requirement to undertake a mini-pupillage, although you will have some explaining to do if your pupillage application is lacking in that respect. There is no 'standard' requirement as to what a mini-pupillage should entail, but if, as you should, you do several of them, you are likely to get the opportunity of:

- Shadowing junior barristers (ie attending court and case conferences with them)
- Talking to pupils and tenants in the set
- Firming-up what areas of the law you can see yourself practising as a barrister
- Getting a feel for how the bar works in practice

Use mini-pupillages primarily to identify which practice area(s) you see yourself working in. Further guidance is given later on in this chapter, when we look at the different types of chambers. Of course, it helps to make a 'dream impression' if you have your heart set on a particular set, but treat that as a bonus rather than your goal, as you won't necessarily get a chance to shine, however brilliant you are. If you do too many mini-pupillages (ie more than six), it may indicate an element of uncertainty as to the direction you are headed. Don't think you are going to amaze anyone with the fact that you've got a dozen notches on your mini-pupillage belt – you can certainly afford to leave the less relevant mini-pupillages off your CV if you have done more than six.

Case study

Not all mini-pupillages start well. The key is knowing that it is within your power to do something about it. Melissa spent almost three days stuck in a room reading papers she didn't understand with a barrister who clearly didn't want her to be there. She eventually plucked up courage to extricate herself from the room to speak to the clerks to see if there was an alternative way she could spend the last two days of her mini-pupillage. The clerks were extremely helpful and after congratulating Melissa for 'lasting that long', they placed her with one of the junior tenants who was only too happy to allow Melissa to shadow him for the remainder of the week, during which she sat in on two case conferences and a short trial.

Not all sets offer mini-pupillages, and most pupils did not do 'mini' at the set where they end up for pupillage. But several do: the BSB Pupillage statistical report dated March 2012 ('PSR') reported that 34.5% of pupils completed a mini in the chambers where they secured pupillage.

Some sets actively use 'minis' as part of the pupillage recruitment process, which can be pretty scary, particularly if you haven't yet started the BPTC. These are known as 'assessed mini-pupillages' during which you will be given you all sorts of advocacy and research tasks to see if you've got the brainpower and raw ability which they are looking for. They know you won't be Rumpole of the Bailey yet, so don't set the bar (!) too high for yourself either. Just do your best: they are looking for accuracy, brevity and clarity – the 'ABC' we mentioned earlier – in both your oral presentations and your written pieces of work. You may spend a considerable amount of time on your own during assessed mini-pupillages, when, for example, you may be sent to the library to produce a research note on some obscure area of the law, although you may do this with one or two other mini-pupils.

Top tip

Make sure you keep as detailed a record as possible of absolutely everything you did, saw and felt during a mini-pupillage.

- Who did you speak to?
- What tips did they give you?
- What pre-trial conferences did you attend?
- What did you learn about the work?
- What did you learn about the role of a barrister?
- What did you like about the place, the work?
- What didn't you like?
- What surprised you?

Applying for pupillage

The chance of your winning the UK lottery is around 14 million to one. At times, an aspiring barrister, even one with the best academic record will be left thinking it's even harder to secure pupillage. The simple fact is that a string of A*s at GCSE and A level combined with a first-class degree (even one from Oxford or Cambridge) will not guarantee you anything, other than a few more tickets than your competitors in 'the pupillage lottery'.

Get used to rejection

Securing pupillage isn't really a lottery, but at times it will feel like one. You will submit what you think is the 'perfect' application supported by almost unbeatable academic credentials, blinding references, highly-relevant mini-pupillages and experience, together with a string of high-achievement in your interests outside the law, and appear to be a 'perfect fit' for the set you have applied to both in terms of your background and personality, yet it's still not good enough. Not even for the reserve list.

The irony is that if you are an aspiring barrister, you're not used to 'failing'. You've always done well. In fact, not just 'well' – you are likely to have excelled at school, at university and you've probably 'achieved' outside your education as well – maybe in sport, music or something else. So, how will you take rejection? Virtually no one secures pupillage without the pain of multiple rejections. So, are you ready for the 'fight'? And are you prepared to take a barrage of punches along the way? If so, here are the numbers:

The Bar Standards Board ('BSB') publishes annual statistics about pupil barristers, although the published figures tend to be two or three years old. Between 2004 and 2011 there were, each year, between 444 and 562 pupils in England and Wales who registered with the BSB as starting their first six, the lowest figure being for 2010-11, reflecting the general state of the economy at the time. Contrast those numbers with the BSB's year-on-year figures for those who completed the BPTC (and its predecessor, the Bar Vocational Course), which amounts to between 1,640 and 1,852 people looking for pupillage. In addition, the PSR reports that there were 2,802 online applications for pupillage via the Pupillage Gateway (which includes unsuccessful candidates from previous years) of which 249 gained pupillage. That's a success rate of less than 9% for applications via the online gateway. Even though the PSR reports that 134 students successfully applied directly to chambers for pupillage (ie outside the gateway), the stark reality is, even if you pass the BPTC, the odds are stacked against you progressing to pupillage. (Bar Standards Board, 2013)

When you take into account the fact that a significant number of pupillages are secured by applicants more than one year after they have been called to the bar (ie over a year after they have passed the BPTC), you have to be prepared for the fact that the transition from education to chambers (even if you get there) will not necessarily be a smooth one: you may have to stall your career progression for a year or two (or possibly more). But that doesn't mean you can't be acquiring valuable experience along the way: you can always be developing your talents, particularly your advocacy skills both in the voluntary sector (eg FRU) and in practice.

Many prospective barristers get a lot of rejections from pupillage applications and still go on to become counsel eventually. Apart from the BSB's requirement that you must start your pupillage within five years of passing the BPTC, it's not as though there's a clear cut off point where rejection means you can't become a barrister any more. At least that's what I tell myself!

You can first apply for pupillage before you start the BTPC - I did, as did many of my peers, and most of us did not succeed at that stage (the standard of application tending to be higher from those who have already completed the BPTC for obvious reasons). I was therefore in good company when I started the BPTC already having failed one round of pupillage applications: experience that's made it easier to cope with later rejection!

Once I had received all my rejections, I sent off a steady stream of applications direct to chambers through the autumn and then repeated the whole process the following year. I was getting legal experience in the meantime (pro bono and paid) so felt the quality of my applications was improving and I did end up getting interviews at sets that had declined to interview me the previous year: because many sets have only one place to offer, just because you get rejected doesn't mean you haven't made a favourable impression. It is by no means unheard of for applicants to be offered pupillage at sets they unsuccessfully applied to in the past (not least because some sets tend to ask the same questions every year - it actually confers a bit of an advantage upon you if you've been around before!)

In my experience, most people who succeed do so in the year of the BTPC, but I've known someone to receive a pupillage offer almost five years afterwards (having applied every year in between). So, there's hope for me yet!

BPTC graduate and current pupillage applicant, London

Pupillage at the employed bar

The vast majority of pupillages are offered in private practice by barristers' chambers (around 95% according to the PSR), but there are a handful of opportunities at the employed bar, including (but not limited to):

- The public sector – eg working for the Crown Prosecution Service ('CPS') and Government Legal Service ('GLS'); and
- The private sector – eg working 'in house' for a large company.

In 2012, after a two-year freeze, the CPS re-launched its Legal Trainee Scheme (LTS), offering 15 pupillages or training contracts for those seeking to complete their legal training and qualify as practising lawyers. It is not clear what the proportion was of pupillages to training contracts, and the process is under review at the time of publication of this title. The Government Legal Service offers around 12 pupillages each year, part of which you will spend with a departmental GLS legal team and part with an external set. However, applicants should note that there is very little prospect of an extended advocacy career at the GLS who state:

> *'It is uncommon for GLS barristers to conduct their own cases in court... many GLS legal teams use the services of external counsel for much of their court work.'*

As a pupil at the GLS, you will be exposed to a wide range of work, attending court (to observe/take notes, rather than act as an advocate), undertaking research and drafting legal opinions.

Pupillage at the independent bar

We will focus on applications to barristers' chambers in this chapter, but many of the tips we recommend will equally apply to those who seek pupillage outside the independent bar.

Pupillage providers are required to advertise vacancies for pupillage on the Pupillage Portal, which is a single website that acts as a hub for all pupillage applications. Some sets require you to apply via the Pupillage Portal, but others prefer direct applications. You can apply to as many sets as you like who invite direct applications and a maximum of 12 sets via the Pupillage Portal.

You should start applying in the final year of your QLD or during the GDL – depending on whether you are a law or non-law graduate. Unsuccessful applicants can still apply again if they don't succeed first time round. Some take two to five years after completing the BPTC before they secure a pupillage, but for the many who can't wait that long or can't handle multiple 'thanks but no thanks' letters, you need to ask what yourself what (if anything) you can do to boost your CV. And if you're left drawing blanks, as many extremely able aspiring barristers do, then maybe it's time to start looking at other career options.

Researching pupillages takes a considerable amount of time, but you must do it properly or you simply won't succeed. And, even if you devote a substantial part of each week over a period of many months (or even years) to your campaign, given the odds of success are so small, it is essential that you make your application stand out.

We will now take you through some of the key decisions which you will need to make before you complete any pupillage application.

What type of chambers?

It is important that you identify what areas of the law interest you and where you can see yourself working, both in terms of the practice area and location. Hopefully, your mini-pupillage experiences will have helped you decide in which areas (both law and location) you're headed.

Then, draw up a shortlist of chambers which specialise in those particular practice areas in your preferred location. Don't necessarily choose the subject you scored best in during your studies, because the practise of law is a world away from academic study. You will obviously need an excellent understanding of the law in that area – that goes without saying – but above all, you need to demonstrate a passion for that subject, both in writing and at interview, so applying to a set which practises in areas which excite and stimulate you must be the right place to start.

You then need to research thoroughly both the chambers themselves, including the profiles of their tenants and the range of their specialist practice areas. Find out what cases they have had reported in the legal press and research those cases, keeping track of any further developments (eg an appeal). Some chambers give an indication of how they assess candidates as part of the pupillage recruitment process and for those who don't, a quick internet search will often reveal discussion boards with useful pupillage gossip which may give you valuable nuggets of information that can sometimes help your preparation.

Exercise 10.1

When you decide you are seriously interested in a particular set, prepare a paper dossier or electronic folder of all the important information you can gather about them. Treat this like a pre-trial research project, for which you are gathering evidence and formulating arguments, ready for the 'trial' itself – the selection process. Your dossier should be prepared over several months (if not longer), well before it's time to apply for pupillage and should include:

- Details of the extent of the chambers' practice areas – ask yourself what their work involves in terms of who the clients are, the fact patterns, the law and the procedures used to try such cases in court/at tribunals
- Biographies of tenants, particularly ones whose path you may wish to follow

- Tenants' reported cases
- Their pupillage recruitment strategy and procedure
- Your well-rehearsed answers in writing to 'Why this chambers?', 'Why this area of law?', 'Why do you think you will fit in here?' as well as any other questions which your research reveals may be asked by this particular set during the recruitment process

Continue to build up, review and revise your dossier, so that, firstly, in your application and, later, at interview, you can demonstrate a deep understanding of the people who are looking at you and the areas in which they practise.

There are a wealth of reports on barristers' chambers in law careers publications such as *Chambers Student Guide*, the *Training Contract & Pupillage Handbook* and *TARGETjobs Law*, all of which should be available in any careers service linked to an institution which has a law faculty. One of the best places to start is by attending the National Pupillage Fair which is held in March of each year, at which you will get the opportunity of meeting a wide selection of practising barristers and pupils, including members of pupillage committees.

You will discover in your research several sets who specialise in one or two very narrow areas (eg family or employment law), and others who undertake an extremely broad range of work. The four most common sets are:

- Chancery
- Commercial
- Common Law
- Criminal

Chancery sets

The fictitious case of Jarndyce v Jarndyce in Charles Dickens' *Bleak House* isn't the greatest advert for Chancery work, but it does gives the reader a flavour of the enormous complexities which Chancery practitioners have to wrestle with. Mercifully, things have moved on in the last 200 years – these days, even the most complex of contested inheritance claims won't remain unresolved for over a generation and ultimately exhaust a large estate of all its funds in legal fees! What hasn't changed is the level of difficulty of the legal concepts which Chancery practitioners are instructed on. Consequently, this area of law tends to attract the more academic lawyers, as they will spend much of their time writing legal opinions on complex areas such as trusts, insolvency and tax. If these areas don't excite you, the Chancery bar isn't for you!

Chancery pupils and juniors don't usually get much big-hitting work early on in their careers. Appearing in court in insolvency proceedings (ie bankruptcy petitions and winding-up petitions) and possession proceedings (to evict squatters) is the norm in the early days and usually doesn't involve particularly difficult areas of the law. But in time (and for some juniors this will come sooner rather than later) you may be invited to assist one of the leaders in your set (a QC) on something much bigger both in value and complexity. That's when the real Chancery work starts.

Commercial sets

Commercial practitioners usually end up specialising in the law relating to a particular business sector, like construction, insurance, media or shipping. It is amazing how quickly you can acquire knowledge of a particular industry if you are living and breathing a heavyweight commercial case for several months. A successful commercial barrister will need to rapidly acquire industry jargon, understand the business of that industry, any relevant scientific processes, and so on. Even in the largest of business sectors, there are relatively few commercial law barristers who have a real understanding of that industry, so if you do an excellent job for one commercial client, news travels fast and the next brief won't be far away, even if you never dreamed of being, say, a leading legal authority on the manufacturing of cement!

Because commercial cases tend to be hugely valuable to those instructing counsel, pupils and newly qualified commercial barristers often have to cut their advocacy teeth on cases which are more typical of a common law practitioner (like personal injury cases). Their first exposure to high value commercial cases will tend to come when they are asked to assist a more senior junior or perhaps a QC at their chambers.

Applications for pupillage from candidates with relevant industry experience is helpful when applying to some chambers, but it won't get you pupillage on its own – all the other factors – not least an impressive academic record and your personality – will be more persuasive when a commercial chambers' pupillage committee makes its decision.

Common Law sets

You will learn in your studies that the 'common law' is law which is established by precedents set in leading cases, rather than law which is created by acts of parliament. Common law litigation is usually founded in contract or tort. So, breach of contract cases (eg disputes between manufacturers and those to whom they sell their goods) and instructions based in negligence (eg personal injury claims) are the regular diet of many common law practitioners.

In your early years in practice, expect to appear in court more days in the week than those you don't, usually on a variety of many small matters. When not appearing in court, you will be asked to 'settle pleadings' (eg drafting a defence) or provide an opinion on the prospects of success for a litigant, or advise as to quantum (eg how much a claim is worth). The latter is often used as a guide to solicitors and their clients to negotiate a settlement in order to avoid the time, cost and uncertainty of a contested trial.

Common Law practice is never boring – the variety of instructions will give you a taste of many different areas of the law. The downside is that it often takes longer for Common Law practitioners to find their 'niche' and develop a reputation for excellence in a particular field. One specialist area is in defending or bringing claims against hospital trusts following an operation or procedure (like the birth of a child) which goes wrong and leads to permanent injury or death.

Criminal sets

Many barristers will admit to being attracted to the bar (at least initially) by the portrayal of a criminal courtroom in literature, or a television or film drama. After all, the wigs, the gowns, the unsavoury characters, the battle of 'good' against 'evil' – the very drama of it all – it's incredibly alluring. However, when arguably more intellectual challenges tempt you in the direction of the Chancery bar, or you realise you can't handle a regular diet of blood-stained fact patterns, you then might decide that Crime isn't for you.

But for some, the attraction never goes away and the Magistrates' and Crown Courts becomes your domain. A pupil in a Criminal set will start with many short hearings each week covering a miscellany of driving offences and bail applications in the Magistrates' Court. In a short time, they move on to petty theft and minor assault cases. It will take a few years before you get your first chunky white-collar crime, rape or homicide case, but you do have a realistic prospect of appearing in the Crown Court before you complete your pupillage or shortly afterwards.

Receiving more than one brief the evening before each hearing, sometimes at different courts, is commonplace for pupils and junior criminal barristers. It's hectic but high octane stuff as well!

Top tip

If you're in a relationship, you need an extremely understanding partner: you both soon learn that you only ever book theatre tickets for weekend shows – unless he or she fancies going on their own when you cancel!

Unlike Common Law and Commercial practitioners, unless you're involved in a complex fraud case, a Criminal practitioner is not as likely to have enormous volumes of lever arch files to pour through as part of their brief. Nevertheless, a key clue as to a party's innocence or guilt may be buried in one of several dozen witness statements, the facts of which you will have to carefully absorb and remember. As well as having a keen eye for the smallest of details, a criminal barrister will also need a wider range of courtroom skills than other practitioners; not only do they need a thorough knowledge and understanding of Criminal Law and procedure, they need to present arguments in a powerful and persuasive manner, not just to a fellow lawyer or JPs on the bench – they need to do so in a language which is both accessible and convincing to a Crown Court jury.

How do chambers select their pupils?

Because they are so scarce, offers of pupillage are only normally awarded to candidates who demonstrate that they have something 'exceptional' to offer. Finding your 'USP' (unique selling point) and then persuading a room full of barristers that you are unique when each of them has already passed the same test is incredibly daunting.

A first-class academic record (often a first-class degree) is a pre-requisite – anything else will be sifted out well before the interview stage unless you are otherwise truly exceptional. But chambers are looking for so much more than that and just to make things harder, they are not all looking for the same thing. A Criminal set will usually be looking for a charismatic, persuasive personality who is able to relate to a wide range of people.

On the other hand, those sets who practise in the area of civil liberties and human rights will want to see evidence of a real commitment to the area from their prospective recruits – you'll need to demonstrate your passion a whole lot more than having attended a few undergraduate talks by a well-known human rights activists or volunteering at Amnesty International over the summer. That shows curiosity, maybe interest, but not passion. Have you travelled half-way round the world to work for a sustained period with charities who support prisoners on death row? Have you researched and had published a paper on how the law treats the rights of transgender persons in different legal jurisdictions? That is just part of the passion and commitment that a human rights set may be looking for.

Top tip

When applying for pupillage, particularly to sets who have a reputation in a highly specialised area, like human rights, shipping, tax or family law, your application needs to demonstrate that you know what the PRICE is... and that you've already paid it!

PRICE =

P assion - you have a passion for the subject

R esearch - you have acquired the requisite knowledge by studying/researching it in depth

I nterest - you are genuinely interested both in the subject and the clients it affects

C ommitment - you can demonstrate an unwavering commitment to the area

E xperience - you have accumulated sufficient experience to know the area is 'for you'

As part of the pupillage selection process, Chancery and Commercial sets may give applicants two or three days to research a particular point of law in relation to a complex set of facts, and to submit a legal opinion – ie a written advice. Those who impress with their opinion may be invited to move onto the next stage, which can be spread over several weeks and can be a gruelling combination of:

- Research tasks
- Advocacy tests
- Written assessments, such as drafting pleadings and legal opinions
- Interviews

Top tips for pupillage applications

Do ...	Don't ...
1. Sell yourself hard but honestly.	1. Sell yourself short.
2. Tailor each application for each set.	2. Cut and paste your last application.
3. Focus on applying to particular sets.	3. Apply to a wide range of sets.
4. Highlight areas which will set you apart.	4. Say what everyone else is going to say.
5. Answer the question, but in doing so, say what you want to say.	5. Second-guess what you think they want to hear.
6. Demonstrate relevant experience.	6. Apply without relevant experience.
7. Fully research each set you apply to.	7. Send a half-baked application.
8. Retain an air of humility.	8. Try to 'show off' or appear arrogant.
9. Show you've paid the PRICE (see above).	9. Imply a lack focus or direction.
10. Double, triple and quadruple check it yourself and then get someone else to proof-read it as well.	10. Rush it or only check it once.

At some stage, if you have jumped through all the hoops and deftly side-stepped the obstacles which have been placed in front of you, you may be invited for a formal interview in front of the pupillage committee. The interview may begin with a test of your oral skills – eg a plea in mitigation at a criminal set or cross-examining a hostile witness at other sets. You may be asked to reflect on the oral exercise, and demonstrate an ability to learn from your mistakes: 'How would you do it differently next time', is a tough question which expects you to identify your weak areas and demonstrate how you would work on them.

Unlike most interviews outside the bar, most of which tend to be before a panel of one to four members, expect a pupillage interview panel to comprise anything from four to twelve members of chambers, although there are some sets who ask everyone who is around to sit in when you're getting very close to the job! That tends to be more common for tenancy applications, but isn't unheard of for pupillage interviews.

The interview may last any time upwards of half an hour during which you will be grilled on a host of subjects – some law-related, and some more personal. Expect to be put under enormous pressure. And then some. The panel want to see how quick you are to formulate ideas and respond to changing and difficult circumstances. You may have seen the interviews in the final rounds of the BBC's *The Apprentice*. Expect the same, but not on a one-to-one basis – probing and provocative questions can be fired at you from all angles. Your CV will be scrutinised and any weaknesses will be exposed, so be prepared to justify why you took a gap year to backpack around Asia, Australia and New Zealand when you could have used the time much more 'constructively'. Rehearse your answer as to why you chose an elective subject on the BPTC, which is not practised by anyone at this particular set.

Your job is to stay calm, and keep a clear head so you can deal with whatever is thrown at you. The chances are some of the punches will hurt, and if they do, show them you have the character to bounce back from adversity while all times keeping your composure.

Pupillage applications to provincial sets

If you apply to a set outside London, they will be keen for you to demonstrate not just a commitment to them but also a commitment to the area. An applicant who has applied and failed to secure pupillage in London over a two or three-year period is unlikely to get anywhere near an interview with a provincial set. If you are from the area or are currently studying there, you have a much greater prospect of convincing a provincial pupillage committee that you're not going to dash back to the 'Smoke' as soon as the opportunity arises. Accordingly, you should emphasise your ties to the area in your application.

Chapter summary

Applying for pupillage requires considerable research, patience and hard work over many months, if not years. Be sure of the practice area you want to specialise in, research thoroughly the sets which undertake that type of work, and only then apply.

Key points

- Do at least two or three mini-pupillages.
- Keep an eye on the closing date for pupillage applications.
- Quality, not quantity: concentrate on focused bespoke applications rather than a scattergun approach.
- Get used to rejection. It's not personal. It's not even fair. It just 'is'.
- Research. Research. Research.
- Prepare. Prepare. Prepare.

Useful resources

www.barstandardsboard.org.uk

www.chambersandpartners.com

www.lawcareers.net

www.prospects.ac.uk

www.pupillagegateway.com

www.targetjobslaw.co.uk

Chambers Student 2013: The student's guide to becoming a lawyer

Training Contract & Pupillage Handbook 2013. 16th edition. London: Globe Business for the Law Society. For more information go to www.tcph.co.uk

References

Bar Standards Board (2013) Pupillage Survey 2010/11. [Online] Available at: http://www.barstandarsboard.org.uk/media/1408372/pupillage-supplementary-survey-201011.pdf [Accessed May 2013]

Government Legal Service (2013) Gradute opportunities. [Online] Available at: http://www.gls.gov.uk/graduate-opps.html [Accessed May 2013]

A day in the life of a mini-pupil

Time	Monday
9:30am	'It feels wrong to be up at this time: not only am I a student (on the BTPC) but it's also the Easter holidays. While my classmates are having a lie-in I'm determined to gain some CV points and a little more knowledge of the bar. I arrive at chambers and explain who I am. The receptionist seems a bit confused. She goes into the next room to speak to the clerks (the people who organise the barristers' diaries) then politely tells me I'll have to wait a while as they're trying to find a barrister for me to shadow. This is my third mini-pupillage and I've come to realise by now that some sets of chambers are better organised than others. My first 60 seconds here tells me this one is not in the 'well-organised' category. That suits me because the barristers tend to be more approachable and the working environment more informal, but on the downside it means they haven't bothered to find someone for me to shadow in advance; so rather than being telephoned on Friday evening and told which court to go to on Monday morning, I'm killing time here while they try to do it now. It does give me the opportunity to look around the building though. On previous mini-pupillages I've spent almost all the time at court (because that's where all the action is), but barristers spend a lot of time in their chambers preparing cases so I get to see a little of that side of things. There are several barristers working in each room and numerous bookcases stretching from floor to ceiling, filled with hefty legal books and bundles of papers from past cases. The whole place feels slightly overcrowded and the rooms don't look like modern offices – more your classic headmasters' study: oak-panelled walls and heavy wooden desks.

Time	Monday
10:00am	I speak to the pupils (the trainee barristers). They are very helpful and keen to answer all my questions. They bemoan the long hours but stress they find the work very fulfilling and the other barristers in the set very supportive.
10:20am	The clerks are still finding it difficult to track down a case for me to watch, but Sarah, a senior barrister in the set, invites me to watch a conference she is about to hold downstairs with a client in an employment case. She gives me a quick summary of the facts before he arrives.
10:30am	The client keeps trying to go off on tangents but Sarah continually (and diplomatically) steers him back on course. She covers a lot of ground quickly and clearly has a full grasp of the facts. I don't know about her client but I feel pretty confident she'll win. Then, no sooner is the defendant out of the door, then she turns to me and asks: 'What do you think: is he lying?' I'm unprepared for this question but luckily I'm saved the difficulty of answering it by one of the clerks – he has finally found a case for me to watch – a burglary trial in a court a short Tube ride away.
11:45am	I reach the court. Jack, the barrister I'm shadowing, tells me the case is yet to start. He is representing the defendant and is in a conference with the barrister for the prosecution about which sections of the witness statements are hearsay (and therefore have to be hidden from the jury).
12:30pm	The case is called into court. I sit in the row behind the barristers, right in the well of the court – as far as any spectators and jurors are concerned I look like a proper lawyer! Before the jury arrive, the barristers tell the judge which pieces of evidence they consider to be hearsay. This is fairly dry and I've just heard the barristers discussing it for thirty minutes, but it's dealt with quickly because everything is agreed between the barristers, and the judge then adjourns for lunch.

Time	Monday
1:00pm	I stick with Jack over lunch – which we share (in the fairly drab canteen at the court) with the barrister for the prosecution and several other barristers. We get a special roped off section in the canteen so no members of the public can sit near us and overhear what we say – I feel like a VIP. I'm introduced to the other barristers – there's quite a range of ages but they all seem to know each other. I'm asked where I am in my studies and receive a few snippets of career advice ('Don't work in Criminal Law whatever you do!'). The conversation is mainly about reforms to legal aid – useful opinions I can pass off as my own in interviews! A very junior barrister also sits with us and discusses the case he is working on – and gets swamped with opinions on what he should do: barristers certainly like the sound of their own voice!
2:00pm	Back in court and the jury are sworn in. The barrister for the prosecution speaks first, explaining the charge to the jury. I don't understand what he's talking about and I've had years of legal training – goodness knows what the jury are thinking. I am prepared to bet good money that the defendant gets acquitted – I just can't imagine the jury will convict if they don't understand what crime he's being accused of.
2:20pm	Now he's taking the first witness for the prosecution through her witness statement. I've already read the witness statement so, again, this is not especially interesting for me to watch. I'm more interested in what Jack is going to do next in his cross-examination.
2:50pm	Jack isn't sticking to the rules we are taught on the BTPC about cross-examining but he still seems to be getting a good result. I make a note of one of his tactics.

Time	Monday
3:20pm	I feel a bit like a freeloader as I have been shadowing all day without much to contribute and I want to get stuck in. While Jack is still cross-examining I idly read through the witness statements in the bundle hoping to find something of interest. Then I do! I notice the witness has lied about her age. I get very excited that I have finally achieved something and pass a note to Jack letting him know. He reads the note then turns around and whispers to me that it's 'not relevant'. Very disappointing.
4:00pm	It's the end of the day for the jury who go home, but the case will continue tomorrow. The barristers stay for another hour to raise points of law with the judge that the jury doesn't need to hear. Jack invites me to come back again tomorrow and I accept – it will be good to watch the case from opening speeches to verdict.
5:00pm	I reflect on the day on the way home. I did my first two mini-pupillages before I started studying law. I found them helpful because they helped me confirm I wanted to become a barrister – but I've decided now! I didn't find today's mini-pupillage as useful but it was helpful to look around the chambers and make some contacts – especially as I have decided to apply for a job here. I liked everyone I met and my application will stand out if I can name-drop a few of the barristers. I resolve to write a thank you letter at the end of the week so they remember me.'

A day in the life of a pupil

Type of chambers firm: Criminal **Stage of pupillage: Second six**

Time	Wednesday
7:30am	'I usually get in at about this time, which is when I believe I do my best thinking. I do all my prep the night before, but fine tune the wording of my trickier submissions in the morning. I usually work a 12-hour day during the week, but it only causes friction with Sean, my fiancé, at weekends. He's in the second year of his training contract with a medium-size law firm. He gets most of Saturday to himself, as I'm often in the Magistrates' Court on Saturday mornings dealing with the carnage of the night before. Being a criminal barrister is never boring, but you have to have a strong constitution to deal with some of the horrific incidents which come across my desk. My sister is training to be a surgeon, so 'blood and guts' must be in the family!
8:45am	I leave chambers to get to the Magistrates' Court which is a short bus journey away. Getting around in London tends to be much quicker on public transport than any other method. I do occasionally jump in a cab if I'm running late, but that's a luxury I try to limit unless my papers for the day are bulkier than usual.
9:15am	I arrive at court and find my instructing solicitor, Leon, who regularly refers work to my chambers, deep in conference with his client, Angus. Angus has been charged with drink driving. When he was breathalysed, Angus' reading was 95mcg. The legal limit is 35 mcg of alcohol in 100 ml of breath. So, not even close! He will be pleading guilty today and my job will be to put forward Angus' plea in mitigation to limit his sentence. We had arranged to meet at 9.30, but Leon catches my eye and invites me to join them in conference. Angus is not much younger than me. He's a 22-year-old painter and decorator and still lives at home with his parents, who know nothing about his brush with the law last month. Angus is keen to get everything 'over and done with' this morning and is desperate to know what his sentence will be. We can't assure him that he won't be given a custodial sentence (suspended or otherwise) but Leon and I know that's unlikely. A period of disqualification is the most likely outcome, but despite Angus 'wanting to know' what it will be, we can't second guess the court.

Time	Wednesday
10:00am	We're listed for 10.00am, but in the Magistrates' Court, so is everyone else this morning. It's a long list and we're in for a long wait. You simply have to wait your turn. We all pile in, the defendants, lawyers and anxious-looking friends and relatives who make for the seats at the back of the court which are reserved for members of the general public. We are two-thirds the way down the list and while he is waiting his turn, Angus gets to see summary justice being dispensed at first hand, as a succession of illegal street traders get their five or ten minutes in consideration for a variety of fines for selling their wares at a local market without a licence. Sometimes I manage to get two or three briefs in the same morning in the same court, but today it's just the one.
11:20am	Immediately before Angus, a young man of about 18 pleads guilty to driving without insurance and is banned from driving for 12 months and fined £500. Their worships seem grumpy today and I'm privately fearful for Angus.
11:40am	The prosecution sets out the case against Angus. The eyebrows of the two justices are raised in unison as the prosecution mentions the figure of 95 mcg. Angus confirms his guilty plea and I am invited to make my plea in mitigation before he is sentenced. I explain that the police had closed off one side of the road which Angus was driving on because of an accident ahead. Angus was directed by a police constable to drive round the accident, but Angus misunderstood the gesture and drove onto the pavement, where he was stopped and breathalysed. It was raining heavily at the time, which made visibility difficult, and I draw this to the court's attention. The retort from the bench is 'it's hardly surprising he couldn't see where he was going, given the amount he'd been drinking!' I change my tack and emphasise that Angus is ashamed he got behind the wheel having drunk so much alcohol, which was out of character for a young man with no previous convictions. I also ask the bench to consider the impact on Angus' livelihood as a painter and decorator when considering the sentence. He is disqualified (as expected) for 24 months but it could easily have been a three-year ban.

Time	Wednesday
1:15pm	I arrange lunch with Sean. We try to meet for lunch once per week, but most of the time one of us has to cancel due to a hearing or meeting over-running. We compare notes as to how our days have gone. Sometimes this is the best 'quality' time we get during the week because we're both in a rush in the morning and one or both of us are usually pre-occupied with a work-related matter in the evening.
Afternoon	I have been asked by my pupil supervisor, Matthew, to pour through several volumes of lever arch files during the afternoon which relate to a complex insider-dealing case in which he's acting for one of the defendants. Matthew asked me to read some other papers on the case a few weeks ago 'out of interest' but I suspect he had it in mind all along that I would peruse the voluminous print-outs of emails between the defendants and various third parties. I have been asked to look for documents which the prosecution are likely to cross-examine our client on. It's fascinating stuff but, unfortunately, it doesn't take long for me to conclude what I am reading looks highly incriminatory to Matthew's client. It's clear that Matthew has been through the papers already because many of the pages have been flagged with post-it notes and key words have been highlighted, but, during the afternoon, I manage to find a few pages which warrant discussion at our meeting which is scheduled for tomorrow afternoon.
6:00pm	Harry, the junior clerk, hands me my briefs for tomorrow. A couple of bail applications in one Magistrates' Court and a pre trial review in another, so I'll be getting plenty of use out of my Oyster card tomorrow. It looks like I'll be burning the midnight candle again. But I don't mind at all. It's what I trained for and I love it. I just have to call Sean and explain that the trip to cinema which we pencilled in for tonight is off. I take out my phone to call him, but there's no need to. He's got his retaliation in first – my phone was on silent while I was in court and I forgot to turn it back on. Had I done so, I would have seen Sean's text message – that he's working late too on a some corporate deal. Oh, the joys of being hitched to lawyer! At least we understand each other even if we seldom see each other!

A career as a lawyer...

BPP
LEARNING MEDIA

Chapter 11

The interview – getting that job

BPP
LEARNING MEDIA

Introduction

You've got an interview! Well done! You must have made a good impression on 'paper', so treat being asked to attend an interview as an enormous vote of confidence in you as a future lawyer. You have probably beaten off 90% of the other applicants to get this far. But you haven't got the job yet. There is still much work to be done.

This aim of this chapter is to assist you in your preparation for that interview – whether it is for a training contract, your first job as a solicitor, for pupillage or for your first tenancy in chambers.

The key to succeeding at an interview is no different to the way you are likely to have secured the interview in the first place – by convincing the interviewing panel that:

- You have as much to offer them as they have to offer you
- You are a 'fit' for each other intellectually and philosophically
- You have the commitment, passion and work ethic to succeed in the position

In this chapter, we will discuss a number of frequently-asked interview questions ('FAQs') for which you need to prepare your own unique answers. We will explain what lies behind some of these questions and we will give you tips on how to prepare to answer them, as well as general advice as to how to prepare for the interview itself.

The A to Z of preparing for an interview

A is for... Appearance

The first judgment any interviewing panel will make about you is how you physically present yourself. You can never go wrong with a smart dark suit tidy hair and modest, well-polished shoes. If you have any visible body art, adventurous hair (facial or otherwise), fabulous heels or multiple piercings, consider your priorities: your right to self-expression or the right to have a chance of getting the job? The legal profession is a conservative one: as much as we like to eulogise about our right to free expression, the reality is that the management of most law firms would prefer it if you didn't stand out for the 'wrong' reasons. You may think that this is pandering to irrational discrimination – and in a way it is. But this is the real world, not college. And to get on, sometimes you will need to compromise. And if it means your wacky hairdo only gets an outing at weekends, that should be a price worth paying.

B is for... Big-headed

If you are arrogant about your achievements and/or give the impression to the interview panel that they would be 'fools' not to give you the position, you won't get the job. Even if you satisfy every other criteria going, if no one fancies the prospect of working alongside you and your ego, they will make sure it never happens. No one likes a big head. On the flip side, unless you 'sell' yourself as part of the interview process, you won't get the job either. That doesn't mean you have to conduct the interview like a second-hand car salesman. Your sales pitch can (and ought to be) a lot more subtle. For example, sometimes all you need to do when answering questions is to expand your explanations by referring to your achievements and experience.

C is for... Commitment

'Demonstrate to me that you have a commitment to... [our specialist practice areas]'.

Demonstrating such commitment requires you to draw upon your personal experience, which your CV and/or application form should have covered already, at least in part. What the panel is usually looking for is an account which shows a consistent theme, initially showing how or why you acquired your interest in the practice area, and, more latterly, specific examples of what you have done to 'commit' from the moment you realised 'that's the area for me!' If the Criminal bar is your calling and you have not been regularly visiting the local Magistrates and Crown Courts, you need to ask yourself how committed you are to a career at the Criminal bar. Alternatively, if you're not regularly reading the *Financial Times* (for those who want a job in the City) or the *Estates Gazette* (if you want to be a Real Estate lawyer), how will you deal with the question the panel might pose about the ground-breaking article which appeared last Monday?

D is for... Downside

'What do you think the downside is of this job?'

This question tests whether you know what you're letting yourself in for! If you don't anticipate the downside of the job, your application will lack credibility. Every job has its 'bad days' and those interviewing you will want to know that you appreciate what they could entail. Examples will include:

- Long hours (but everyone says that, so try to be more original!)
- Irregular hours

- Working weekends and evenings
- Having to put work ahead of family/personal commitments
- Losing a case for a client/when a judgment goes against your client
- Losing a regular client
- Complaints
- Making a mistake

The usual follow-up question is **'how would you deal with the underlying cause of such a bad day**?' If you discuss the loss of an important client, there are a number of supplementary questions which law firms and chambers may pose so that you demonstrate an understanding of the commercial implications of losing a client (eg loss of revenue and reputation), and what you would do to minimise the risk of any repeat occurrence (eg investigating the underlying cause which led to the client going elsewhere and putting appropriate systems or measures in place to avoid a repeat occurrence).

E is for... Ethics

Legal ethics is a complex area and, consequently, pupillage and tenancy applications, in particular, will often include a question asking you how you would extricate yourself from an ethical dilemma. Solicitors and barristers will have already studied professional conduct as part of the LPC or BPTC, so it is worth brushing up on this area before your interview. Conflicts of interest, your duties to the court and confidentiality and disclosure problems are particular favourites of interviewing panels.

F is for... don't Fidget!

Most people are completely unaware of how they come across physically in interviews. Body-language plays a significant and under-rated part in the initial assessment that interviewers make about you before you have even opened your mouth. So, fidgeting, putting your hands through your hair, 'playing' with jewellery or an item of clothing will show you are particularly nervous. The panel will expect you to be nervous, but it is best to try to avoid any nervous tics you may have. Above all, maintain eye contact not just with your questioner, but with each and every member of the interviewing panel. Not only does this portray confidence, it also means that you don't just sell yourself to the more vocal members of the panel. In fact, some of them may say very little (and some nothing at all) but they are all, potentially, as important as each other, when your suitability for the position is discussed by the panel once you leave the interview room.

G is for... Geography

'How committed are you to a career in [town/city]?'

This is a particular favourite for firms and chambers located outside London, particularly if your CV suggests that you have previously been drawn to the capital. Having a close family connection looks good, as does the fact that your relationship partner may already be working there, but try to avoid name-dropping the aunt you haven't seen for ten years, or you may create a hole you cannot escape from. Equally, if your CV suggests no previous connection with London, be prepared for the question; 'What makes you think you'll enjoy living in London?' Being a Spurs or Arsenal fan, however important it may be to you personally, doesn't count. Interviewers may need to be convinced that you are ready for the hustle and bustle of the capital.

H is for... Honesty

Interviewing panels have a very finely-tuned nose for exaggeration and outright lies. Don't get yourself into an apparent anecdote, which you're actually making up as you go along simply because you can't think of any other way to answer the question. It's perfectly acceptable to ask for a few moments to gather your thoughts. Occasionally, saying 'I don't know' may sometimes be your best answer. As soon as interviewers get a whiff of embellishment or worse, you've blown it. By asking whether you can come back to a question later on, and doing so when you've found a good answer, shows that you're able to manage a difficult question and skilfully resolve it without losing credibility. You won't necessarily be re-asked the question if you 'park it' in that way: interviewers won't be that impressed if you just duck the question. Instead, the panel may be looking for you to use your initiative to resolve the unanswered question yourself.

I is for... Inspiration

'Who is your inspiration? How have they inspired you?'

This is a question that enables you to demonstrate your passion for the law and a particular practice area as well explaining one of the reasons for your chosen career. Making your answer personal will interest the panel – they're not necessarily looking for you to say your inspiration is a famous politician, activist or lawyer. It may be that a member of your family, a friend or a schoolteacher is your inspiration. Whoever your inspiration is, make sure you are able to demonstrate what you have learned about that person and/or what it is about this person that you identify with. Then, in your answer, explain how what you have learned from that person will help you in your career as a lawyer.

My role model was the late Norman Selwyn, who was a great friend of my parents. Norman was the author of Selwyn's Law of Employment, which is a market leading textbook that many of the readers of this title will come across during their studies. I talked to Norman several times before I applied for my place on a law degree course and, until his passing in 2010, Norman maintained a keen interest in my progress through law school, practice and academia, not least because it was the same path he had forged some years earlier.

What did I learn from Norman? His wit, turn of phrase and the fact that he understood his audience meant that he was able to break down complex legal concepts into something which was instantly more digestible, yet still comprehensive. Norman taught me that the best way of communicating – whether it is in writing, in a meeting with clients, or at at interview – is to truly engage your audience.

Jonny Hurst

J is for... Jokes

An interview is a serious matter. A considerable amount of time and money will be invested in your career development, so now isn't the time to show off your sense of humour – it isn't a romantic date or an audition for the Comedy Store. There usually isn't much opportunity for levity during the interview process, so don't try to engineer a situation whereby you get a chance to demonstrate why you went down so well at the university law society comedy revue. Resorting to comedy may be perceived as a sign of nervousness or a lack of focus on the 'important things'. On the other hand, if you have an outgoing personality and you have an opportunity of demonstrating 'the real you', don't stop being yourself in the interview, but hold back on the stand-up routine until the office Christmas party.

K is for... Knowledge

'Tell me what you know about... this firm/this set.'

This is a very open-ended question which expects the interviewee to draw upon what they have learned from researching the interviewer's website and any other research (eg from careers publications like *Chambers Students Guide*.) Those posing the question expect you to add value to what you have read on their website, not just regurgitate it. So, researching the legal press, like the *Lawyer* and the *Law Society Gazette* may give you more discussion points, as well talking to past and present employees, pupils and tenants. This is when you may get the opportunity of referring to your mini-pupillage or vacation scheme, if you have had previous experience of the firm/set.

L is for... the Law

'Why did you choose law?' is a probably the most common question which is asked at interviews for places on LLB courses. It is also frequently asked of newly qualified solicitors and barristers seeking their first post following qualification. It is incredibly difficult to avoid clichéd responses like 'because I find it fascinating' or 'I want to work in a challenging and stimulating environment.' The key to answering this question is to do so in a novel way which the interviewing panel has not heard before. The key is to personalise your answer: say what event, experience or person(s) inspired **you** to consider law as a career and what was it (during your studies) that confirmed to you that the law was where you were headed. You can weave in the 'usual' 'it's fascinating' and 'I love problem-solving' answers if you really want to, but make your answer more of a personal story, which effectively explains why you're here in this interview today. If the firm or set have a reputation for a particular area of the law and you genuinely share a passion and commitment for it, you can build this into your answer as well, but make sure you back it up with supporting evidence.

M is for... Mock interview

In the same way that a diligent student prepares for an actual assessment by attempting a mock assessment, you should practise being interviewed by arranging a mock interview. Often careers departments at universities may help to arrange such a mock. One of the ingredients to preparing well for the actual interview is preparing equally well for any mock interview you arrange.

Exercise 11.1

In preparation for your mock interview, write down onto a set of postcard-size flashcards as many relevant questions you think you could be asked by your interviewers. Prepare your answers, initially, in writing. When you are happy with how the answers look on paper, practise them out loud. Record yourself and then review your answers, refining any which need further work.

When you're happy with your preparation, shuffle the flashcards randomly and ask a friend (or friends) to pose as the interviewing panel in order to ask the questions – adding supplementary questions to your answers, where your friend(s) think(s) is appropriate, which you may not have thought of. You can start preparing for this exercise by adapting the questions set out in this chapter.

N is for... News

Keep up to date with the news in relation to:

- The legal profession, generally – what subjects are dominating the legal press? Make sure you have a strong grip on those stories and, if they are controversial, try to summarise the pros and cons of each side's argument. Be prepared to commit to one side if asked, but don't feel compelled to do so; it may be more appropriate to say it's impossible to reach a proper conclusion without all the evidence.
- The firm or chambers with whom you have an interview – check the website for any news which is posted on the morning of your interview.
- Current affairs – pupillage committees and law firms are sometimes known to ask an interviewee to put forward arguments on behalf of an almost impossible premise in the news, to test your sharpness, creativity, and, above all, how well you would do for a client even if the odds are stacked against you. For example, what would be the BBC's best case against the charge that the corporation presided over decades of rumours about Jimmy Saville's alleged child abuse, but did nothing to properly report or investigate it?

O is for... On time

Don't be late for your interview, even if it's not your fault (eg due to problems with the weather or public transport). You may not get a second chance, or even a first chance if you miss your allotted time. Mitigate against factors which are outside your control: if you are travelling a long way or anticipate bad weather or transport problems, stay overnight within walking distance or a short journey from the interview.

P is for... Passion

'Demonstrate your passion for the law/specialist practice area' is a test of your genuine interest and commitment, particularly in highly specialised areas like Family Law, Human Rights, or Immigration. Your personal experience or knowledge of real-life cases will help to demonstrate your passion. On a no-names basis (as you must at all times preserve client confidentiality!) briefly summarise the facts to contextualise your account, but spend most of your answer explaining **why** you feel compelled to practise as a lawyer in this particular area.

Q is for... Questions

The interview isn't just a forum for you to be asked questions. Make sure you have your own questions for the panel. In a law firm, don't be afraid to ask questions about career progression within the law firm – ie the various steps there are from newly qualified solicitor to partner. For example, some promote you to 'associate' as a stepping stone to partnership. How is the partnership structured? Why do barristers choose to leave your chambers? Be prepared to answer the supplementary **'Why do you ask?'** so it doesn't look like your question is just avoiding an uncomfortable silence. Asking such questions implies you're looking beyond just getting the job – that you're interested in possibly making more of a long-term commitment. Equally, you should be asking more short-term questions as well – ask for more detail about the extent of any mentoring you may receive from more senior colleagues. Raising such a question can appear like you lack confidence, but you can justify it on the basis that you want to be a sponge and to learn as much as you possibly can from a more experienced colleague.

Case study

Rebecca is a student on the LPC and has had several training contract interviews to date, but no offers. The questions she has been asked have varied from demonstrating examples of the firm's key competencies to discussing issues in the financial press. Her interviews have not had a rigid structure – the interviewers have allowed the discussion to digress in order to get a real feel for what Rebecca was about. Rebecca doesn't believe she has had a chance to shine at interviews yet; partly due to a lack of confidence but also because she needs to improve her commercial awareness. She is hoping that a subscription to the Economist and a good dose of self-belief will help her clinch the deal!

R is for... Reported cases

Especially when applying for any position in chambers or in a large litigation department, a common question is **'Tell me about any recently reported cases you may have read about which has involved this firm/counsel practising from these chambers'.** A good answer to this question will demonstrate that:

- You have a genuine enthusiasm in both the firm/chambers and the work they undertake
- You are able to discuss the key legal points coming out of a reported case in a succinct way

Be prepared for the supplementary question: '**What did you learn about**...' the reported case or any experience which you end up recalling during an interview. Interviewers are keen for you to show that you are aware that, as a lawyer, you are 'always learning'.

S is for... Supplementary questions

Be prepared for supplementary questions, so if you have an answer prepared, consider what follow-up question the interviewers may ask. For example if you have passion for Family Law because you feel your calling is to protect the interests of children, how do you reconcile that principle with your obligation to act in your client's best interests? In other words, suppose you were instructed by a father who is seeking a residence order (what used to be called 'custody') in respect of his seven-year-old son in circumstances where you personally believe that the son will be better off living with his mother, seeing his father at weekends and in the holidays? How do you reconcile Section 1 of the Children Act 1989: that 'the child's welfare shall be the court's paramount consideration' with your professional duty to act in the father's best interests?

T is for... Talent

'What talents and skills do need to succeed in this job? Tell me why you believe you have these attributes to succeed.'

It is incredibly easy to answer this question in the same way everyone else does. But your academic record and professed work ethic will only get you so far. Being a good 'team-worker' is vacuous unless you can provide relevant examples to support your statement and justify why that ability is important for this particular position. Again, gear your answer to your personal experiences but also give it some context. If the firm/chambers have described the type of individual they are looking for (which they often do), it's a good place to start with their criteria. Your application should have covered their criteria, at least in part, so by all means re-state any nuggets which you've already told your interviewers about, but don't stop there. This is your opportunity to add value to your application which was probably subject to a space or word limit. Interviewers want to see depth to your answer with highly relevant examples to support your assertion that you are the person they have been looking for.

U is for... Unexpected questions

By definition, there is little one can do to prepare to answer unexpected questions. But you should at least mentally prepare for them. If you're really stumped for an answer, have a device available to 'park' the question until later in the interview. But make sure you come back to it. There's nothing wrong with replying 'that's an excellent question' or asking for a few second to work out your answer. But don't engage mouth before brain!

V is for... Video-recording

As cringe-worthy as it sounds, recording any mock interview(s) will be incredibly helpful, so that you can pick up on any presentation tics which you need to manage (see 'F is for... don't Fidget' above). Are you maintaining eye-contact? Are you fidgeting? Are you addressing the whole panel or just the questioner? Listen to how you sound as much as to what you are saying. Do you sound confident? Do you vary the pitch and tone of your voice? How animated is your voice?

W is for... Weaknesses

'What are your weaknesses? How may they hold you back in this position?'

This is a really difficult question to answer. On the one hand, you don't want to give the panel a reason to reject your application, but they will expect you to show an element of openness and genuine humility. If you only mention something trivial, the panel may question your honesty. The key to getting the balance of your answer right is to make a 'positive out of a negative'. Saying 'I'm a bit of a perfectionist' can be seen as a positive statement – but it is still a weakness if you acknowledge that perfectionism can compromise the timing of the delivery of a task. You will be expected to explain how you would manage your weaknesses and/or eliminate them.

Top tip

Be prepared to discuss more than one weakness. Most interviewees are ready for the question, but are not prepared for **'What are your other weaknesses?'**

X is for... the X factor!

Don't worry, it's extremely unlikely that your karaoke skills will be tested at this stage! But remember, the interviewing panel is usually looking for someone who is different to most other applicants – someone who has something 'special' to offer. If you have a unique selling point (USP) or at least a rare talent (eg a useful foreign language or a strong science background), which is relevant to the position, make sure you don't leave that interview without reminding the panel. You should have made a point of emphasising this on your application form, but even if you did, there is no harm in dropping in such a reference at a convenient moment – but be careful about overplaying that card.

Y is for... be Yourself!

Be yourself. Don't be someone you're not, as those interviewing you will see through the charade. There's a positive side to being yourself as well – if you get the opportunity of showing 'the real you' to your interviewers, then do so. But you will rarely get that chance as the formality of the interview won't give you many opportunities, other than to demonstrate that you're intelligent, articulate and cool under pressure.

Z is for... Zero or hero

The outcome of a job interview is all or nothing – zero or hero. And not a lot in between. The key is not to overreact either way: Kipling advises that when you meet Triumph and Disaster, you 'treat those two impostors just the same.' Getting the job will be a huge achievement, but it's only the start of the journey, whereas failing to get the job this time round may be devastating, particularly when you consider the time and effort you will have invested, but it never has to be the end of the road. Just keep the outcome of the interview in perspective, whichever way it goes.

Exercise 11.2

Assume you are invited for an interview by a law firm or set of your choice.

In no more than a page each, write honest, personal answers to the questions raised in this chapter. Take no more than ten minutes for each question. Come back to your answers a week later and re-read them.

DON'T READ ANY FURTHER IN THIS EXERCISE UNTIL YOU'VE WAITED A WEEK

Look at what you wrote. How many of your answers appear clichéd? Do you think you came up with the same answer as everyone else – or a version of a similar theme?

Now spend more time tailoring your answers to make them stand out. It may mean you need to think deeper or make the answers more personal. Speak to people who know about you and/or the legal profession. By all means be creative, but, above all, stay honest.

My first interviews were filled with nerves and a sense of foreboding, as I had no idea what was expected of me, or how I would be challenged. Would it be a law-based interview? Would it be an interview that was purely about me? I found them difficult to prepare for and my self-confidence was minimal.

It took a few interviews before I started to believe that each interviewer knew how I felt. They almost always began by distracting me from why I was there. This tactic made me feel more comfortable and enabled them to see as much of the 'real me' as was possible, in a small bracket of time.

Some of my interviewers placed me at the centre of the discussion. We talked about my schooling, my university experiences, work I had done for charities and work I was doing for an events company. We talked about why I have pursued law as a career, where I thought my strengths would lie, and what I expected from a training contract. Other interviewers tested my legal knowledge and commercial awareness. They gave me hypothetical situations to work through, asking me about VAT and giving me a list of daily tasks that I had to re-number in terms of priority.

My very last interview was undoubtedly my best. Exhausted after a long summer of interviews and rejections, I had begun to feel desperate. I went into the interview as if I had already received my rejection letter. But I remained calm, professional and confident and felt like I was testing them, rather than the other way around. I received an email for a second round interview within fifteen minutes of leaving the office!

India Corbin, LPC student

Chapter summary

Prepare for an interview like your life depends on it. (It doesn't, although you may feel like it does!). If you prepare well, and remain committed, confident and composed in the interview, you may keep yourself in the reckoning. But if you don't get the job try to get feedback as to where you fell down, or maybe you will know that from the interview. As Bram Stoker said, 'We learn from failure, not from success.'

Key points

- Research your interviewers thoroughly
- Prepare answers to the FAQs we have mentioned in this chapter
- Arrange mock interviews to practise your interview technique
- Keep your mind clear for (and expect) a question for which you don't have a rehearsed answer

Useful resources

www.lawgazette.co.uk

www.chambersandpartners.com

www.lawcareers.net

www.prospects.ac.uk

www.rollonfriday.co.uk

Chambers Student Guide 2013: The students guide to becoming a lawyer, Chambers and Partners Publishing, London 2013

Training Contract & Pupillage Handbook 2013. 16th edition. London: Globe Business for the Law Society. For more information go to www.tcph.co.uk

Chapter 12

Private practice or elsewhere?

BPP
LEARNING MEDIA

Introduction

The vast majority of lawyers start their careers in private practice, whether it is as a solicitor working for a law firm or a barrister at the independent bar. Indeed, a large proportion of them will stay in private practice for their entire careers. However, compared to the number of pupillages and training contracts, there are many more opportunities for lawyers to practise law outside private practice once they have qualified.

As the years go by, you will notice that the people you originally trained with all tread their own unique path. Some will achieve their 'life's ambition' of becoming a QC or a partner in a law firm, but after having spent a few years in private practice, other qualified lawyers may look for somewhere else to ply their trade.

Why is private practice not for everyone?

Stress/health issues

Stress is one of the main reasons why many lawyers leave private practice. As law firms emerge from the recession, they are looking to grow their businesses, but with a leaner and meaner workforce. Initially, most members of staff embrace the challenge, but there comes a point where even the most diligent and able of lawyers cannot deliver any more, and that is what separates the firms which are well-managed from those which are not: the former have adequate systems and strategies in place to support their fee earners who are asked to increase their workload. Unfortunately, fee earners would not leave private practice in the numbers they do if all firms just had 'challenging-but-realistic' expectations.

Most fee earners in law firms will have their own personal billing targets, which are usually set on an annual basis. Heads of department and partners will track fee earners' profitability on a monthly if not week by week basis, part of which will include an analysis of the time each fee earner spends on fee-earning work. Yes, law firms require you to account for almost every minute of your working day, achieving a minimum number of 'chargeable hours' per day – ie time which you spend which will be charged to clients. Depending on the firm, this will be around six hours per day, which sounds easy enough to achieve if you work an eight-hour day, but actually, it's not! Interruptions from work colleagues, departmental meetings, marketing, non-chargeable legal research, attending training courses, making cups of tea, comfort breaks, and daring to nip out to grab a sandwich all eat into your chargeable working day. Having one or two large matters to work on makes the target much easier to achieve, as opposed to a multitude of tasks, provided you can justify spending significant amounts of time on one file.

Recording time on a client matter which is, ultimately, not charged to the client, is time which has to be 'written-off' by the firm, and that affects your personal profitability. Consequently, firms closely monitor how much of your recorded time actually gets billed to clients. It's easy to see how hard-working solicitors who are slightly under-performing (financially-speaking) can be put under pressure by their managers even if they are doing a fantastic job for their clients.

Clients can also be incredibly demanding; they are, after all, paying your firm several hundred pounds per hour for the benefit of your time and expertise, so not surprisingly, they want their money's-worth. But clients can, at times, be unreasonable, and so managing them doesn't help stress levels either.

Of course, solicitors don't have a monopoly on high stress levels; barristers face their own fair share as well. Imagine having a succession of clients and instructing solicitors who are not happy with the outcome of their litigation. This can lead to a loss of work from those instructing you and clerks may (consciously or not) direct some briefs which you would have normally expected to come your way to other members of chambers, which could lead to cash flow issues, ultimately jeopardising your tenancy.

Long hours/work-life balance!

Don't go into law unless you expect to work hard! There are few cushy legal jobs inside or outside private practice. However, the volume of work undertaken by solicitors and barristers in private practice does tend to be larger and the hours are usually longer. There is much less of a 'long hours culture' outside private practice, where leaving the office before 6.00pm does not tend to be met with so many raised eyebrows. However, few employers are going to object if their in-house lawyers work beyond 7.00pm, as many of them do. Some solicitors do manage to work a 'nine to five day' in private practice, but only usually for small firms, where there is less of an expectation to work late. Many lawyers who move away from private practice report 'getting their lives back' as the demands of their old job left them exhausted and time-poor. A fresh challenge in a different environment, with less of a time commitment will often bring an imbalanced work-life equation back to equilibrium.

Need a change/loss of job satisfaction/office politics/career options limited

Sometimes it's just a question of being a little bored or frustrated with private practice. Maybe you have been overlooked for partnership, you don't get the same buzz as you used to, or you could just be bored of the work you're doing and/or the people you work with.

A career as a solicitor in private practice

If you impress sufficiently during your training contract, you may offered a job on qualification. If you are, it takes a very brave lawyer in the current economic climate to reject such an offer, unless you have something else lined up, or the type of work on offer is not what you see yourself doing at the start of your career. But you may not get an offer to stay at the firm, in which case you will need to apply for a job elsewhere if you wish to stay in private practice. There are many places to look – try the *Lawyer*, the *Law Society Gazette* and the numerous specialist recruitment agencies which advertise vacancies in the legal press and on their own websites. You should also check out the websites of law firms, most of whom will publicise their vacancies. Some firms say they entertain speculative applications, which is worth a punt, particularly if you are looking to build your career in a highly-specialised practice area.

A career as a barrister in private practice (at the independent bar)

Securing a permanent place in chambers by way of a tenancy is almost as competitive as the battle to secure pupillage. You may be offered a tenancy from a set where you spent time as a pupil. Most newly qualified barristers would choose to accept such a tenancy, which means that you become self-employed sharing your chambers overheads (ie premises, utilities, clerks and administration costs) with other members of chambers. If you don't secure a tenancy after pupillage, if you want to practise as a barrister at the independent bar, you will need to apply to chambers directly and respond to advertisements in the legal press and online.

Top tip

If it is looking likely that you won't find a paid job immediately on qualification, try to get experience when you're not pursuing your target of finding a job as a qualified solicitor or barrister – eg by working part-time as a lawyer in the voluntary sector at a law centre, the citizens advice bureau or the Free Representation Unit. This will look much better than a gap on your CV and will continue to develop your general legal skills.

Careers outside private practice

In the remainder of this chapter, you will find short summaries of some of the alternative careers which exist outside private practice for qualified lawyers who wish to continue to use their legal background. These opportunities are not only open to newly qualified solicitors and barristers, but also to those who wish to leave private practice at any stage of their career.

Government Legal Service ('GLS')

'We have only one client: but that client is the British Government' (GLS, 2012). The GLS employs around 2,000 lawyers working in separate legal teams across 30 Departments of State, regulatory bodies and other government organisations. The work undertaken by GLS lawyers will largely depend on the nature of the government department to which they are seconded. Consequently, the work is incredibly varied, covering 'the armed forces to zoology and anything in between' and includes:

- Agriculture
- Charities
- Commercial and procurement work
- Constitutional issues
- Education
- Environment
- Finance
- Health
- Human rights
- Justice
- Social security
- Taxation
- Trade

GLS lawyers will:

- Draft legislation
- Advise government ministers on the legality of proposed policy
- Represent the government in high profile litigation cases, although the advocacy itself is usually contracted out to the independent bar

Although the salary is considerably lower than you would expect to command in private practice, many lawyers choose to work for GLS for all sorts of reasons:

Flexible hours and terms

It isn't easy in many areas of private practice to work part-time without putting in many extra hours in your own time to 'get the job done' – which defeats the object of working part-time in the first place! GLS is generally able to accommodate those with young families and others who wish to work reduced hours and/or a day or two per week from home. Consequently, over 20% of GLS lawyers work part-time.

The ability to move departments every three to four years

By the time you are three or four years into your career in private practice, the chances are that the type of work you do has 'settled down', and there is a degree of familiarity and predictability about the work, albeit that your experience permits you to gradually take on more complex work. The ability to switch to a completely different department in a law firm is very difficult at this stage, whereas, this is common practice every three to four years at GLS.

I presently work as a legal adviser to an enforcement team at OFGEM (the Office of the Gas and Electricity Markets). OFGEM supports the Gas and Electricity Markets Authority – the regulator of the power industry in this country. This is an in house role – and I work as part of a team comprising lawyers and non-lawyers.

OFGEM has various teams dealing with different aspects of the energy market regulation and each has a team of lawyers attached. My legal team works as part of a wider team containing policy and enforcement specialists and economists as well as lawyers. Our work focuses on checking and investigating the compliance of energy suppliers with various legal regimes, in the interests of consumers. Cases can be pursued that may lead to the imposition of large financial penalties.

Both civil and criminal cases may be pursued. For example, we check that:

- *consumers are treated fairly when they are sold products;*
- *they are aware of their rights to information about the services they are paying for;*
- *transfers between suppliers and billing is dealt with fairly;*
- *where vulnerable consumers run into debt this is dealt with sensibly, taking into account those consumers' ability to pay.*

I work with policy colleagues to interview witnesses and obtain written evidence. I will draft pleadings or requests of suppliers for disclosure of data. I will also instruct Counsel to appear in larger hearings and to advise on more complex areas of law.

> *As a public body much of our work is carried on subject to possible Judicial Review if we get decisions wrong, or act unreasonably or contrary to ways we have said we will act. My role often involves steering a case around possible risks of challenge on these grounds. We also have to think about freedom of information requests – which is potentially tricky given that much of our work relates to market-sensitive activities by blue-chip companies who are rightly concerned to ensure that our investigations do not unfairly or unduly affect their financial position in stock markets and in relation to their profitability and reputation.*
>
> *The role is challenging and different every day – and so very stimulating. It can be nerve-wracking too – often we are asked to advise senior clients who have to take decisions about multi-million pound transactions – so the advice has to be right!*
>
> Richard Morgan, Legal adviser at OFGEM

Local government lawyer

Local authorities employ around 2,000 solicitors and like GLS lawyers, local government lawyers only have one client – the particular council they work for.

Local government lawyers fulfil a wide variety of roles. For example, local authorities employ large numbers of staff, so there is a considerable amount of work for employment lawyers advising the council in relation to a full compliment of employment law matters, such as disciplinary and tribunal proceedings. In addition, managing the terms and conditions of the contracts of such a wide and diverse workforce is a major challenge for councils, particularly in the light of the recent high profile equal pay claim against Birmingham City Council: Birmingham City Council v Abdulla and others [2012] UKSC 47.

There is also plenty of property and litigation work for local government lawyers. The property work may include drafting tenancy agreements and leases both in relation to the council's social housing stock (eg council flats) and commercial properties which are let to business tenants. The range of litigation to which the council may be party is vast – from personal injury claims for someone tripping up on a pavement to judicial reviews of key council decisions.

Proceedings involving children, debt recovery, licensing (eg of public houses) and planning are just some of the other specialist areas you can work in as a local government lawyer.

The experience and expertise which local government lawyers gain can prove to be an excellent platform to later working in-house or going back into private practice.

In-house

To work in-house for a company, public body, charity or trade association, it is helpful to have a background in at least one of the following:

- Corporate work
- Commercial work
- A similar to area to the business of the organisation (eg medical negligence experience if you work in-house for an NHS Trust)
- Compliance/regulatory work

Those working in-house will manage relationships with the management of their organisation (eg board of directors in a company) as well as lawyers in private practice whom the organisation will instruct from time to time. Where there is expertise and capacity within the in-house legal team, the organisation may choose to keep the dispensing of legal services in-house. For example, large retail chains will have extensive property portfolios consisting mainly of leasehold interests in shopping centres, high streets and retail parks. Leases need negotiating for new sites, old leases need renewing and issues will arise in relation to these properties where the input of lawyers is required – eg if the retailer wishes to make physical alterations to the premises which may require the landlord's consent. Some retailers will send all such work out to private practice, whereas others may deal with part or all of the work in-house.

Definition

The 'in-house' head of legal affairs is commonly referred to as **General Counsel.**

An in-house survey was published in 2012 by inhouselawyer.co.uk in conjunction with *Legal Business.* The majority of the respondents were the UK General Counsel in top UK and American companies. Around 75% of their in-house legal departments had less than ten qualified legal staff, so most in-house jobs will mean you work as part of a small team.

Crown Prosecution Service

The Crown Prosecution Service ('CPS') is the government department responsible for prosecuting criminal cases in England and Wales. Its responsibilities include:

- Advising the police on cases for possible prosecution
- Preparing criminal cases for court
- Presenting criminal cases at court

Solicitors tend to fill the first two of these roles whereas those representing the Crown in court are often (but not exclusively) trained barristers.

The CPS employs around 8,000 staff and calls itself 'the largest law firm in the country'. Like GLS, the salary of CPS employees is generally lower than private practice, but again, like GLS, CPS staff enjoy more flexible workable arrangements.

Law Centres and Citizens Advice Bureaux (CABs)

The main aim of Law Centres and CABs is to provide access to professional legal and financial advice to members of the local community who are unable to afford the services of a lawyer or other adviser on a commercially viable retainer. Areas regularly covered include social housing, welfare benefits, debt management, immigration and employment law. Professionally qualified staff are employed as well as volunteers, the more senior ones being responsible for managing and organising the training of staff members as well as providing advice on the more complex instructions.

Other careers

Having a legal background is an excellent stepping stone to careers which do not involve the practise of law, but still draw upon your legal training and knowledge, such as being a court reporter or law lecturer. In addition, large law firms employ a number of 'professional support lawyers' (PSLs). PSLs do not, generally, have a fee-earning role, but they do important work in ensuring that their fee-earning colleagues are up to date with changes in the law and legal practice. Much of a PSL's role will involve legal research and training. Some PSLs move into education (eg teaching at universities on law degrees, GDL and LPC courses). Equally, those who teach for a while sometimes decide to pursue a PSL role. For an example of a PSL's day, see the feature at the end of this chapter.

But of course, just because you have a legal qualification, it doesn't mean that you have to become a lawyer or work with lawyers. Having a legal qualification means that you will have acquired a number of transferable skills – arguably as many (if not more) than any other qualification. Journalism, social work, business and banking are just a few of the other options.

Chapter summary

There is a whole world of work out there – even in recessionary times. Prospective employers, both within the legal profession and outside, are looking for variations of the same theme: committed, enthusiastic and intelligent people. Your legal background will impress (even if it is 'just' a law degree) and should open more doors than most. The rest is up to you. Good luck!

Key points

- Most law students head to private practice following their legal education.
- A career in private practice isn't for everyone – there are plenty of other options in the law and outside.
- Keep an open mind to those options outside private practice – don't assume that because everyone else is heading off to the City, you should do so as well.

Useful resources

www.citizensadvice.org.uk

www.cps.gov.uk/careers

www.gls.gov.uk

www.inhouselawyer.co.uk

www.lawcentres.org.uk

www.localgovernmentlawyer.co.uk

References

Government Legal Service (2012) *What is the Government Legal Service?* [Online] Available at: www.gls.gov.uk/index.html [Accessed May 2013]

In-House lawyer (2012) The In-House Survey 2012. [Online] Available at: http://www.inhouselawyer.co.uk/index.php/the-in-house-survey-2012 [Accessed December 2012]

A day in the life of... a professional support lawyer

Type of law firm: Large | Department: Real Estate

Time	Monday
9:00am	I arrive at the office, park my bicycle in the basement and head up to my desk. I'm slightly addicted to my Blackberry and am already checking my emails as I walk down the corridor. The professional support lawyer's (PSL) role involves ensuring that the rest of the department are kept up to date with changes in the law, so it is important that I spend some time scanning through the daily email updates I receive. These updates report on new cases/ legislation and any relevant business or political news. Every PSL in the firm will probably be doing a similar thing in their subject area. I spot that the government has announced a consultation on some new legislation which I know will affect one client in particular. I email the information to that client, keeping Adam, the partner responsible for that client, informed, so that he will know about the topic if the client rings him. I am also waiting for the judgment in an important Court of Appeal case to come through because when it does, I need to quickly draft an email to all the department's clients advising them of the decision and its impact. A PSL from another firm (I am part of a large group of PSLs from different firms who get together every two months to discuss legal developments in our area of law) has just emailed our PSL group to say that he has heard the judgment will be out tomorrow. That is good news for me as I know I have a busy day today and that tomorrow will be clearer!
10:00am	I'm delivering some training for the paralegals (people who work in law firms but who are not qualified solicitors) who assist the lawyers in my department. The training is on licences for alterations, documents which permit tenants to carry out alterations on their premises and which are negotiated between landlords' and tenants' solicitors.

Time	Monday
	I devised the training session last week, which involved me thinking back to when I was a transactional lawyer in practice. I needed to break down into small steps how I would have dealt with drafting and negotiating the contents of a licence. I also needed to think about what specific legal knowledge the paralegals would require as many of them will have done a law degree but not the LPC. This training session involves the paralegals practising their drafting skills, so there is plenty of heavy paperwork for me to carry to the training room, but my PA, Gary, has been a star preparing all the different bundles of documents for me.
11:30am	I get back to my desk after the training and see that I have a couple of emails and a voicemail asking for my help. Another part of the PSL's role is to advise the transactional lawyers on tricky points of law or procedure. I usually get asked questions when others don't know the answer and am sometimes treated like a walking encyclopaedia! When junior members of the department are asking it is often something I can answer off the top of my head, thinking back to my time in practice. When senior people ask me questions, it can be more tricky. If the question is about a recent case or change in the law, then it is probably something I have been studying and following closely, so the answer will be at hand. However, it might be something quite esoteric which will involve me doing some research using our online legal database which contains all law reports, practice notes and many textbooks. Going to the library, as I often used to when I was a trainee, is now a thing of the past. This shows how the PSL role differs from the transactional lawyer in practice as the people I deal with most are other lawyers in the firm, rather than external clients.

Time	Monday
12:30pm	I am running a lunchtime training session for the department's trainees. This session is about drafting a lease and gets repeated every six months when we get a new set of trainees in the department, so I am fairly familiar with this session. The trainees are a fun bunch and ask lots of questions, keeping me on my toes. They are keen to show that they are interested in the topics as some of them wish to qualify into the Real Estate department. I particularly enjoy the training side of my role. When I was a transactional lawyer in practice, the part of my job that I enjoyed the most was supervising and training the trainees, so moving into the PSL role which focuses on those skills, seemed a natural step for me. After the training finishes, I get chance to go to the firm's café before it stops serving lunch and grab some Thai prawns with noodles – the catering here is varied and quite delicious. I bump into Emma, a partner from the Corporate department, whom I used to live with when we were trainees together, and we sit down for a good gossip.
2:00pm	I spend some time preparing for my half-yearly appraisal tomorrow morning. I make a list of all the department projects I've been involved with over the last six months (training projects, writing articles for real estate publications, improving the department's intranet/ knowledge management systems etc) and then a list of the cross-departmental projects (working with PSLs from other departments on firm publications for clients, marketing and networking projects, general induction training for trainees and newly qualified solicitors etc). My appraisal will be with Anjuli, the head of the PSLs in our firm, although I don't have much day-to-day contact with her because the majority of the work that I do is for the Real Estate department and she was previously a PSL in litigation. I therefore need to make sure that I also ask a selection of the people that I've worked for (which has ranged from the head of the department to trainees!) to provide feedback on my work.

Time	Monday
	The PSL role is quite unique in that at some point or other you will work with everyone in the department across each of the firm's offices, as they will all have queries at some stage. There is less of a sense of hierarchy and almost everyone in the firm will treat you as their equal. Career-wise, the role often sits outside the firm's main structure and it is up to each individual PSL as to how they might want to see their career develop. It is unlikely that a PSL will become a partner, though.
3:30pm	I now head up to the meeting rooms to deliver a training session to a client on some recent case law developments. The client has been using our offices to hold a training day for its staff and PSLs from different departments of the firm have been delivering slots. I am also taking an eight-year qualified lawyer with me who knows the client well and who will be helping with some of the interactive parts of the training.
5:00pm	I pop back to my desk and there are a couple more emails asking me legal queries. I can answer one quickly and for the other I reply, acknowledging the message, giving an estimate of when I will be able to get back to that person.
5:30pm	I would normally finish my working day between 6-7pm, but tonight I am heading out for drinks and a meal with the client that I provided training for this afternoon. There are about ten of us from this firm and fifteen from the client (most of whom are booked into a city centre hotel, so this might prove to be a late night!). I'm hoping I can slip away by about 10.00 pm, though, as I've got to catch a train to one of our other offices tomorrow (I try to work in each office a couple of times a month) and I know that I'll need to have a clear head to write an email about the results of that important Court of Appeal case being released tomorrow.

Extract from the electronic diary of a Commercial Property partner (to be read with the Week in the Life feature below)

	Monday	Tuesday	Wednesday	Thursday	Friday
08 00	Weekly dept team meeting: Imran to present	Fee earning work	Fee earning work	School assembly	Meeting with Amy
08 30					
09 00	Review and distribute post	Review and distribute post	Review and distribute post		Review and distribute post
09 30	Fee earning work	Fee earning work	Review work in progress, unpaid bills		Fee earning work PLUS Completions day for: 1) Land at Ritter Heights 2) Arlow Park 3) 12 Carrow Place
10 00					
10 30				Review post	
11 00			Fee earning work	Fee earning work	
11 30		Travel to Hart & Co			
12 00		Meeting at FW Hart & Co with Clive Owen re: Option over land at Milton Grange			
12 30			Meeting with finance partner	Travel to partners mtg	
13 00	Lunch with Tim		Integration committee meeting	Partners' meeting	Lunch with Sian Blackstone and directors of GW Developments (London) Ltd
13 30					
14 00	Jerome Garner Potential new client?	Travel back to office	Quarterly review meeting with NRT (Properties) Ltd		
14 30		Fee earning work To exchange contracts re: Bailey & Co portfolio			Fee earning work
15 00	Fee earning work				
15 30			Fee earning work		
16 00					
16 30					
17 00	Review outgoing mail	Review outgoing mail	Review outgoing mail		Review outgoing mail
17 30					
18 00	Fee earning work	Fee earning work	Fee earning work	Travel back to office	Friday drinks
18 30				Fee earning work	
19 00	END WORK FOR THE DAY		Reception at H & F		END WORK FOR THE DAY
19 30					
20 00					

Figure 12.1

A week in the life of a commercial property partner

Introduction

'I am one of the partners in the commercial property department of a 50-partner firm of solicitors. I specialise in property acquisitions and sales for property developers and property investment companies. I work in my firm's central London office, which is the largest of our four offices, two of which are outside London on the M4 corridor. One of the firm's trainees, Amy, currently shares my office. Most of the work she does is for my clients.

MONDAY

Monday: 8:00-9:00am Departmental team breakfast meeting

We hold a departmental breakfast/team meeting on the second and fourth Monday of every month. We usually timetable 20 to 30 minutes for one of the team to present a mini lecture on recent changes in property law or practice. One of the department's assistant solicitors, Imran, recently attended a commercial property course as part of his continuing professional development. Today he provides us with highlights of that course, including new land registry forms and procedures, some significant changes to the law affecting the adoption of drains by local water authorities and some recently reported landlord and tenant cases.

The meeting is an opportunity for the five property partners to monitor:

- Fee earners' workloads
- Which deals are likely to complete this month (which our finance partner will want to know later in the week)
- Who has spare capacity; and
- Any potential new client leads which the team may have.

The meeting also has a slot for the team's collective brains to be picked by anyone who has an unresolved query on property law or practice. Amy knows that if we don't resolve any query in the meeting, it will usually be added to her in-tray to research and provide an answer by the end of the day.

Monday: 9:00-9:30am Review and distribute the post

Part of the role of a partner is to review his/her department's incoming mail and to distribute it to the team. The first part of our firm's references (which are quoted in all correspondence) contain the initials of the supervising partner. The post room has already sorted the mail into piles for each partner, so we review and distribute our mail to the team members we supervise. Today, one of my partners will not be in until lunchtime as she is visiting clients out of town, so I carefully peruse her incoming mail before distributing it to the relevant fee earners. This is a good way of partners keeping in touch with the stage each transaction has reached, and, on occasions, this exercise helps us to identify problems which need actioning. In today's post, there two new instructions from one of our investor clients. I pass these to Siobhan, who completed a large deal at the end of last week, as she now has some spare capacity.

Monday: 9:30am-1:00pm Fee-earning work

As well as managing my team in the commercial property department, I undertake fee-earning work as well. Both I and my team members (including Amy) have personal billing targets, which require partners to record at least five and non-partners to record at least six chargeable hours against client matters each working day. I must also ensure that, collectively, my team meets its monthly billing targets as well. I start by answering my post and outstanding client emails, which is all chargeable to the relevant client files. I answer some of the internal emails which only need quick replies (like confirming I will be attending the integration meeting on Wednesday). I make a mental note of reading the other internal emails later in the day. I aim to record in excess of three hours of chargeable time on Monday mornings, which I comfortably achieve today once I complete reviewing the complex planning history of a site which one of the firm's major clients is acquiring, before dictating a report which my secretary will type up. I usually do much of my own typing having mastered touch typing (at last!) a couple of years ago. However, I do find I get through my work quicker by dictating most of the longer documents. A few internal and external calls interrupt my morning's work, but not many; Monday mornings are relatively quiet and allow me to 'get my head down'.

Monday: 1:00-2:00pm Lunch with Tim Sharman (mergers and acquisitions partner)

Tim and I go back several years. We are both around the same age and joined the firm within a year of each other. We share a common outlook on most things, so we like to go to lunch together at least once a month. As well as sharing confidences and exchanging office gossip (mostly acquired by his well-connected secretary), Tim frequently refers work to my team. Today, Tim tells me that he has been instructed on the acquisition of a large private company which owns several commercial properties. Tim would like my team to undertake due diligence on the target company's properties, because they form a significant proportion of the value of the company. Property departments often provide this type of corporate support, and this is usually something I delegate to one of my team's assistant solicitors. We start to discuss yesterday's big game and the disputed penalty when my secretary calls; my 14.00 appointment has arrived early, so I leave Tim to pay the bill and promise I'll return the compliment next time.

Monday: 2:00-3:00pm Meeting with Jerome Garner (potential new client)

When I arrive at the office, Amy has already shown Jerome Garner to a meeting room. I met Jerome last month at a property investment conference where we were both delegates, and he has also been recommended to the firm by one of our existing clients. Jerome explains that his current solicitor is retiring shortly. Jerome does not feel that the remaining lawyers at his current solicitor's firm will serve him as well. He has a small investment deal which he would like to try us out with, which I say Amy will handle under my close supervision. We agree a fee for the job and I leave Amy with Jerome at the end of the meeting to perform the usual 'Know Your Client' checks, which we are obliged to undertake when taking on any new client.

Monday: 3:00-5:00pm Fee-earning work

During this time, I debrief Amy on the Jerome Garner instruction. I ask her to open the file and prepare a client care letter to send to Jerome. This is a standard letter written to all new clients confirming details of the firm's fees, complaints procedures, who is acting and supervising the matter and so on. I then work on my existing client files. One job I complete is perusing and then amending a draft contract on one of my clients' latest deals, before emailing my suggested amendments to the solicitor on the other side.

Monday: 5:00-6:00pm Review outgoing mail

During this hour of the day, I read (and amend where necessary) my own outgoing mail which I have previously dictated and which is presented to me by my secretary at 5:00pm each day. I also review the outgoing post of members of my team. This is part of my supervisory role and it allows me to keep in touch with the progress on each deal. On occasions, I may question the content of an outgoing letter or a contractual provision, which may need to be amended by the team member before it is sent.

Monday: 6:00-7:00pm Fee-earning work

I complete another hour's fee-earning work at the end of the day once the outgoing post is sorted. On the way home, I open up and read the internal emails on my Blackberry which I have not yet had time to read in full, responding where necessary. My wife has a regular commitment on a Monday evening, so I make sure that I'm home before 8:00pm.

TUESDAY

Tuesday: 8:00-9:00am Fee-earning work

I'm usually one of the first to arrive in the commercial property department, although Sandy is almost always the first – I like to get the breakfast ready at home and make sure the kids are dressed for school by the time I leave. Sandy's kids are at university now, so he's usually in by 7.15. Sandy is fantastically connected and spends many a lunchtime and afternoon cultivating his vast network of contacts and his penchant for vintage clarets. I spend most of the hour drafting a certificate of title for one of our lender clients.

Tuesday: 9:00-9:30am Review and distribute the post

Tuesday: 9:30-11:30am Fee-earning work

I complete the certificate of title which I was working on earlier and then spend 20 minutes chewing over a complex query which Sandy has on a legal title which he was investigating earlier in the morning. Responding to my routine mail (which I like to get out of the way first) seems to take forever today, as I'm interrupted by a succession of phone calls and unscheduled visits from colleagues on a variety of matters ranging from my views on the proposed venue for the firm's Christmas party to a performance issue relating to one of the secretaries in my department.

Tuesday: 11:30am-noon Travel to Hart & Co

I have a meeting at noon with one of my property developer clients, Clive Overton. Clive arrives at my office and we travel together to the meeting by taxi. We have been planning for this meeting for several months, so we use the travelling time to rehearse our tactics. Clive is trying to negotiate the terms of an option he would like one of his companies to take to purchase various plots of land at Milton Grange which are all jointly owned by three family members who don't get on and who each have their own solicitors. Normally terms would be negotiated directly between the sellers and buyers or via real estate agents, but the personalities and complexities of this transaction mean that the only way a deal will be struck is by getting all the parties around the negotiating table with their lawyers.

Tuesday: Noon-2:00pm Meeting at Hart & Co with Clive Overton

We knew the meeting would be tough, and in that respect we weren't disappointed. Only one of the sellers said that he really wanted to sell, but Clive and I suspected that the other two were playing a game of brinkmanship, trying to hold out for the best possible terms. After around half an hour, one of the sellers postured to walk out of the meeting as Clive's opening gambit was 'so off the mark, he was wasting everyone's time.' However, after a two-hour chess game, we reached a meeting of minds on 90% of the contentious issues, but we were still some way apart on price. We left the meeting with an agreement that I would draft heads of terms, which we hoped would act as a catalyst to reaching agreement on price and the other outstanding issues shortly afterwards.

Tuesday: 2:00-2:30pm Travel back to office

Clive and I reflect on the meeting, which we agree went well, in the end. He still has plenty of ground to give on price (if needed) – the meeting had achieved the desired outcome: to agree as much as possible except the price in order to get all three sellers psychologically committed to the deal.

Tuesday: 2:30-5:00pm Fee-earning work

I dictate the draft heads of terms for Clive and while my secretary types this up, I make the final check and then exchange contracts on the sale of the Bailey & Co portfolio. My secretary emails me the draft heads of terms which she has now typed up. I tinker with it slightly and then send an email to Clive seeking his approval, which comes back by return, following which I email the document to each of the sellers' solicitors.

Tuesday: 5:00-6:00pm Review outgoing mail

Tuesday: 6:00-8:00pm Fee-earning work

During the last hour, I have received an email from the solicitor for the 'willing' seller of Milton Grange with a few suggested amendments to the heads of terms, which are not contentious. More importantly, this seller wants to re-open the negotiations over price and confirms she will accept a lower sum for her interest if the others sellers will agree. Clive instructs me not to accept or reject that offer – rather, he tells me to enquire whether the other sellers will agree to sell at that price. The appropriate emails are sent just before 8pm.

WEDNESDAY

Wednesday: 8:00-9:00am Fee-earning work

Clive is on the phone at ten past eight, but there is no news overnight. He wants to chase one of the 'unwilling' sellers directly. I recommend patience – try not to look too keen – we need to see if the sellers will all take the bait of the heads of terms and, then, hopefully, move on price. I also take the time to catch up with some of my other fee-earning work; the focus on Clive's deal has meant other matters have not received the attention they should have in the last couple of days; I pass the more urgent files to Imran and Siobhan to make progress on today.

Wednesday: 9:30-11:30am Review work in progress and unpaid bills

The end of the month is drawing near and I have a meeting with the finance partner later in the morning to discuss how my team's monthly billing figures are looking. I have access to a considerable amount of financial data, such as how many unbilled chargeable hours each fee earner in my team has recorded this month, and the value of the work in progress of each matter. I check with each fee earner which matters are billable this month and estimate the likely bill for each matter. I also check our list of unpaid bills in readiness for my meeting with the finance partner.

Wednesday: 11:30-12:30pm Fee-earning work

Wednesday: 12:30-1:00pm Meeting with finance partner

We start by checking the list of unpaid bills. In the commercial property department, our debtors are relatively low compared to those of other departments, mainly because most commercial property matters get billed and paid at completion – and if the client wants the deal to go through, he or she has to pay us first! There is one outstanding bill (which has been unpaid for over 60 days) which is causing the finance director (and me) some cause for concern – one for £10,000 plus VAT for the costs of an aborted purchase which our client NRT Properties Ltd ('NRT') withdrew from due to a failed planning application. I am meeting the directors of NRT later in the day for our quarterly review, following which I hope to have news for the finance partner. This month is looking like a good one for the team – we will probably hit our numbers. However, the property market has been slow for some time, and, as a consequence, the team is a little behind our annual target at the moment. Having said that, we usually accelerate to and through the annual target towards the end of the financial year, which the finance partner seems happy to accept for the time being.

Wednesday: 1:00-2:00pm Integration committee meeting

A little under a year ago, the firm merged with a smaller eight-partner London firm. A committee of partners and staff from both firms was formed following the merger to smooth over the integration of the cultures and practices of both firms. Although the smaller firm has, effectively, been absorbed by my firm, there are issues of conflict which need to be resolved. Many are dealt with at partnership level following consultation with the Integration Committee, such as the payment of Christmas bonuses, the amounts for which 'we' have always paid on merit. In contrast, our new partners' old firm did not link the bonus to performance, paying all members of staff a fixed percentage of their gross salary.

Wednesday: 2:00-3:30pm Quarterly review meeting with NRT Properties Ltd ('NRT')

I meet with most of my larger clients on a quarterly basis. NRT is a house builder and we review the status of each file at these meetings. In reality, the client is up to date with all current transactions, but these meetings are a useful forum for the clients (as well as me) to take a look at the 'bigger picture' – to discuss potential deals in the near future and any problems on existing ones, like the unpaid £10,000 bill I discussed with my finance director earlier in the day. The clients moan a little at the size of the fee, but that was what we agreed when the matter aborted three months ago, so I hold my ground and am told that the monies will be paid by a bank transfer by the end of the week.

Wednesday: 3:30-5:00pm Fee-earning work

Wednesday: 5:00-6:00pm Review outgoing mail

Wednesday: 6:00-7:00pm Fee-earning work

Wednesday: 7:00-9:00pm Reception at H & F

I crack through my outstanding mail and review a couple of reports on title which Amy has drafted, following which I attend a reception at the firm's accountants with Tim and one other partner. It is the usual fare of champagne and canopies. I dish out a few business cards to potential clients. There are a few property people at the reception, one of which is an overseas investor who I agree to call next week. When the same unclaimed canopies come out for the fourth or fifth time, like the uncollected luggage from an airport carousel, I take that as my cue to slip away.

Thursday

Thursday: Before 10:30am – school assembly

I don't see enough of my kids. But I do try to make an effort to attend at least one school event per year for each of them. Today my daughter is taking the lead role as Florence Nightingale in a school assembly, which I couldn't miss, even if I wanted to. I'm glad I didn't miss it: she was delightful.

Thursday: 10:30-11:00am Review post

My team has already received their post but copies have been made for me in case there is something I wish to discuss.

Thursday: 11:00am-12:30pm Fee-earning work

An email comes through from Felix Arrowsmith, one of the solicitors for the 'unwilling' sellers on Clive Overton's deal. Apparently, he'd like to talk about the price. I check with Clive if he has heard anything since we last spoke (which he hasn't) and I then contact Felix Arrowsmith. After a rambling introduction, he spits out the reduced amount which he says both his client and the other unwilling seller are prepared to accept. I am pretty sure this will be acceptable to Clive, but cannot confirm this without Clive's instructions. Whilst I seek Clive's instructions I ask Felix to ensure that all three sellers' solicitors confirm by email their respective client's agreement (in principle) to the amended heads of terms and the reduced price (subject to contract). The emails materialise within 45 minutes and Clive has one last attempt to push the sellers down on price even further. It goes down badly with one of the 'unwilling' sellers, who, again, postures to pull out of the deal. We don't believe the threat, but Clive (and I) realise that these are the best terms he is going to secure, so the heads of terms, including the price of the option and various other sums payable are now finalised.

Thursday: 12:30-1:00pm Travel to partners meeting

We hold a partners' meeting every month in a hotel near Paddington station so partners travelling from our offices on the M4 corridor don't have far to travel once they arrive in London for the meeting. I travel to the meeting with Tim, reminding him that I've not yet seen the instructions on the corporate support job which he said would be coming my way when we met earlier in the week.

Thursday: 1:00-6:00pm Partners meeting

The managing partner delivers a report as to how the firm is performing financially and gives details of lease renewals on office premises and a few significant personnel changes. Sometimes we invite a guest speaker, but this week we workshop some strategic issues in mini groups made up of partners from different offices. We then run a plenary discussion to give the senior management of the firm ideas to move forward from. This time, we focus on the firm's marketing strategy, and in particular, how we can improve the cross-selling of our services across the firm's departments and offices.

Thursday: 6:00-6:30pm Travel back to office

Thursday: 6:30-8:00pm Fee-earning work

There's no sign of the draft option agreement yet on Clive's deal, but the papers on Tim's corporate support job were couriered during the afternoon and I start to read through them and work out how the work will be shared by the team. There are 43 properties involved, which means we need 43 reports on title. That's quite a lot of work to distribute.

Friday

Friday: 8:00-9:00am Breakfast meeting with Amy

We meet at this time every fortnight to review Amy's caseload and her general progress. I take the opportunity of telling her that she will be preparing a report on title in respect of the more straightforward titles which I identified last night on Tim's corporate support job. Amy is showing much promise and has a good instinct for where the problems are on a property deal, although her drafting of letters and documents still needs further development – but that is usual for a trainee in her second six months of a two-year training contract.

Friday: 9:00-9:30am Review and distribute the post

Friday: 9:30am-1:00pm Fee-earning work

I have three deals completing today. Amy will administer them while I peruse the draft option agreement which has arrived at last. Completion days are relatively straightforward (in most cases) – it's simply a question of ensuring that all the relevant documents have been signed in advance and the money changes hands by electronic bank transfers. All three deals complete before noon. I spend much of the morning on the phone with Clive discussing the minutiae of the option agreement.

Friday: 1:00-2:30pm Lunch with GW Developments ('GWD')

GWD send most of their work to another firm, but I have been courting their business for some time. I get the feeling that their directors are looking at several other firms at the moment as well. They are keeping their cards close to their chest, and I'm not sure how much progress I've made in winning their work. I learn that one of the directors travels in on the same line as me each morning, which may give me a further opportunity to find out more in the near future.

Friday: 2:30-5:00pm Fee-earning work

By the end of the afternoon Clive confirms he is happy with my suggested amendments to the option agreement and I email the sellers' solicitors. I look at a one of the complex titles on Tim's corporate support matter and start to draft the report on title. I check on the team's progress on the rest of these reports, mainly to see if there are any issues or complications which require my input. I call Tim to confirm the team's progress.

Friday: 5:00-6:00pm Review outgoing mail

Friday: 6:00-7:00pm Friday drinks

It has been a good week. A regular crowd from the firm go to the pub after work every Friday. I only go around once a month, but I go today because one of my former assistant solicitors (who now works at another firm) will be there. I normally leave after buying the first round of drinks. Like most Fridays, I leave central London with a file or two which I will look at on Sunday evening. But only after Downton Abbey has finished.'

And finally... let's talk about Kevin.

Kevin's story should inspire all law students – wherever you are in your studies, whatever career path you ultimately choose. Kevin's account of his achievements to date should particularly appeal to students who, like Kevin, do not set the world on fire with their academic record.

I taught Kevin on the LPC in 2008-9. By the time you get to the end of his account, you'll realise why I have taken a keen interest in his career development since he left law school.

Jonny Hurst

I over indulged during my A levels and law degree. It was only when I attended the Legal Practice Course that I focused on my career and started looking for a training contract - I hadn't realised the uphill struggle I had before me.

I had tremendous support during law school from both peers and tutors which was invaluable: it helped me to focus on what I could offer a law firm, with very little experience and less than desirable academics.

After passing my LPC, I obtained a job as a paralegal in a provincial law firm. Regrettably, the work was slow and it ultimately resulted in my redundancy after only 6 months. It had, however, provided me with an insight into how a law firm works, the importance of billing and being viable as a fee earner in your own right.

Most importantly, being made redundant at such an early stage provided me with the motivation to ensure I was never in a similar situation again. I realised that in order to progress my career and get that elusive training contract, I needed to be able to bring new clients into a firm and, effectively, become self sufficient.

Having gaps on your CV never looks good so I took unpaid work experience with another provincial firm which specialised in personal injury, while I looked for another paralegal position. I quickly realised that a focus on marketing would make me useful to this firm, and I made that one of my main goals (as well as working on securing a training contract with the same firm). Over a six month period, while I worked as a paralegal at the firm, under supervision, I built up my own client base in a niche Personal Injury area, helping to develop the firm's practice. As a consequence of this achievement, I secured a training contract with the firm.

During my training contract I focused a lot of my time on product liability. I am now one year qualified and I run a department at the firm with a small team. I am also focusing on new concepts to develop product liability law and put these concepts into practice. As a result of this, I have been fortunate to win a number of national industry awards and been interviewed, reported and quoted widely in the media.

From the uphill struggle I faced to qualify as a solicitor during a recession, there are several things which are now clear to me which should apply to everyone looking for a training contract:

- *Academics should not be underestimated. Having less than desirable grades makes the process of getting your foot in the door extremely tough. Take it from me, I know!*
- *Everyone has extra-curricular activities, but these are only really relevant if they show how an individual has the skills which a firm is looking for.*
- *Commercial acumen is an ambiguous phrase. Yes, many City firms want to know an individual understands the business of their clients, but more importantly, I think, it is for the individual to show that they do not just understand a firm's clients, they should also appreciate how the law firm works, and how it makes money. The focus should be how that individual can show they will help to make a firm profitable while, at the same time, understanding where they will fit in as a trainee and beyond.*
- *Applicants need to understand how the legal world is changing. I am a firm believer that all lawyers need to focus on innovative ways to provide their service to clients and also have an innovative approach to the law. It's easier said than done, but something to try and work on.*
- *Standing out from the crowd. It's an over used phrase, but if you demonstrate all of the above, you may just land that training contract. It worked for me.*

Kevin Timms, solicitor.

Glossary

BPP
LEARNING MEDIA

Glossary of legal acronyms used in England & Wales

Acronym	Stands for	In a few words...
AIM	Alternative Investment Market	A market in the London Stock Exchange which allows small and growing companies the opportunity of raising capital
BCAT	Bar Course Aptitude Test	A competence test which all BPTC students must pass before starting the BPTC.
BLP	Business Law and Practice	LPC module
BPTC	Bar Professional Training Course	Barristers' professional exams
BSB	Bar Standards Board	Regulatory body for barristers
CPAs	Core Practice Areas	Main compulsory modules on the LPC: BLP, PLP, Civil litigation and Criminal litigation
CPD	Continuing Professional Development	Post-qualification education
CPE	Common Professional Examination	Graduate conversion course
CPS	Crown Prosecution Service	Administers and conducts criminal prosecutions.
CSR	Corporate Social Responsibility	Community projects run and paid for by business
GDL	Graduate Diploma in Law	Graduate conversion course
CILEx	Chartered Institute of Legal Executives	Governing body for legal executives

Acronym	Stands for	In a few words...
FRU	Free Representation Unit	Provides real-life advocacy experience
JP	Justice of the Peace	Magistrate
LLB	Bachelor of Laws	The most popular law degree
LLM	Master of Laws	Master's degree
LLP	Limited Liability Partnership	Type of (law) firm where the partners' exposure to creditors of the firm is limited
LNAT	National Admissions Test for Law	Used by some universities
LPC	Legal Practice Course	Solicitors' professional exams
PLP	Property Law and Practice	LPC module
PSL	Professional Support Lawyer	Non-client-facing lawyer in private practice
QC	Queen's Counsel	Top barrister
QLD	Qualifying law degree	Approved degree to start LPC or BPTC
SRA	Solicitors Regulation Authority	Regulatory body for solicitors
UCAS	Universities & Colleges Admissions Service	Central hub for university applications

Glossary of terms used in this book

Term	In a few words...
Academic stage of training	A QLD or the GDL.
The bar	The profession of a barrister, which comprises the independent bar plus the employed bar.
Barrister	Professionally qualified lawyer who is a member of the bar – a specialist advocate, most of whom work at the independent bar
Black letter law	Basic legal principles
Brief	Documents comprising a barrister's instructions on a case
Chambers	A collection of independent barristers who share premises and overheads (like clerks) but who are all self-employed. Often referred to as a 'set of Chambers' or just a 'set'
Counsel	Barrister
Employed bar	The collective term used to refer to barristers who are employed in commerce, industry and in the public sector, rather than in private practice
Equity partners	Owners of a law firm
Foundations for Legal Knowledge	The compulsory core subjects of study on QLD and GDL courses
General Counsel	The 'in-house' head of legal affairs at a company or other organisation outside private practice
Independent bar	The collective term for self-employed barristers who work in private practice
In-house lawyer	Term used to when a solicitor or barrister works for a company or other organisation, rather than private practice
Inns of Court	Gray's Inn, Inner Temple, Lincoln's Inn and Middle Temple. By ancient tradition, these have exclusive power to create barristers

Term	In a few words...
Junior	A barrister in private practice who is not a QC
Law Society	Solicitors' representative body
Magic Circle	Five of the leading City law firms: Allen & Overy, Clifford Chance, Freshfields Bruckhaus Deringer, Linklaters and Slaughter and May
Mini-pupillage	A short work-experience placement in chambers for prospective barristers
Mooting	A hypothetical case which is debated by law students by way of a mock trial
Paralegal	Someone working as a lawyer (often with some legal training) who is neither a barrister or solicitor
Pleadings	A formal statement setting out a client's claim or defence in legal proceedings
Practice area	Specialism
Pro bono	Work done at no or little charge 'for the public good'
Pupillage	For prospective barristers, a year's training in private practice after the BPTC
Pupillage Gateway	Website for online pupillage applications
Right of audience	The right to appear as an advocate in court
Seat	A period of time in a department of a law firm during a training contract
Set	See Chambers
Silk	Term used to refer to a QC (because of their silk robes)
Six	Period of six months during pupillage (hence: 'first six' and 'second six')
Solicitor	Professionally qualified lawyer who usually works for a law firm if in private practice

Term	In a few words...
Statute books	These are legal reference books containing acts of parliament, statutory instruments, and a variety of rules and regulations. These materials are usually collated in subject-specific books – eg Butterworths Company Law Handbook
Tenant (in a barrister's context)	Barrister who is a member of a set of chambers and works from there
Training contract	Traditionally, a two year legal apprenticeship for trainee solicitors, usually commenced immediately after the LPC
Vacation Scheme	360° placement at a law firm, which is a combination of work experience and a lengthy job interview, where they take a look at you and you take a look at them! Commonly referred to as a 'Vac Scheme'

Table of Cases

BPP
LEARNING MEDIA

Table of Cases

Birmingham City Council v Abdulla and others [2012] UKSC 47
Donoghue v Stevenson [1932] AC 532
R v Ahluwalia [1992] 4 AER 889
Rylands v Fletcher [1868] LR 3 HL 330
Salomon v A. Salomon & Co Ltd [1897] AC 22

Index

BPP
LEARNING MEDIA

A

B

C

E

F

G

H

I

L

S

T

U

V

W